MICHIGAN WOMEN:
FIRSTS AND FOUNDERS
VOLUME II

1920 to 1995

Celebrate 75 Years of Women's Suffrage

RACHEL BRETT HARLEY
and
BETTY MACDOWELL

MICHIGAN WOMEN'S STUDIES ASSOCIATION, INC.

IN CELEBRATION OF

THE 75TH ANNIVERSARY OF
THE NINETEENTH AMENDMENT

Ratified on August 26, 1920
ending a 72-year struggle for American women's right to vote
begun in 1848 at Seneca Falls, New York

*"All honor to the small army of noble women
who were brave enough to face and fight prejudice;
who overturned old ideas and upheld new,
standing for that liberal spirit of equal human rights."*

Clara B. Arthur, President
Michigan Equal Suffrage Association

Rachel Brett Harley, Ph.D., is an Associate Professor in the Department of Music and the Women's Studies Program at Eastern Michigan University. She is also a member of the Michigan Women's Studies Association Board of Directors and co-author of <u>Michigan Women: Firsts and Founders</u>, Volume I.

Betty MacDowell, Ph.D., is a Research Associate and Director of the Michigan Stained Glass Census at the Michigan State University Museum. She is also a member of the Michigan Women's Studies Association Board of Directors and co-author of <u>Michigan Women: Firsts and Founders</u>, Volume I.

TABLE OF CONTENTS

MICHIGAN, MY MICHIGAN

(Sung to the tune of "O Tannenbaum.")

Oh, women of this sovereign state,
Michigan, My Michigan,
Oh, rally to emancipate,
Michigan, My Michigan,
From worn traditions, stale and old,
And limitations manifold,
Come sisters, join our army bold,
Michigan, My Michigan.

From home, from shop and college hall,
Michigan, My Michigan
Come work for freedom, one and all,
Michigan, My Michigan,
For "Votes for Women" let us stand,
A strong, undaunted fearless band
Until the women of this land,
Sing, Michigan, My Michigan.

Since we must needs obey the laws,
Michigan, My Michigan,
Though well we know they have their flaws,
Michigan, My Michigan.
Oh, let us do the woman's share
To guard our homes from every snare.
To us entrust our children's care
Michigan, My Michigan.

And if we cannot fight for thee
Michigan, My Michigan
We bear the men who make thee free,
Michigan, My Michigan,
And if we cannot go to war,
The men who do, we suffer for,
We, too, have known the veteran's scar,
Michigan, My Michigan.

Oh, be as just as thou art great
Michigan, My Michigan.
And let us trim the ship of state
Michigan, My Michigan.
For we would with our brothers stand,
And serve and love thee, hand and hand,
And make of thee, a glorious land,
Michigan, My Michigan.

From the <u>Michigan Suffragist</u>, December 1914.
Author unknown.

FOREWORD

As President of the Michigan Women's Studies Association, I am honored to introduce to you Volume II of <u>Michigan Women: Firsts and Founders</u>.

This volume recognizes the achievements of more than five hundred women who have been the first women (or first persons) in their fields or who have been the founders of movements, programs, organizations or institutions that have benefitted our society.

It pays tribute to such diverse women as Irene Auberlin, founder of World Medical Relief; Waunetta Dominic, Native American activist; Willie Hobbs Moore, African American physicist; Betsy Graves Reyneau, Suffragist imprisoned for picketing the White House, and a great many others, both contemporary and historic, who have made contributions to our state and nation.

This volume also celebrates the 75th Anniversary of the passage of the Federal Suffrage Amendment. It includes an expanded chronology of Michigan women's history that highlights Suffrage events, photographs of Suffrage activities, and a Michigan Woman Suffrage Honor Roll that lists by county more than 3,000 women and men who supported the long struggle for women's right to vote. We all owe much to Rachel Brett Harley and Betty MacDowell for the energy and time they devoted to the research that made it possible.

Proceeds from the sale of this book will benefit the continued development of the Michigan Women's Historical Center and Hall of Fame at 213 W. Main Street in Lansing. The Center was created by the Michigan Women's Studies Association to give visibility to the achievements of Michigan women and to restore them to their rightful place in history.

We invite you to visit the Center and learn more about the roles that Michigan women have played in the development of our state and nation.

Gladys Beckwith
Michigan Women's Studies Association, Inc.

INTRODUCTION

This volume, like the first volume of <u>Michigan Women</u>: <u>Firsts and Founders</u>, gives recognition to several hundred women who have been pioneers and pathfinders in entering fields once closed to women or in finding new ways of overcoming social, economic and political injustice. Many of these women contributed in various ways to their local communities; the achievements of numerous others had state, national or worldwide impact.

Almost immediately after the first volume was published three years ago, we began to hear from readers who told us about other women who should be similarly recognized for their achievements and contributions. We also continued to discover additional women "firsts" and founders in newspaper and magazine articles, obituaries, books, and other sources. We soon realized that many historic women were still unrecognized for the roles that they played in our state and nation and that contemporary women were still breaking through barriers and helping to find new solutions to social problems. This realization motivated the present volume.

A second volume of <u>Michigan Women: Firsts and Founders</u> also seemed the most appropriate way in which to celebrate the 75th Anniversary of the Suffrage Amendment, which became law on August 26, 1920. We have included entries for many Michigan women who were active in the long struggle to secure the right to vote for all American women. Their stories reveal the dedication of these women to the cause of equal suffrage.

Scattered throughout the pages of this volume are some quotations drawn from the statements of those who supported the Woman Suffrage cause and women's claim for equal rights. At many local Suffrage meetings, it was customary to have a "Suffrage Salad Bowl" holding slips of paper that contained such quotations and sentiments. Each person present would draw a slip of paper from the bowl and read aloud its statement, thus helping to strengthen the courage and commitment necessary for the struggle.

The Michigan Woman Suffrage Honor Roll included in this volume was created by requesting from each county the names of women and men who had been involved in the Suffrage movement on the local, state or national level, and by searching through publications and papers to identify Michigan leaders and supporters of equal suffrage. The Honor Roll contains more than 3,000 names from 80 of Michigan's 83 counties. We will add more names and counties as they are found or provided.

This volume also includes an expanded Chronology of Michigan Women's History that brings the Chronology in the first volume up to the present year. It highlights significant events in Michigan's Suffrage activity. The List of Sources identifies places, publications and individuals that furnished information for the biographical entries. The Index organized by category is provided to facilitate finding women in a particular field of work or area of interest.

We hope you will enjoy reading about these Michigan women as much as we have enjoyed discovering them and sharing information about their achievements and contributions.

ACKNOWLEDGEMENTS

This compilation of women who were firsts and founders has been drawn from many published and unpublished sources. We are indebted to the staffs of the Burton Historical Collection at the Detroit Public Library, the State of Michigan Library in Lansing, Nancy Bartlett of the Bentley Historical Library at the University of Michigan, Maria Davis of the Eastern Michigan University Library, Gordon Olson of the Grand Rapids Public Library and Linda K. Panian of the John M. Longyear Research Library in Marquette for their assistance in our research. We are also grateful for the help of numerous individuals and historical societies that told us about many of the women included in the biographical entries and the Michigan Woman Suffrage Honor Roll. We especially thank Edith Ash of Osseo, Rose Collamer Bauman of Midland, Esther Brown of Howell, Jo Ellyn Clarey of Grand Rapids, William Fagal of Berrien Springs, Elizabeth Giese of Lansing, O'Ryan Rickard of Kalamazoo, and Virginia White of Okemos for providing much information about women who were firsts or founders and for helping to assemble the Michigan Woman Suffrage Honor Roll. To our husbands, Ted Harley and Harlan MacDowell, we express our gratitude for their encouragement and aid. Lastly, we deeply appreciate the financial support of John H. and Martha N. Aldinger, Gladys Beckwith, the Consumers Power Company, Helen Jones Earley, Louise Heck-Rabi, Marian McCracken, Jane Kay Nugent and an anonymous donor.

Rachel Brett Harley and Betty MacDowell
November 1995

KEY TO ABBREVIATIONS

The following abbreviations are used for organizations that are listed in the biographical entries.

AAUW	American Association of University Women
ACLU	American Civil Liberties Union
AMA	American Medical Association
BPW	Business and Professional Women
DAR	Daughters of the American Revolution
GAR	Grand Army of the Republic
LWV	League of Women Voters
MEA	Michigan Education Association
MWSA	Michigan Women's Studies Association
NAACP	National Association for the Advancement of Colored People
NCSEE	National Coalition for Sex Equity in Education
NEA	National Education Association
NOW	National Organization for Women
NWSA	National Women's Studies Association
OES	Order of the Eastern Star
PTA	Parent Teachers Association
UAW	United Auto Workers
UNICEF	United Nations Children's Fund
WCTU	Women's Christian Temperance Union
WPA	Works Progress Administration
WRC	Women's Relief Corps
YMCA	Young Men's Christian Association
YWCA	Young Women's Christian Association

MICHIGAN WOMEN: FIRSTS AND FOUNDERS
VOLUME II

****

*"If the first woman God ever made was strong enough
to turn the world upside down all alone, these women together
ought to be able to turn it back and get it right side up again!
And now they are asking to do it, the men better let them.."*
Sojourner Truth of Battle Creek, 1851

****

ADAMS, FRANCES (FANNY) HARRIS, of Southfield Township; first woman to be a township treasurer in Oakland County, elected as treasurer of Southfield Township in 1932. She served as treasurer until 1934 when she became the Southfield Township Clerk, a position she held until 1969. Ref.: 209; 212

ADELMAN, SUSAN HERSHBERG, of Southfield; first woman to be president of the Michigan State Medical Society in its 124-year history, elected in 1990. Adelman, a physician, was also the first woman to be president of the Wayne County Medical Society and in 1992 was the first woman elected to the American Medical Association Council on Medical Service. Ref.: 24 (Oct. 1992, 8); 81 (Jul.-Aug. 1990, 18)

AIKEY, MARY, of East Lansing; former executive director of the YWCA of Greater Lansing and founder in 1974 of the first biennial Diana Awards Dinner, to honor the contributions of women to the Lansing area. Aikey was honored with a special Founders Award at the Diana Awards Dinner in 1994. Ref.: 57 (May 26, 1994, 3C)

AIRRIESS, MARY, of Clawson; first woman to be mayor of Clawson, from 1984 to 1993. A real estate broker, Airriess served for more than a decade on the Clawson City Council before becoming mayor. Ref.: 24 (Oct. 1993, 55, 58)

ALDINGER, ELLA HOUGH (1879-1952), of Lansing; first woman to be president of the Lansing School Board, from 1920 to 1921; co-founder of the Ingham County LWV in 1921. A New York native, she moved to Lansing in 1908 and taught high school before her marriage to Rev. Frederick C. Aldinger, a Unitarian minister. Both were ardent believers in votes for women. In 1916 she was elected to the Lansing School Board, where she served until 1932, advocating equal funding for elementary schools and night school

for business women. In 1917 Aldinger joined the more militant
National Woman's Party in picketing the White House, to pressure
President Woodrow Wilson into giving his support to the suffrage
cause. Her Michigan picketing colleagues included **Betsy Graves
Reyneau** and **Kathleen McGraw Hendrie** of Detroit and **Mrs. G. B.
Jennison** of Bay City. Aldinger's picketing activity was criticized in
Lansing, but she withstood attempts to remove her as president of
the board and was re-elected in the next election. After her election
as the second president of the Michigan LWV in 1921, she
monitored legislative action on issues related to women and
continued to fight for social reform. She was also a member of the
Lansing Women's Club, the DAR, and the AAUW. Ref.: 22 (Sunday
Supplement, May 6, 1917); 38 (10); 112 (Feb. 18, 1995, 10A)

ALLISON, JANICE, see **COLLAMER BAUMAN, ROSELLA E.**

ALVARADO-ORTEGA, YOLANDA G. HERNANDEZ, of East Lansing;
founder in 1988 of Hispanic Women in the Network of Michigan,
providing state conferences and leadership workshops for Hispanic
women. A native of Texas, she came to Michigan in 1969 and
served on the Human Relations Commission of Holland. She joined
the Lansing State Journal as a reporter from 1974 until 1987, when
she became a copy editor. During this time she earned a degree
from Spring Arbor College and served as president of both the
National Newspaper Guild in Michigan and the Mujeres Unidas de
Michigan, a Hispanic women's organization founded by **Delia
Villegas Vorhauer**. (See Michigan Women: Firsts and Founders,
Vol. I). Appointed by Governor William Milliken to the Michigan
Women's Commission, she edited its newsletter, Michigan Women.
She also coordinated the Michigan State University Hispanics in
Journalism Program and served as vice president of the Michigan
Coalition of Concerned Hispanics from 1987 to 1991. As a result
of her daughter's illness, she became active in the Michigan
Handicappers Association and the Alliance for the Mentally Ill in
Michigan and developed two handbooks for families in crisis:
Mental Illness: A Family Resource Guide (1989) and The Wrap-
Around Service Model (1993). She also developed a training
program to help law enforcement personnel deal with the mentally
ill. In 1990 she was co-coordinator of Women for Meaningful
Summits, a coalition of women's groups to identify women's issues
for a meeting between U.S. President George Bush and Soviet
leader Mikhail Gorbachev. She served as chair of the children's
committee on abuse and violence and was a member of the ethnic
women's delegation that met with the Women's Soviet Commission
in Moscow. She has also served on the board of the Michigan
Protection and Advocacy (of rights for the mentally ill) and the
Michigan Civil Service Comparable Worth Task Force. As the
newsroom community outreach coordinator at the Lansing State
Journal, she promotes diversity in coverage and staff sensitivity.
Her awards include the Diana Award in Communications from the
YWCA in 1985, the National Newspaper Guild's Distinguished

Service Award in 1986, the Sondra Berlin Award from the Michigan Handicappers Association in 1989, and a Life Achievement Award from Hispanic Women in the Network in 1990. In 1987 she was named one of the top 100 Hispanic Women in Communications by Hispanic Magazine. She was inducted into the Michigan Women's Hall of Fame in 1995. Ref.: 95 (12-14); 184

ANDERSON, KATHERINE, see **THE MARVELETTES**

ANDREWS, BARBARA (1936-1978), of Detroit; first woman ordained in the American Lutheran Church, in 1970. Her first pastorate was at a church in Minneapolis. Confined to a wheelchair due to paraplegia, Andrews died in a fire caused by defective wiring. She was acting pastor of Resurrection Lutheran Church in Detroit at the time of her death. Ref.: 22 (Apr. 5, 1978, 12C); 103 (20); 184

ANGELL, ALICE (1870-1961), of Adrian; co-founder and first chair of the Lenawee County Equal Suffrage Association, in 1918. An 1888 graduate of Adrian High School, Angell was the owner of an insurance business from the 1920s until her retirement in 1953. Ref.: 21 (Mar. 4, 1995, A3); 177

****

"We shall fight for the things we have always carried nearest to our hearts -- for democracy. For the right of those who submit to authority to have a voice in their government."

Banner carried by **Ella Hough Aldinger** of Lansing
when she picketed the White House in 1917

****

ASHBAUGH, DELPHINE DODGE (d. 1936), of Detroit; founder and president of the Salvation Army Auxiliary; first woman appointed to serve on the Detroit Recreation Commission, in 1913; founder and first editor of the periodical, The Detroit Club Woman. She also served as president of the Detroit Review Club, the Detroit Federation of Women's Clubs, and, from 1914 to 1916, the Michigan State Federation of Women's Clubs. During World War I, she was the director of Red Cross for Michigan and state chair of the Women's Liberty Loan Drive. She was a life member of the Michigan Equal Suffrage Association and active in the Equal Suffrage League of Wayne County. Ref.: 49 (191-192); 77 (Jun. 1915, 9; Aug. 1915, 5)

ATKIN, KAREN HALLER, of Grand Ledge; founder in 1989 of the Grand Ledge Children's Theatre and co-founder, with **Jane Goebel** of Grand Ledge, of Lansing's first professional dinner theater company, Act-On Productions, in 1992. The Grand Ledge Children's Theatre conducts school year workshops and summertime "Play in the Park" drama camps that result in productions done by children for children. Atkin and Goebel perform in and direct the Act-On shows. Atkin, a Detroit native with a degree in theater from Western Michigan University, has appeared in movies and television. Goebel, who once ran Alpena's Thunder Bay Theater, also founded TaleSpin Theatre, for which she writes and presents one-woman shows at Michigan schools on such topics as self-esteem, women in history, and Indian legends. Ref.: 56 (Oct. 1994, 11, 15); 57 (Nov. 6, 1993, 6D; Jun. 26, 1995, 4B)

AUBERLIN, IRENE McGINNIS, of Detroit; founder in 1953 of World Medical Relief, which she directed as a CEO without pay for 32 years until her retirement in 1985. With the help of a Board of Directors and hundreds of volunteers, the organization has provided medical supplies and equipment to hospitals and clinics throughout the world for more than 40 years. In 1994 alone, 459 volunteers shipped $16,000,000 worth of medicines and equipment from Detroit to 28 countries worldwide and provided $400,000 worth of prescriptions and supplies to the elderly poor in the Detroit area. In recognition of her work for the sick and needy of the world, Auberlin has received more than 50 awards, including the William Booth Award in 1972, the National Jefferson Award for Outstanding Public Service in 1981, the President's Volunteer Action Award and Silver Medal in 1984, and the Stanley S. Kresge Award for outstanding community service in 1994. She was inducted into the Michigan Women's Hall of Fame in 1995. Ref.: 184

AVERY, BLANCHE (1881-1967), of Pontiac; co-founder of Pontiac Junior College, where she was Dean in 1926; co-founder of the Pontiac chapters of Kappa Alpha Phi Sorority in 1898 and the AAUW in 1922. A graduate of the University of Michigan, she taught in Pontiac High School and Pontiac Junior College. She was also active in the Woman Suffrage Movement with her mother, **Lillian Drake Avery**. Ref.: 180; 191

AVERY, LILLIAN DRAKE (1856-1930) of Farmington and Pontiac; founder and first president of the Chautauqua Circle History Class (which became the Pontiac Woman's Literary Club) in 1892; founder and first president of the Oakland County Equal Suffrage Association. As the only woman appointed to the 1916 Oakland County Centennial Celebration Committee, she was in charge of the Women's Day activities and played a leading role in the Suffrage pageant held on the steps of the Oakland County Courthouse. For the Centennial Day parade, she organized a large contingent of marchers for equal suffrage. She was also a member of the Ladies' Library Board, which opened a free public library in 1898, and a charter member and the first regent of Pontiac's General Richardson Chapter of the DAR. In 1904 she became the DAR state historian. Drake located and marked the graves of Revolutionary War soldiers buried in Oakland County and was the author of <u>Revolutionary Soldiers of Oakland County</u>, published as part of the Michigan Pioneer and Historical Collections. She served as vice president and secretary of the Oakland County Pioneer and Historical Society and published six volumes of Oakland County pioneer history, marriage records, and cemetery inscriptions. In 1915 she organized the Pontiac Federation of Women's Clubs, which lobbied for nurses in public schools. During World War I she led the registration of women for war work. Under her leadership, the Pontiac Federation of Women's Clubs joined with the National Women's Party in 1922 to lobby for the Women's Bill of Rights. In 1928 Drake wrote <u>Memories of a Farmington Childhood</u>, illustrated with her own watercolor paintings. She was the mother of **Blanche Avery** and **Lucile Avery Whitfield**. Ref.: 33 (2-8); 180; 191

AVERY WHITFIELD, LUCILE (b. 1883), of Farmington and Pontiac; founder and first president of the Oakland County League of Women Voters in 1921; first woman elected to serve in Oakland County government, elected as Register of Deeds in 1922 and re-elected in 1924. Avery operated her own real estate and insurance agency in Pontiac. Like her mother **Lillian Drake Avery**, she was active in the Woman Suffrage Movement. Ref.: 33 (8); 180; 191

BACH, ANNA BOTSFORD (d. 1915), of Ann Arbor; first woman to be president of the Ann Arbor School Board, in 1896. She was also the president of the Charitable Union and on the boards of the Ladies' Library Association and the YWCA. In 1900 Bach founded the Old Ladies' Home Society to raise money for a women's retirement home in Ann Arbor that opened in 1909, was named the Anna Botsford Bach Home in 1919, and moved to its present location in 1927. **Emma Eliza Bower**, editor of the <u>Washtenaw County Democrat</u>, was elected to the Ann Arbor School Board in 1894 and as president in 1899. **Sarah Bishop** was the first woman elected to the Ann Arbor School Board in 1883. (See **Bishop, Sarah** and **Bower, Emma Eliza**) Ref.: 11 (67); 124; 203

BALL, LUCY (1861-1936), of Grand Rapids; co-founder of the Grand Rapids Historical Society in 1894; first professionally-trained head librarian for the first public library in Grand Rapids; organizer of the library's card catalog system and, in 1894, the School District Libraries in the Grand Rapids schools. Ball, youngest daughter of Grand Rapids pioneer John Ball, began as an assistant at the Grand Rapids Public Library in 1886. She graduated in c. 1890 from Library School in Albany, New York, and served as head librarian in Grand Rapids from 1891 until 1900. Ref.: 136; 183

BALLARD, L. ANNE (1848-c. 1938), of Lansing; co-founder of the Lansing Medical Society in 1882. Ballard, a physician and surgeon, served the Society as director for seven years and as president for one year. She attended Abigail Rogers' Female College in Lansing and taught school for two years before entering Women's Medical College of Chicago. (See **Rogers, Abigail** in <u>Michigan Women: Firsts and Founders,</u> Vol. I.) Ballard received her medical degree in 1878 and established her practice at Lansing the following year. She was also active in the Lansing Industrial Aid Society, the Lansing Women's Club, the WCTU and the YWCA. In 1887 she led a successful drive for changing state legislation to raise the "age of consent" from ten to fourteen. Ref.: 104 (1)

BALYEAT, MABEL LANDIS (1883-1985), of Grand Rapids; founder and first president of the Kent County Library System in 1934. She devised a "library system" to provide books for rural school children and began the first library with a handful of books displayed at the Grand Rapids YMCA. Balyeat then convinced the Depression-era Federal Emergency Relief Administration to provide funding for space and utilities, a supervisor and seven librarians. "Book Showers" stocked the library shelves and family member-ships were available for a dozen eggs. Within three years the Kent County Library Association had 23 branches throughout the county and was one of just three such library systems in the country. In 1936 the Kent County board of supervisors officially recognized the association and formed a five-member board, including Balyeat, who served as president until her retirement in 1946. Fifty years after its humble beginnings, the Kent County Library System boasted the highest circulation of any library in Michigan, allocated the highest percentage of its annual budget for new books and materials, and held the fourth largest collection in the state. Ref.: 41 (May 16, 1984); 136; 183

****

"LET OUR MOTHERS VOTE"
1918 Labor Day Parade Banner
Grand Rapids Equal Franchise Club

****

BANYAI, PAULINE ILLICH (1920-1992), of Madison Heights; co-founder of the Michigan Hosta Society; developer of the "Gold Standard" hosta variety. A certified Master Gardener, Banyai was active in the Royal Oak Farmers Market since the 1940s. She was a charter member of the American Hosta Society and was known as "the Hosta Lady," because of her success in developing award-winning varieties of hosta, including the popular "Gold Standard." At times her garden contained as many as 200 hosta plants. Ref.: 22 (Jun. 11, 1988, 1B; Dec. 22, 1992, 18A; Jul. 4, 1993, 1J)

BARBER, MARY ISABEL (1887-1963), of Battle Creek; founder in 1923 and director for 25 years of the Kellogg Company's Home Economics Department; hosted the first in-flight airline passenger meals in 1930; first person named to the National Home Economists in Business Hall of Fame; first "dollar-a-year" woman in the nation during World War II, appointed in 1941 as Food Consultant to the Quartermaster Corps, to assist with menu planning for the U. S. Army, and as Expert Food Consultant to the Secretary of War. In 1953 she was appointed to the National Advisory Committee on Women in the Armed Services. A native of Pennsylvania, Barber graduated from Drexel Institute in Philadelphia and in 1920 from Columbia University, where she then taught dietetics. She was hired by W. K. and John L. Kellogg in 1923 to organize a Home Economics Department and to incorporate scientific information into Kellogg's advertising and recipes. On April 8, 1930, during a flight on Ford Motor Company's "Tin Goose" trimotor plane, Barber supervised the serving of the first airline passenger meals, provided by the Kellogg Company, to 15 presidents of Detroit women's organizations. A nationally-known dietician, she served as president of the American Dietetic Association, Michigan Dietetic Association, and Michigan Home Economics Association, and as vice president of the American Home Economics Association. She received an honorary doctorate from Drexel Institute in 1942, the Emblem for Exceptional Civilian Service from the U. S. Army in 1945, and the Marjorie Hulsizer Copher Award from the ADA in 1956. Ref.: 61 (272-275); 122

BARFIELD, CLEMENTINE, of Detroit; founder in 1987 of Save Our Sons And Daughters (SOSAD), an organization to eliminate the causes of youth violence and to aid families of the city's victims of violence. After her own sixteen-year-old son was shot and killed in 1987, Barfield turned her grief into a mission of protecting other young people through violence prevention training, anti-gun and anti-drug campaigns, and victim advocacy programs, as well as offering grief counseling and bereavement support. She is a graduate of Wayne State University. Ref.: 4 (September 3, 1994, A6); 117 (Summer 1993, 14-15)

BARNES, AMANDA WATSON FLEMING (1825-1921), of Lansing; co-founder in 1875 of the Ladies' Library and Literary Association, which helped to establish Lansing's first public library in 1882; co-founder in 1896 of the Women's Hospital Association, the parent organization of Lansing's Sparrow Hospital. Born in Romulus, New York, she came to Michigan in a covered wagon with her family in 1844, settling on a farm near Albion. After her marriage in 1852 to Orlando M. Barnes, the couple lived in Mason until 1875, when they moved to Lansing, where Orlando became a prominent lawyer, legislator and mayor. The Ladies' Library and Literary Association was originally formed to maintain a library for its members. Barnes addressed the Michigan legislature for permission to purchase property on the Capitol grounds but her request was denied. The library was housed in various rented locations until 1882, when the Association offered its books to the Lansing school district on condition that a free public library be established. The Women's Hospital Association opened a hospital in 1896, after Lansing had been without a hospital for three years. Barnes, as president of the Association in 1899, appealed to the "generous men of the community" to help with the construction and equipment of a new hospital. She was also a member of the U and I Club and the Lansing Woman's Club, which she served as president. Ref.: 48 (Vol. 3, 542); 57 (Oct. 26, 1921); 74 (Jul./Aug. 1986, 18-23); 170

BARNEY, VIOLET JANE LOCKWOOD, of Ann Arbor; founder of a Michigan Department of Public Health program to train and register all nursing home aides in the state and to combine community volunteer service with nursing home administration; founder of the Community Councils Association (CCA), a non-profit organization that trains nursing home volunteers and supports community councils at nursing homes. Born in Boston, Barney graduated from Wellesley College and Union Theological Seminary. After twenty years with the Episcopal Diocese in New Hampshire, she and her husband came to Michigan in 1956 to work at the Parishfield Community, where Episcopal laypersons receive training. Following a move to Ann Arbor, she earned a master's degree in Social Work and a Specialist in Aging Certificate in 1970 from the University of Michigan, where she joined the U-M Institute of Gerontology as liaison to organizations concerned with aging issues and as co-director of the Pilot Geriatric Arthritis Program. Barney received an award from the American College of Health Care Administration for her contributions to improved nursing home care. Ref.: 184

BARSAMIAN, GLADYS, of Detroit; founder of the Wayne County Juvenile Court's Youth Assistance Program for children at risk of becoming delinquent, a diversion program for shoplifters, the court's Citizen's Advisory Council and an intensive probation program. Barsamian served as judge in the Wayne County Juvenile Court for eighteen years before her retirement in 1992. She was among the first lawyers in Michigan to specialize in juvenile court work during the 1960s, when the United States Supreme Court gave abused, neglected or delinquent children the right to be represented by an attorney in juvenile or family court hearings. She co-authored court rules for probate judges statewide to use in cases of abuse and neglect. Barsamian has served on the boards of the YMCA of Metropolitan Detroit, Aurora Hospital (a private psychiatric hospital for children and young adults), the Wayne County Children and Youth Initiative, United Community Services, the Boys and Girls Club of Southeastern Michigan, and the Michigan Women's Forum. She has also been active in the Armenian community. Ref.: 22 (Dec. 1, 1992, 3A)

BARTHWELL, GLADYS WHITFIELD (c.1906-1993), of Detroit; co-founder of the Delta Home for Girls, while president of the Detroit chapter of Delta Sigma Theta. A native of Greensboro, North Carolina, where she graduated from Bennett College, Barthwell earned her master's degree in education from the University of Michigan. She and her husband Sidney were African American pioneers in Detroit retailing, at one time owning thirteen stores and an ice cream company that gave employment to many people. After earning her master's degree in library science from Wayne State University, she worked as a Detroit Public Schools librarian until her retirement. Barthwell was a lifetime member of the NAACP and was active in numerous organizations, including Girl Scouts, Cub

Scouts and her church. An advocate of the arts, she organized trips to the opera and theater for her community. Ref.: 22 (Feb. 25, 1993, 4B)

BATES, M. E. CRAM (first name not known) (1839-1905), of Traverse City; co-founder of the Ladies' Library Association of Traverse City in 1869. Born in Northville, Cram moved with her parents to Traverse City in 1863. After her marriage to Thomas Bates in 1867, she and her husband edited the <u>Grand Traverse Herald</u>, for which she was the associate editor. She also edited the Home and Sunshine departments of the paper. Ref.: 116 (71)

BATES, MRS. MORGAN (first name not known) (d. 1872), of Traverse City; co-founder and leader of the Ladies' Library Association of Traverse City in 1869. Bates, the wife of the lieutenant governor of Michigan, called eight women together to form the Association. Known for her organizational abilities and resourcefulness, she was undaunted when a hundred-pound squash was presented as a joke to the Association. Bates turned the squash into many pies, announced a squash pie social at her home, and raised twenty dollars for the Association through the event. Eventually the Association raised enough funds to build and stock a brick library building. Ref.: 116 (25)

****

The suffragette is a peaceful suffragist grown despairing and aggressive, and so many are there of her that she forms a union or political party of over 100,000 members."

Clara B. Arthur of Detroit

****

BATES, OCTAVIA W. (d. 1911), of Detroit; first and only American delegate to speak at the International Council of Women at London in 1899. Bates' address on "Women and the Law" prompted great public discussion and was reprinted in nearly every city newspaper in Europe and America. The London papers reported that Queen Victoria, who invited her to the palace for tea and questioning, "was deeply impressed with the spirit of progressiveness of American women." Bates, who received an A.B. in 1877 and a law degree in 1896 from the University of Michigan, bequeathed sizeable portions of her estate to the U-M Law Library and Literary Department. She was also active in the Woman Suffrage Movement. Ref.: 68 (77)

BECKER, AGNES JANE GRAY (1889-1983), of Saginaw; co-founder of the Saginaw County Health Unit, with Dr. U. K. Volk and Ottilia Frisch, in the 1930s. Becker was president of the Otto Roeser School PTA (1920s), Bridgeport Village School PTA (1920s), and Saginaw County PTA, charter member and president of the Saginaw County Crippled Children's Society, volunteer camp director of the Saginaw County Crippled Children's Summer Camp Program from the 1930s to 1950, and founder in 1950 of the "Second Wind Club," a senior citizens group at St. John's Episcopal Church. She was also active in the Boy Scouts, Campfire Girls, Home Extension Club, 4H work, and the Bridgeport Order of the Eastern Star. She served as Matron at the Home for the Aged in Saginaw from 1950 until 1959. Ref.: 165

BECKER, CRISTIE J., of Troy; first woman in Michigan to be a pediatric diagnostic interventional radiologist, in 1987. An interventional radiologist uses x-rays to both diagnose and begin immediate treatment of medical problems. A 1983 graduate of Wayne State University Medical School, where she is an assistant professor, Becker is affiliated with Children's Hospital of Michigan in Detroit. Ref.: 127

BELL, MARY L. TEAKS (1901-1995), of Detroit; owner, president and chair of the first black-owned and operated broadcasting company to be licensed by the Federal Communications Commission, the Bell Broadcasting Co., which established WCHB-AM in Inkster in 1956 and WCHD-FM (now WJZZ-FM) in Detroit in 1960. A native of Tennessee, Bell came to Detroit in 1922. She inherited her husband Haley Bell's controlling interest in the company in 1973. Known for her support of many charitable and civic causes, Bell was involved especially with the United Negro College Fund and the NAACP. She served on the boards of several national organizations, including the World Wide Council of the YWCA. In 1994 she was inducted into the International Heritage Hall of Fame at Cobo Center, in recognition of her contribution to international and multicultural understanding in the community as a whole. Ref.: 22 (May 25, 1994, 2B; Mar. 28, 1995, 2B)

BENANE, ANNA (dates not known), of Iron River; first teacher at the Nash School at Iron River, in 1894. Because seven children were required to open a school, four-year-old Amie Nash was enrolled to fill the quota. Ref.: 34 (109)

BERGH, IDA JARVE (1889-1972), of Eagle River; first woman to be sheriff of Keweenaw County, from 1939 to 1946. Born in White City, she attended school at the quarry town of Jacobsville, and then taught lower grades there and at the fishing village of Betsy. After her marriage to commercial fisherman William Bergh, they moved to Bete Gris and then to Copper Harbor. When William was elected as sheriff of Keweenaw County, they relocated their family to Eagle River. Ida was appointed to finish out William's term when he died in January of 1939. She was then re-elected for three more terms, during which she applied her philosophy of kindness and cleanliness to the courthouse and jail, which were kept spotless. During her tenure the crime rate for Keweenaw County declined, due perhaps to the great respect given to Ida Bergh. Ref.: 35 (147-148); 149

BERGT, MARILYN, of Detroit; co-founder in 1983 of Wellness Networks, the first and largest volunteer-based AIDS service organization in Michigan; co-founder in 1988 of the AIDS Interfaith Network, an agency to provide spiritual counsel to people with AIDS and guidance for clergy and congregations in dealing with the disease. Bergt, a Catholic nun, serves as co-chair of the Aids Community Alliance, an association of eight Detroit AIDS organizations. A Detroit native, she joined the Sisters of Divine Providence in 1963 and lived for many years in its community at Pittsburgh, where she taught high school biology. She returned to Detroit in 1982 to staff the Newman Center at Wayne State University. After helping to lead a seminar on human sexuality, she was asked to join others in forming an organization that would help those afflicted with the newly-named AIDS disease. The founders and first board of the Wellness Networks included Bergt, an infectious disease doctor and eight others, mostly gay men. She became president of the board in 1986. Her experience with AIDS patients and concern for their relationship with religious organizations led her to found the AIDS Interfaith Network.
Ref.: 22 (Nov. 28, 1993, 1F, 4F)

BERNHARDT, MARCIA WEBSTER, of Caspian; founder and first co-chair of annual art shows, begun in 1958; co-founder of the Iron County Historical and Museum Society in 1962; first curator of the Iron County Museum, 1968 to the present; co-founder in 1985 of the Northland Historical Consortium, comprised of over 40 historical organizations from the Western Upper Peninsula and Northern Wisconsin; first woman in the Upper Peninsula to win an ATHENA Award, in 1986; co-founder of the Iron County Writers' Guild in 1991. She has also served as exhibits coordinator, newsletter editor, publicity chair and researcher for the Iron County Historical and Museum Society. As a high school English and Humanities teacher, Bernhardt has produced and directed plays and films with her students. She has written or edited numerous historical books, pamphlets, and feature articles for newspapers. She has been an officer of the West Iron County Youth Center, Iron County Library Board, West Iron District Library, Twentieth Century Women's Club, and Delta Kappa Gamma educational society, a member of the Michigan Museums Association, Historical Society of Michigan, MEA and NEA, advisor and pageant director for the Junior Historical Society, chair of Ferrous Frolics (a local arts fair), tour leader for Clark University's program of European travel for High School Students, and director of the Historic Sites Survey for Iron County. In 1984 she chaired the Carrie Jacobs-Bond House Committee which raised funds to restore the home and establish programs in recognition of the Michigan composer. (See **Jacobs-Bond, Carrie**) In 1971 Bernhardt was named "Community Minded Woman of the Year" by the Twentieth Century Women's Club and in 1980, with her husband Harold O. Bernhardt, she received the Charles Follo Award from the Historical Society of Michigan for preserving Upper Peninsula history. In 1993 she was elected the

U.P. Writers' Association "Writer of the Year." Ref.: 34 (353-354); 128

BETTS, KATRINA, of Milan; youngest member of the USA Women's Wrestling team to compete at the first international Klippan Cup tournament, held in Sweden in 1994. Eleven-year-old Betts won four consecutive matches to capture a Junior Division (35 kg weight class) title and gold medal. The daughter of former wrestling champion Mike Betts, she has been winning wrestling matches against both girls and boys since she was six years old. (The Amateur Athletic Union or USA Wrestling do not yet separate wrestlers by gender, as is done in Europe.) Also at the Klippen Cup tournament, two-time world champion wrestler **Patricia McNaughton Saunders**, formerly of Ann Arbor, took a gold medal in the 50 kg weight class (see **Saunders, Patricia McNaughton**). Ref.: 4 (Mar. 2, 1994, D5; Apr. 22, 1994, B1)

****

"If my cup won't hold but a pint, and yours holds a quart, wouldn't ye be mean not to let me have my little half measure full?"

Sojourner Truth of Battle Creek, 1851

****

BIGNELL, ANN H., of Howell; first woman to both own and manage a radio station in Michigan, WHMI-AM in Howell in 1961. After she and her husband Frank bought the station, Bignell served as vice president and worked in the news and sales departments until his death in 1972. She then became president and general manager, positions she held until she sold the station in 1989. She added an FM frequency in 1977 and constructed a new building to house the two stations. Bignell was the first woman to complete the National Association of Broadcasters' management course in the early 1970s. In 1984 she became the first woman to be president of the Howell Chamber of Commerce and the first woman to be named their Citizen of the Year. She was also the first woman to head the Howell United Way Campaign and the first woman to be a member of the Howell Rotary Club. In 1987 she received the first Life Achievement Award given by the Detroit Chapter of American Women in Radio and Television. Bignell has also served on the Livingston County Mental Health Board, and the boards of the Livingston Area Council Against Spouse Abuse, Livingston Community Food Bank and McPherson Community Health Center. Ref.: 58 (Jun. 10, 1987)

BIRMINGHAM, EMILY M., see **GREENWOOD, MABEL S.**

BISHOP, SARAH (dates not known), of Ann Arbor; first woman elected to the Ann Arbor School Board, in 1883. Women property owners had received the right to vote in Michigan school elections in 1881. Many new women voters joined the Prohibition party, which supported women's rights and gave women full power in its councils. This alliance of women voters and Prohibitionists helped elect Sarah Bishop and other women to school boards in Michigan. Ref.: 12 (66)

BLACK, CAMILLE, of Lansing; swimmer who set a new world record of 1:54.79 and won a gold medal in the 100-meter breaststroke at the 1992 Paralympic Games held at Barcelona, Spain. Black also won a silver medal in the 50-meter freestyle, fourth place as a member of the 4x50 freestyle relay, and fifth place in the 100-meter freestyle. The Paralympics Games is an international competition for paraplegics, quadriplegics, amputees and athletes with cerebral palsy. Black is a dwarf due to achondroplasia, a genetic disability. The 1992 competition was her first try at the Paralympic Games, held every four years since 1960 in conjunction with the Olympics. Ref.: 57 (1992, 1C)

BLACKWELL, CATHERINE CARTER, of Detroit; founder of the African American Studies program for the Detroit Public Schools, which she incorporated into her teaching career from 1960 to 1994. A graduate of Howard University with a master's degree in social work and an internationally recognized authority on Africa, Blackwell was an African/African-American Instructional Specialist in the Department of Social Studies of the Detroit Public Schools at the time of her retirement. She has traveled to Africa 60 times, earning the unofficial title of "Detroit's Ambassador to Africa." The Detroit Board of Education has recognized her contributions to education by naming one of its schools the Catherine C. Blackwell Institute of International Studies, Commerce and Technology. She was inducted into the Michigan Women's Hall of Fame in 1993. Ref.: 22 (Oct. 7, 1994, 3D); 25 (Oct. 24, 1993, 1A, 12A)

BLAQUIERE, THERESA, of Detroit; founder and director of the non-profit Core City Neighborhoods group on Detroit's west side in 1984. Core City serves a three and one-half square mile area, bounded by West Grand, Martin Luther King and Rosa Parks Boulevards. The group organizes community projects such as cleaning vacant lots and patrolling the neighborhood on Devil's Night. It also rehabilitates buildings for rental units and develops new rental units. To finance the rehabilitation of 37 rental units in 1992, Blaquiere and her staff raised $2.04 million from state and city loans, banks, religious and charitable groups, and foundation support. Ref.: 22 (Dec. 17, 1992, 12F)

BOLDI, LANA, of Kentwood; first woman to be a skilled trades apprentice at General Motors' Fisher Body plant in Kalamazoo, as well as in all of General Motors Corporation, in 1972; first woman officer in Local #488 of the United Auto Workers. Boldi began on the assembly line at Fisher Body in the early 1970s, after stints as a model, as the first woman to be a Reno casino dealer, and as a bartender. She became a journeyman in welding, equipment maintenance and repair and is now an International Representative and Education/Community Action Program coordinator of United Auto Workers for Region 1-D in Grand Rapids. A graduate of

Western Michigan University, Boldi has served since 1989 on its
Board of Trustees, became vice chair in 1994, and was named
chair of the Board in 1995. Ref.: 84 (Nov. 11-16, 1994, 2; Apr. 2-
15, 1995, 10)

BOLT, MILDRED A. (d. 1922), of Detroit; founder and principal of
the Detroit School of Expression in 1888; founder and first director
of the Shakespeare Study Club, from 1906 to 1922. Bolt studied
elocution (public speaking) with Moses True Brown of Boston,
S. H. Clarke at the University of Chicago, and **Edna Chaffee Noble**
at the Detroit Training School of Elocution and English Literature.
(See **Noble, Edna Chaffee** in Michigan Women: Firsts and
Founders, Vol. I.) Bolt's school offered lessons in elocution,
English literature, philosophy, voice training, dramatic reading,
physical culture, deportment, calisthenics and general literature.
Ref.: 19 (Vol. 15, Sept. 1922, 20); 20 (167, 209); 45 (39)

BONDE, DEBRA, of Livonia; founder and director of Seedlings, a
nonprofit publishing business that specializes in affordable Braille
books for blind children. Bonde, who took a course in Braille at
the Grosse Pointe War Memorial, began her business in 1984,
operating in her home. By 1991 the company was based at the
Bentley Center in Livonia and was selling thousands of books in
the United States and ten other countries. Other Braille publishers
in the country tend to print expensive textbooks and classics.
Operating with grants and donations, Bonde is able to print popular
children's books for comparatively low prices, using a Braille
computer printer, two part-time employees and many volunteers.
The company's name was chosen because of the similarity of Braille
dots to seeds. Bonde compares putting a book in a child's hand to
planting a seed. Ref.: 23 (Jun. 22, 1992, 5F)

BONNEMA, MARGUERITE, of Grand Rapids; co-founder with **MARY
DE BOER VANDEN BOSCH** of the Bethany Christian Home (for
children), at Grand Rapids in 1944. Bonnema, a nurse from
Cleveland, and De Boer, from Denver, were students at the
Reformed Bible Institute in Grand Rapids when they decided to
establish a home for homeless children. Bethany Christian Home
was begun in 1944 and incorporated in 1945. The original single
home has now become Bethany Christian Services, with offices in
58 locations nationwide, a staff of 390 and a 1994 budget of over
$18 million. Its focus is now on adoptions, assistance to pregnant
women, foster care, and family counseling. Ref.: 125; 136; 183

BOVING, RENEE LAYA, see **TILLEY, BARBARA**

BOWER, EMMA ELIZA (1849-1937), of Ann Arbor; first woman to be
owner and editor of the Washtenaw County Democrat, succeeding
her father and brother in 1888. A graduate of the University of
Michigan medical school in 1883, Bower practiced medicine in
Detroit until 1888. In 1893 she was elected Great Record Keeper of
the Ladies of the Maccabees, serving until 1929. In 1894 she was

elected to the Ann Arbor School Board, serving as its president in
1899. (See **Bach, Anna Botsford**) Bower was a member of the Old
Ladies' Home Society and was president of the Michigan Women's
Press Association, Honorary Supreme Commander of the
Maccabees, and active in the Woman Suffrage Movement.
Ref.: 203: 204 (Box 2)

BOYNTON, MARCIA, see **FERGUSON, JOAN**

BOYSE, ALICE (1911-1995), of Clio; first woman elected to the Clio
City Commission, in 1973. Before her appointment to the
Commission in 1972, Boyse had retired after 41 years of teaching
Latin and English at Clio High School. In 1989 she was appointed
mayor, a post she held until her death. Ref.: 22 (Apr. 5, 1995, 2B)

****

"Around me I saw women overworked and underpaid,
not because their work was inferior but because they were women.
With all my heart I joined the crusade for 'equal rights.' "

Anna Howard Shaw of Big Rapids

****

BRATER, ELIZABETH S., of Ann Arbor; first woman elected as
mayor of Ann Arbor, serving from 1991 to 1993; founder in 1991 of
the Washtenaw County Chief Elected Officials Intergovernmental
Summit, a bimonthly meeting of mayors, township supervisors and
village presidents. A graduate of the University of Pennsylvania
with degrees in History and American Civilization, she has been a
lecturer in English and in Public Policy at the University of
Michigan. Brater was first elected to the Ann Arbor City Council in
1988. In 1994 she was elected from the 53rd District to the
Michigan House of Representatives, where she serves on the Mental
Health, Higher Education, and Conservation, Environment and
Great Lakes committees.   She was chair of the U.S. Conference of
Mayors Advisory Council on Composting in 1992 and has served
on numerous other governmental and political committees and
boards. Ref.: 1 (Mar. 1993, 1); 130

BRAWN WAY, JULIA TOBY (1816-1889), of Bay City; first woman to
be keeper of the Bay City lighthouse at the mouth of the Saginaw
River, from 1873 to 1889. A native of Hallowell, Maine, Brawn
moved to Bay City with her husband Peter and their family in 1864,
to care for the lighthouse. Because her husband was crippled, she
was responsible for much of the work involved. After her
husband's death in 1873, she continued as lighthouse keeper, with
the help of her son. Although she married George Way, a Great
Lakes pilot, in 1875, Brawn Way kept the Bay City lighthouse until
her death in 1889. Ref.: 121 (6)

BREITUNG, CHARLOTTE GRAVERAET KAUFMAN (1876-1936), of
Marquette; co-founder of the Seamen's Church Institute of New York
City, the YWCA of New York City, and the New York Orthopedic

Dispensary and Hospital; donor of the first automobile ambulance equipped with X-ray to the United States Army in France, accepted by General John J. Pershing; sponsor and producer of more than twenty successful New York plays (including "Good Luck Sam" and "Yip, Yip, Yaphank") to raise funds for families of U.S. soldiers awaiting transportation to Europe; founder of a club for sailors of all the Allied nations; organizer of many social events to honor groups of American officers departing for France; sponsor and patron of benefits for needy music and art students. The League of the Allies awarded her the Carter Gold Bag in 1917 in recognition of her wartime work. She was also honored by the Italian government for her service to the Italian Red Cross during the war. A native of Marquette, she moved to New York City after her 1892 marriage to Edward Breitung, a mining engineer, banker and owner of many shipping firms. When her husband died in 1924, she gave up her social activity to take over his shipping business, which was failing due to wartime shipping losses. Within two years she had restored the business to solvency. Breitung was also active in the Woman Suffrage Movement, serving in 1915 as the first chair of the Michigan Branch of the Congressional Union, which later became the National Woman's Party. Ref.: 193

BREWER, MABEL E. OVERETT (1884-1985), of Stambaugh; first Matron at the Wakefield Hospital; first matron at the Stambaugh General Hospital, in 1931. Born in Surrey, England, she received her nurses training, including midwifery, in England. As Mabel Overett, she worked in London hospitals, became a British Army nurse, and served in Turkey and Germany during World War I. After coming to this country, she served on the staff at St. Luke's Hospital in Duluth, before coming to Michigan where she was the first matron at the hospital in Wakefield until moving to Stambaugh. During those early years, a matron was head of the hospital staff and lived at the hospital, along with some of the nurses. Overett was known for her English tea table set with her finest linen and china. During her stay at Stambaugh, she delivered most of the babies in the county. She continued her work at the hospital until she married William Brewer, who also was from England. Ref.: 34 (228); 128

BRODBENT, MILDRED CAROLYNE YOUNG, formerly of Fowlerville; first woman to become a member of the American Legion Post at Hulbert, in 1976; first woman to be Commander of Devereaux Post 141 of the American Legion at Howell, in 1985. A native of Milwaukee, she joined the U.S. Air Force in 1950 and served until 1951, the year of her marriage. She came to Michigan in 1952. As Commander of Post 141, she established the Robert E. Myers Award given to outstanding members and emphasized the meaning of Flag Day. In 1989 she received an Associate Degree in Applied Science from Oakland Community College. Ref.: 131

BROWN, ESTHER M. LYNCH, of Howell; first woman to be elected mayor of Howell, serving two terms from 1985 to 1989; founder of the Howell City Farmers Market in 1979. A native of Ann Arbor, Brown moved to Howell in 1974 and was elected to the City Council in 1977. She has also served on many boards, including those of the Michigan Association of Mayors, LWV, Salvation Army of Livingston County and Howell Carnegie Library, in addition to serving as City Planning Commissioner, on the Livingston County Criminal Justice Council, and as chair of the Livingston County American Cancer Society, Livingston County United Way, and Michigan Municipal League, Region II. Ref.: 133

BROWN, JUDITH L. (JUDI), of East Lansing; first American woman to win a silver medal in the 400-meter hurdles at the Olympics, in 1984. As a track athlete at Michigan State University, Brown won twelve Big Ten championships, a 1983 NCAA Championship, and two Pan-Am gold medals. In 1987 she was named a Sports Illustrated Sportswoman of the Year. Since 1992 she has been the women's track and field coach at MSU and in 1995 was inducted into the MSU Athletics Hall of Fame. Ref.: 57 (Jun. 25, 1995, 1G)

BROWN, MARY CARNEY, of Kalamazoo; recipient of the first "Woman of the Year Award" from the Kalamazoo Women's Festival, in March of 1995. The annual award honors a woman who has demonstrated continued support for the advancement of women and sensitivity to women's issues. Brown served from 1977 to 1994 in the Michigan State House of Representatives, where her legislative work included gender equity legislation, family day care registration, school age parents' programs, a married women's property act, prohibition of probation in rape cases, expansions of the displaced homemaker act and mandated consideration of retirement benefits in divorce settlements. A graduate of Syracuse University, she has taught at Western Michigan University. She is a member of the AAUW, Kalamazoo Area LWV, Kalamazoo Women's Network, Michigan Democratic Women's Caucus, and NOW. Brown has also been honored for advancing the status of women by the Women Lawyers Association of Michigan, the Michigan Association of Women Deans, Administrators and Counselors, the Kalamazoo Chapter of NOW, and the Kalamazoo YWCA. Ref.: 84 (Apr. 2-15, 1995, 10)

BRUNSON, ROSE T., GERTRUDE LEE and **INA MAJORS**, of Lansing; founders of the Lansing Association of Colored Women's Clubs, in 1945. The women's first goal was to provide a nursery school for the black community. With contributions from various groups and individuals such as R. E. Olds, they purchased a house to serve as both a nursery and clubhouse. It was the first group in the area to offer prenatal classes and among the first to provide dinners for senior citizens, in addition to a Sunday morning story hour for children, arts and crafts classes, teenage parties and community forums. In 1968 the group changed its name to the

Lansing Association of Women's Clubs. The Association, which now occupies a clubhouse on Butler Street, celebrated its 50th birthday in April of 1995. Ref.: 57 (Apr. 28, 1995, 3B); 98

BRYANT, AGNES HARDIE, of Detroit; co-founder, with her husband Warren, of the Detroit NAACP Youth Council, 1968; organizer of Women's Equality Day celebrations in Detroit, 1975 to 1986. A native of Springfield, Massachusetts, Bryant was the first woman in her family to receive a degree, from Howard University in Washington, D.C. In Detroit she headed the Consumer Research Advisory Council and the Detroit Water Department, before her appointment in 1975 as head of the city's Human Rights Department, where her responsibilities included Women's Equality Day celebrations. In 1968, as vice president of the local NAACP chapter, she formed a committee for consumer education in low-income communities. An activist for peace and justice, she served for seven years as president of the local Women's International League for Peace and Freedom and as a member of the national board. She is also active in the YWCA, the LWV, the Women's Economic Club of Detroit, the Women's Conference of Concerns and the Women's Forum. Ref.: 22 (Aug. 26, 1993, 1C, 4C)

****

"VOTE for Woman Suffrage, FIGHT for Democracy at Home."

Suffrage poster during World War I

****

BUCHALTER, ALICE, of Freeland; founder of a gymnastics program at Freeland High School in 1969. She started the program because there were no sports for girls in the community. Since 1974, either her team or one of her individual gymnasts has reached the state finals every year. Her girls' gymnastic team won the 1983 and 1985 state championships, one girl (Jamie Nieman) became a national high school individual champion in 1988, and Buchalter has been Michigan high school Coach of the Year three times and national Coach of the Year twice. Ref.: 22 (Jan. 31, 1994, C8)

BULSON, FLORENCE BRECK (1857-1924), of Jackson; founder of the Jackson County Federation of Women's Clubs, in 1914. A graduate of Paw Paw High School and Ypsilanti Normal School (now Eastern Michigan University), she moved to Jackson after her marriage to Albert Bulson. In 1896 she became president of the Jackson Tourist Club, which she was instrumental in renaming the Jackson Woman's Club. Bulson served as secretary of the Michigan State Federation of Women's Clubs from 1897 to 1898, as its director from 1898 to 1900, and designed the Michigan Federation pin adopted officially at the Fifth Annual meeting in Jackson in 1899. She also served as vice president of the State Federation from 1914 to 1916 and as president from 1916 to 1919. In addition, she was a member of the Commission on National Defense for Michigan, the War Preparedness Commission, the

Women's Liberty Loan Committee and the DAR, and assisted in organizing Red Cross units. She was also active in the Woman Suffrage Movement. Ref.: 49 (193)

BURDICK, WINIFRED G., see **GREENWOOD, MABEL S.**

BURGESS, LAUREN COOK, formerly of Grand Rapids; first woman to portray a male Confederate soldier in a 1989 re-enactment of the 1862 Battle of Antietam at Sharpsburg, Maryland. When Burgess, a Civil War historian, was seen coming out of the women's restroom, she was told by National Park Service officials that she was not allowed to portray a male soldier because they wanted to preserve the authenticity of the original battle. Knowing that many women disguised as men fought in the Civil War, including at least five at Antietam, she sued the National Park Service for sexual discrimination and won. A federal judge ruled in 1993 that individuals could not be prohibited from participating in Living History events at Antietam "because of their gender." Burgess, now living in Fayetteville, North Carolina, is the editor of The Uncommon Soldier, a collection of letters written by Sarah Rosetta Wakeman to her New York family, while she was disguised as Union Army private Lyons Wakeman. (The first Michigan woman who fought in the Civil War as a male soldier was **Sarah Emma Edmonds** of Flint. See Michigan Women: Firsts and Founders, Vol. I.) Ref.: 4 (Jul. 18, 1994, B2); 22 (Mar. 18, 1993, 18A); 108 (Jan. 1994, 96-104)

BURNS, FRANCES EMILY SANFORD (1866-1937), of St. Louis (Michigan) and Detroit; first woman to be elected head of any state fraternal congress, as president of the Michigan Fraternal Congress; founder of the Frances E. Burns Home in Alma, for aged women of the Maccabees organization. Born and raised in Ionia, she taught school in St. Louis, where she lived after her marriage to John Burns in 1887. Active in the Ladies of the Maccabees, she was elected Great Commander of the order in 1896 and re-elected at every convention until 1926, when the Ladies of the Maccabees merged with the men's Maccabees, after which she served as Assistant Supreme Commander of the Maccabees. Following the death of her husband, she moved to Detroit in 1926, where she continued active in the Maccabees throughout her life. Her dream of establishing a home for aged women members of the order was realized with the founding of the home at Alma. An ardent supporter of equal suffrage, Burns was a pioneer member of the National American Woman Suffrage Association and was present when Governor Albert E. Sleeper signed a bill granting presidential suffrage to Michigan women in 1917. She served many years on the State Committee of the Department of Public Health. She was also a member of the Michigan Women's Press Association, State Central Democratic Committee, OES, and Women's Benefit Association, and was president of the Michigan Federation of Women's Clubs, recording secretary of the National Council of

Women, vice president of the National Fraternal Congress and treasurer of the Michigan Department in the Council of National Defense during World War I. Ref.: 110 (Nov. 25, 1937, 1)

BURTON, HARRIET GUILD (1813-1895), of Grand Rapids; member of the first pioneer family to remain with the Campau family in 1833, making Grand Rapids a permanent white settlement; first pioneer woman to marry in Grand Rapids, to Barney Burton on April 13, 1834; first pioneer woman to adopt a child, Keziah Lincoln, son of another early settler; co-founder and life member of the Union Benevolent Association, in 1848. (See **Campau, Sophie de Marsac**.)   Ref.: 136; 183

BUSBY, CLARA CALDWELL (1894-1994), of Lansing; co-founder of the United Mothers Club of Greater Lansing in 1929; first black woman hired by Reo Motor Car Company, where she worked as a police matron in the late 1930s; first black owner and operator of a Lansing women's shop, the West Side Apparel Shop, in the 1940s; with her husband, operated the first black full-service restaurant, the Black Forest Restaurant, in the 1950s; and was the first black licensed woman realtor in the Lansing area. A native of Mounds, Illinois, Busby and her husband came to Lansing in 1927. For many years the Busbys mentored hundreds of black people who migrated to the Lansing area. In the 1930s, they opened their home to black students at Michigan State College who could not find places to live. When black laborers could not get housing, the Busbys bought and renovated homes for them, often allowing the renters to stay free until they had steady work. In 1955 the local African Methodist Episcopal Church honored Clara Busby for providing decent housing to the black community. In 1957, at age 62, she was ordained as a minister in the AME Church, founded Oak Grove Community Church and served as its pastor for over two decades. As president of the Greater Lansing United Mothers Club in 1970, Busby led a drive to send 1550 pounds of clothing to flood victims in Fayette, Mississippi, and persuaded Oldsmobile to provide trucks for transport. She was honored by the Wolverine State Baptist Convention as the Humanitarian of the Year in 1982. Ref.: 57 (Jul. 28, 1994, 2B; Jul. 29, 1994, 2B)

BUSH, ELIZA POWELL (dates not known) of Lansing; teacher of the first school in Lansing, which opened in 1847 with ten pupils. The school building had one door and one window without glass, both needing to be propped open for light and air. A native of Oneida, New York, who had attended Olivet College, Eliza Powell was paid a salary of $2.00 per week, plus board. She married John Bush, a Lansing alderman. Ref.: 104 (2)

CALVERT-BAKER, GWENDOLYN, formerly of Ann Arbor; first woman and first African American to be president and chief executive officer of the U.S. Committee for UNICEF, appointed in 1993. Through education, immunization, medical and nutrition programs, UNICEF provides help to millions of children and women in developing countries. Calvert-Baker has begun a pilot program in Michigan to involve more schools in national UNICEF month, so that children can learn about and help children in other parts of the world. Formerly a second grade teacher at Ann Arbor's Wines School, she was executive director of the national YWCA for nine years before her appointment. Calvert-Baker holds bachelor's, master's and doctoral degrees in education from the University of Michigan, where she was an assistant professor and head of the affirmative action programs. She has also served as vice president and dean for graduate and children's programs at the Bank Street College for Education in New York City and director of the Minorities and Women's Program at the National Institute of Education in Washington, D.C. Appointed to the New York City school board in 1986, she was elected president of the board in 1990. Ref.: 4 (Jul. 21, 1993, C1); 84 (May 14-27, 1995, 7, 14)

CAMPAU, SOPHIE DE MARSAC (1807-1869), of Grand Rapids; first pioneer white woman on the site that became Grand Rapids, in 1827. She assisted in the operation of the first trading post in Grand Rapids and welcomed new settlers from the East into her home. Ref.: 136; 183

****
"WHO CAN'T VOTE! Children, Insane, Idiots, Aliens, Criminals
and Women. IS THAT A SQUARE DEAL FOR WOMEN?

Poster used by the Michigan Equal
Suffrage Association in their 1918 campaign
****

CAMPBELL EAGLESFIELD, CARINA BULKLEY (b. 1855), of Monroe; co-founder in 1883 and first president of Friends in Council, a women's club in Monroe organized "to develop and maintain interest in reading and study and to assist in the general cultural advancement of the community." Campbell, who graduated from the University of Michigan in 1879, married and moved to Indianapolis in 1885. Among the nineteen founders were **Emily Lewis**, who originated the idea, and **Josephine McBride Van Miller**, who succeeded Campbell as second president. Strict club rules limited membership to thirty and required research, social or officer assignments. Friends in Council, which celebrated its centennial in September of 1983, has met continuously since its founding. Ref.: 145

CAMPBELL, JEAN WINTER, of Ann Arbor; founder and first director of the University of Michigan Center for the Continuing Education of Women (now known as the Center for the Education of Women), in 1964. Born in Chicago, Campbell earned degrees in science and education from Northwestern University before coming to Ann Arbor in 1946. In the 1960s she saw the need for a continuing education program to prepare women for professional and occupational fields and also help them balance their work schedule and private lives. The Center was the first in the United States to combine direct services, advocacy and research. Under Campbell's leadership, it has helped thousands achieve educational and career goals, provided research on issues related to women, and promoted reforms in the work place, such as part-time and flexible work schedules. Campbell, who retired in 1985, was inducted into the Michigan Women's Hall of Fame in 1993. Ref.: 184

CAMPBELL, LOUISE (dates not known), of East Lansing; founder of the first annual Farm Women's Week at Michigan Agricultural College (now Michigan State University), in 1928. As the Home Demonstration Leader at MAC from 1921 to 1930, she expanded and strengthened the MAC Cooperative Extension program in home economics. The first Farm Women's Week brought 200 farm women to campus for lectures on home management, health, citizenship, and farm economics. Eventually the event developed into the present College Week for Women, which includes programs for many women. Campbell Hall on the MSU campus was named in her honor. Ref.: 102

CARGO, RUTH (1893-1974), of Adrian; first woman to serve on the Adrian City Commission, in 1957. She began teaching home economics at Adrian College in 1920, then switched to teaching government and history in the 1940s. In 1955 she was asked to help design a new city charter, which led to a commission-city manager form of government. Elected to the new City Commission in 1957, Cargo continued to teach at Adrian College until 1961, when she retired from both teaching and city government. She received an honorary doctor of humanities degree from Adrian College, which in 1964 named Cargo Hall in her honor. Ref.: 21 (Mar. 31, 1990, 5); 177

CARLSON, ANNIE M. (dates not known), of Marquette County; first woman to be a lighthouse keeper at the Granite Island Light on Lake Superior, from 1903 to 1905. Ref.: 18 (163)

CARLTON, RUTH, of Detroit; originator of the Detroit News weekly series, "A Child is Waiting," which she began on August 18, 1968. Her Sunday column picturing children available for adoption, especially those hard to place, was the first regularly-appearing adoption column in the United States. Since its inception it has resulted in the adoption of hundreds of children and has influenced many hundreds of other adoptions. Her writing has led to reforms in state adoption procedures, including the revision of the Michigan Department of Social Services adoption policies and manual. She has also helped enact a state law providing for adoption subsidies and placement, so that many parents previously rejected for financial reasons are now able to adopt. She has helped other newspapers begin adoption columns and has been field consultant for the North American Center on Adoption in New York, working to create adoption agencies for hard-to-place children across the country. Carlton, a feature writer and news editor at the Detroit News for 26 years until her retirement in 1976, continued her Sunday adoption column until 1987. Among her awards are the Women in Communications national Headliner Award in 1970, the Michigan Citizen of the Year in 1972, and the Woman of Achievement Award in 1973 from the National Federation of Press Women. Carlton was inducted into the Michigan Women's Hall of Fame in 1994. Ref.: 184

CARLTON, S. B. (dates not known), of St. Joseph; first woman to be a lighthouse keeper at the St. Joseph's Light on Lake Michigan at the entrance of the St. Joseph River, replacing her husband, M. G. Carlton, in 1861. Ref.: 18 (164)

CARTER, BETTY (LILLIE MAE JONES), formerly of Detroit; founder of the Bet-Car label in 1969 for her own jazz singing; founder of the "Jazz Ahead" festival in 1992 at Brooklyn, New York, for young jazz musicians. Carter won a 1988 Grammy for her album, "Look What I Got," and received a $20,000 lifetime achievement award from the National Endowment of the Arts and the American Jazz Award in 1992. Born in Flint, she grew up in Detroit, where she won a talent show at the Paradise Theater in 1946. She sang with Lionel Hampton's band from 1948 to 1951, and has also worked with Miles Davis, Ray Charles, and other leading musicians. A resident of Brooklyn, New York, since 1948, Carter began the annual "Jazz Ahead" festival for young performers and helps young jazz musicians to develop their careers. Ref.: 22 (Sept. 14, 1990, C1; Sept. 4, 1992, C1)

CARTER, MARY L. (dates not known), of Alpena County; first school teacher in Alpena County, in School District 1 of Fremont Township in 1858. The school was housed in a small cooper shop made of rough boards, the best building available. She was the daughter of **Sarah L. Carter**. Ref.: 166

CARTER, SARAH L. (dates not known), of Alpena; co-founder of Alpena and first physician in Alpena County, where she practiced medicine from 1856 to 1862. Before coming to Alpena County, she had become skilled as a nurse and in the use of medicines. After her arrival, her services were continually in demand. She was the mother of **Mary L. Carter**. Ref.: 166; 204

CASSIN, CAROLYN FITZPATRICK, of Grosse Pointe Park; first director of Good Samaritan Hospice Care, a community program in Battle Creek, in 1981. Funded by the W.K. Kellogg Foundation, the program became nationally-known for quality care. She received a national leadership fellowship in 1984 from the Kellogg Foundation to study health-care systems around the world. In 1988 Cassin was appointed president and CEO of Hospice of Southeastern Michigan (HSEM), then approaching bankruptcy. Under her leadership the hospice was changed from a 48-bed hospital to a financially sound home-care program serving 460 persons a day. HSEM also operates the first residential hospice in the Midwest for AIDS patients. In recognition of her achievement, Cassin received the 1993 Executive of the Year Award given annually to the executive of a nonprofit organization by United Community Services of Metropolitan Detroit. She holds a BA in Political Science from Miami University in Ohio and an MA in Public Administration from Western Michigan University. Ref.: 22 (Jul. 4, 1993, M4)

CHALOU, MARGARET (PEGGY) RISK (1912-1995), of Harper Woods; first woman elected to the Harper Woods City Council, in 1951, serving until 1955. She had formerly been a police officer and public school teacher in Gratiot Township, and had operated a day care center until retiring in 1991. Ref.: 22 (Jan. 7, 1995, 7A)

CLARK, CHLOE A., see **CLARK, MARY H.**

CLARK, MARY H. (1813-1875), of Ann Arbor; co-founder, with her two sisters, **Chloe A. Clark** (1817-1880) and **Roby Clark**, of the Clark School, the first and best-known private boarding school in Ann Arbor, which operated from 1839 to 1875, using ideas from the school of Emma Willard in Troy, New York, where the three sisters were educated. A fourth sister, **Jessie**, was a pupil in the school, which was housed in several different buildings over the years. Two girls formed the first graduating class in 1841. By 1848 there were ninety-seven pupils, coming from Michigan cities and from other states. The school closed with the death of Mary Clark, its director. Ref.: 109 (113-121)

****
"MAKE MICHIGAN WOMEN REAL CITIZENS"
1918 Labor Day Parade Banner
Grand Rapids Equal Franchise Club
****

CLARK, ROBY, see **CLARK, MARY H.**

COBBIN, GLORIA, of Detroit; first African American woman to be president of the Detroit Board of Education, first elected in 1986 and re-elected twice. A 20-year member of the Board, representing District 2 in southwest Detroit, Cobbin has advocated education programs to benefit all children. She has also served as secretary-treasurer of the Metropolitan Detroit AFL-CIO and as international vice president of American Federation of State, County and Municipal Employees (AFSCME). Ref.: 22 (Mar. 29, 1994, 3B)

COHA, AMY L., formerly of Ypsilanti; one of the first two social workers (with **R. Hedy Nuriel**) to testify as an Expert Witness in court cases involving battered women, in 1983. As of 1995, she has qualified as an Expert Witness in more than 45 cases concerning battered women or child custody, often testifying at murder trials on behalf of women who had killed in self-defense. A graduate of the State University of New York and the University of Michigan, Coha served as director of Ann Arbor's Women's Crisis Center and as associate director of the Domestic Violence Project/SAFE House in Ann Arbor from 1983 to 1995. She is the co-author (with **Susan McGee** and **Kathleen Hagenian**) of Fighting for Justice for Battered Women: A Law and Advocacy Manual, published by the State of Michigan Domestic Violence Prevention and Treatment Board in 1991. Her work has been honored by tributes from the Michigan State Legislature and a NOW Achievement Award. Ref.: 4 (Oct. 6, 1989); 137

COLE, EDNA (dates not known), of Harrisville; first county librarian for Alcona County. After moving from Detroit to Alcona County during the Great Depression of the 1930s, Cole became a county coordinator for the Works Progress Administration (WPA). One of her main concerns was the promotion of libraries in communities throughout the county. Eventually nine branch libraries were established, in addition to the library in the county building at Harrisville. Ref.: 36 (71)

COLLAMER BAUMAN, ROSELLA (ROSE) E., of Midland; co-founder and director of the Chrysallis Center at Midland in 1968; co-founder of the Bay City Women's Center; founder of the Saginaw Humanities Series in 1981. The other co-founders of the Chrysallis Center were **Janice Allison, Donalda Doan, Flora Goggin** and **Jean Griffin**. Working with faculty from Saginaw Valley State College, the five Midland women, all of whom had changed careers, began offering career change classes in their homes, adopting the Latin form of a name suggesting a time of transition. They were joined in their efforts by committee members from Saginaw and Bay Counties. In 1973 the Center was given official status by the SVSC Board of Control and relocated at the College. Peer counseling was a major thrust of the Chrysallis program. Its clients, many of whom were pursuing higher education, supported each other by discussing classroom problems, personal and career issues. Chrysallis provided its clients, predominantly women, with a self-inventory testing program and individual counseling when needed and offered a variety of courses and workshops on such topics as life style and change, media effects on role expectations, job opportunities for women, writing, and entrepreneurship. The Center's published survey of programs, services and courses of special interest to women, offered by Michigan institutions of higher education, provided up-to-date information about educational opportunities in the clients' communities. By 1978, 15,000 clients had been reached through workshops, counseling, TV and radio programs. The Chrysallis Center continued until 1989, when its committee members requested that it be closed and the name retired, inasmuch as many of its original functions had been absorbed by more conventional areas of Saginaw Valley State University. Collamer Bauman serves on the board of directors of the Michigan Women's Studies Association and is a staunch supporter of the Michigan Women's Historical Center & Hall of Fame. Her awards include the 1978 Distinguished Alumni Award from SVSC, the 1983 Woman of the Year Award from the Zonta Club of Saginaw, the 1990 "Wonderful Old Woman" Award from the

Midland Chapter of NOW, and an award in 1990 for founding the Saginaw Humanities Series. She has also been honored by both the National and Michigan AAUW, the International Management Club of Bay City, and by SVSU which awarded her Professor Emeritus status in 1993. Ref.: 139

COLONE, ELIZABETH, of Pinckney; first woman elected to executive office in Livingston County, elected as president of the Village of Pinckney in 1985. Formerly she was the village assessor for two years and village clerk for fourteen years. During her two-year term as president, Colone oversaw the celebration of Pinckney's 150th anniversary. Ref.: 140

COLWELL, JOSEPHINE FRENCH, see **COWLEY, MRS. B. P.**

COMET, CATHERINE, of Grand Rapids; first woman to direct a professional orchestra in the U.S., as music director of the Grand Rapids Symphony Orchestra, in 1986; first woman to conduct a full subscription concert with the Philadelphia Symphony Orchestra, in 1988; first woman to conduct the Chicago Symphony Orchestra, in 1990. Born in France, Comet decided to become a conductor after attending her first orchestral concert at age 4. At age 12, Comet asked to study with Nadia Boulanger, the teacher of many noted conductors. Impressed with Comet's understanding of Beethoven's "Eroica" Symphony No. 3, the 70-year-old Boulanger accepted her as a student. At age 15, Comet enrolled at the Juilliard School of Music in New York, earning both bachelor's and master's degrees in 3 years. She has guest-conducted virtually all major U.S. orchestras, as well as orchestras in Europe and the Pacific. During her tenure several new concert series have been added, doubling the number of concerts and attendance. She has led the Grand Rapids Symphony to two awards from the American Society of Composers and Publishers for adventuresome programming of contemporary American music, as well as the Governor's Arts Award. Comet herself has received a Seaver/National Endowment for the Arts Conductors Award. Ref.: 41 (Oct. 1, 1995, H1); 136

COMEY, LOUISE (1946-1993), of Ann Arbor; co-founder of First Step, a counseling and shelter program for battered women and survivors of rape in Western Wayne County, in 1978. She held a BA from Kent State University and an MSW from the University of Michigan, where she was pursuing a Ph.D. in Urban and Regional Planning and Public Administration. During her years of social work at Family and Neighborhood Services for Wayne County, she served as Program Director of Special Services from 1981 to 1984, supervising many of its programs and developing the Downriver Human Service Center, which is composed of several social service agencies. She was on the board of directors and was chair of First Step, helping the program grow into a permanent facility to house 32 women by 1988. Comey was also a flutist with the Washtenaw Community College Jazz Band, performing at the Montreaux Jazz Festival in Detroit and at Carnegie Hall. Ref.: 4 (Mar. 3, 1993, E3)

COOK, HARRIET A. (dates not known), of Grand Rapids; first woman elected to the Grand Rapids Board of Education, in 1888. The Equal Suffrage Association was a factor in her election. A new law had granted suffrage to women with schoolage children or taxable property. In the 3rd ward caucus, a motion was passed allowing three candidates for voters to choose from at the polls. After a male candidate was selected, the caucus immediately adjourned. Outraged women present announced that they would vote for Harriet Cook as an independent candidate. She served for two years after her victory. Ref.: 136; 183

COOLEY, KAREN, of Milan; first place winner in the National American Armwrestling Association Championships women's competition, at McLean, Virginia, in August, 1992. In November of 1992 she finished seventh at the World Arm Wrestling Championships in Geneva, Switzerland, and in 1993 she took second place at the world competition in Edmonton, Alberta. Ref.: 4 (Nov. 27, 1993, B8); 115 (Sept. 11, 1992, 1A)

****

"Never shall we have the truly womanly woman
until she is made free to think her thoughts and look at the world
with her own eyes, and add her verdict to that of man
upon the things of life which affect her and her children
often far more poignantly than they affect him."
Caroline Bartlett Crane of Kalamazoo

****

CORNELL, HANNAH TRASK (dates not known), of Kalamazoo; first librarian of the Ladies' Library Association, in 1879. Only eighteen, Cornell headed the library that was housed in the first building in the United States erected in 1879 by and for a woman's club exclusively. Ref.: 51 (Jan. 1952, 25)

CORY, JERRE, of Lansing; co-founder and first executive director of Ele's Place, a non-profit children's center in Lansing that gives support for grieving children and their families, after the loss of a family member or friend. Ele's Place began in 1991, when Cory and **Betsy Stover** of East Lansing recognized the need for a place where children could share their grief with others and receive support from peers, professionals, and trained volunteers. Stover's infant daughter Ele had died in 1989 and her other children had struggled with grief over their sister's death. Cory, a social worker who was teaching a class on children and grief at Lansing Community College, joined with Stover to establish the center named for Ele. (The name also serves as an acronym for "embracing loss effectively.") Supported by the Junior League of Lansing, Ele's Place opened with 75 trained volunteers and 35 children and their families. By 1994 there were 150 volunteers, including facilitators trained to work with families, and a team of professionals who donate their services. Several hundred children and their families have been helped since the opening of the Ele's Place, one of few such centers in the country. For her work with grieving children, Cory received the Diana Award from the YWCA of Greater Lansing in 1994. Ref.: 55 (Aug. 1994, 30-32); 57 (May 26, 1994, 3C)

CORYELL McBAIN, EVA DIANN (1857-1927), of Williamston; first woman to graduate from Michigan Agriculture College (now Michigan State University), in 1879. Born in Minnesota, she moved as a child with her parents to Williamston, where she began teaching at the age of 15. She entered MAC in 1875 as a sophomore and graduated in 1879. While teaching in Grand Rapids, she met William McBain, whom she married in 1881. Ref.: 53 (123-124); 104 (3-4)

COWAN, BELITA, formerly of Ann Arbor; founder in 1972 of Herself, a women's newspaper published in Ann Arbor until 1976; founder in 1972 of Advocates for Medical Information (a watchdog group to oppose use of the dangerous drug DES on the University of Michigan campus); founder in 1974 and first executive director (from 1978 to 1983) of the National Women's Health Network (the only national consumer organization devoted to women's health); founder and president of the Lymphoma Foundation of America in 1987; author in 1987 of the first comparative listing of doctors' fees published in the U.S., covering the five most common procedures in each specialty for all doctors in Maryland. Advocates for Medical Information organized after it was discovered that campus doctors were giving DES to unknowing clients as part of a research study that concluded DES to be safe. When the study was published in the Journal of the AMA, Advocates for Medical Information exposed its conclusions as erroneous, giving the issue national attention. Cowan testified on the dangers of DES before Congressional committees and the Federal Drug Administration in 1975 and 1980. She also led the successful campaign to keep the controversial hormonal drug Depo Provera off the market and worked for mandated package information in all estrogen drugs. Cowan graduated from Ohio State University in 1969 and the University of Michigan in 1971. She is the author of Your Rights as a Woman in Michigan, published by the Michigan Women's Commission in 1973, Women's Health Care: Resources, Writings, and Bibliographies (1977), Health Care Shoppers Guide: 59 Ways to Save Money (1988), and Nursing Homes: What You Need to Know (1990). The Health Care Shoppers Guide received the national award for excellence in consumer education from the FDA and in 1990 was the most popular consumer guide ever published in the U.S. In 1980 Ms. Magazine named Cowan one of its "Women to Watch in the 80s." Ref.: 143

COWLEY, MRS. B. P. (first name and dates not known), of Harrisville; co-founder and first president of the Ladies' Literary Club of Harrisville in 1889. Other founders and officers were

Josephine French Colwell, Mrs. George Rutson, Lilley McLelland, and **Annie Duggan.** Ref.: 36 (49)

CURRELL, ANNE-MARIE J. DALMASSO, of Lapeer; founder of the first woman-owned and operated martial arts school in Michigan, in 1975. Born in Provence, France, during the German occupation, she first became interested in martial arts as a child. Although trained as a seamstress, she was dissatisfied with her occupation. After her marriage to an American sailor in 1964, she and her husband moved to Lapeer, where she learned English, earned her high school diploma, took college courses and taught French adult education classes. In c. 1970 she and her husband began training in the martial arts and eventually assisted their master teacher at seminars throughout the country. Currell also conducted seminars in France and in 1975 opened her own "Dojang" (school) in her home. When her Dojang outgrew her home, she renovated a condemned building to house her Korean Martial Arts Institute, where she teaches traditional Chang-Hun TaeKwon-Do to adults, youth, and children, including those with physical and learning disabilities. Her class in Wee TaeKwon-Do is for children four to five years old. Currell became a Master Instructor in TaeKwon-Do in 1980, received her 1st degree Black Belt in Shim Soo Do (sword) in 1986, and her 6th degree Black Belt in TaeKwon-Do in 1993. She has been a state representative of the International TaeKwon-Do Association and has written many articles on the martial arts. Ref.: 217

DeBOER VANDEN BOSCH, MARY, see **BONNEMA, MARGUERITE**

DECKER, EMMA AMY ADAMS (1847-1917), of Mt. Clemens; first woman to be a physician in Mt. Clemens, from 1879 to 1890. Born in Macomb County, Decker graduated from the University of Michigan Medical School in 1878. She specialized in the diseases of women and children. Ref.: 45

DENNING, BERNADINE NEWSOM, of Detroit; first African American (second woman) to be director of the Office of Revenue Sharing for the United States Department of the Treasury, from 1977 to 1979; founder of an interracial consulting firm, DMP Associates, that emphasizes education and leadership training, in 1989. After receiving a degree in physical education in 1951 from Michigan State Normal College (now Eastern Michigan University), she taught in the Detroit public schools until 1959, when she became an administrator of several programs for the school system. She received her Ed.D. in curriculum development from Wayne State University in 1970, then became an administrator and assistant professor of education at the University of Michigan. In 1975 she was named director of the Civil Rights Office for the Detroit Public Schools, where her performance led to her position with the Treasury Department. As director of the Office of Revenue Sharing, she was responsible for the distribution of federal funds to over 60,000 state and local governments and the enforcement of civil rights laws prohibiting federal funding to any unit practicing racial discrimination. After returning to Detroit, she served as the executive director of the School-Community Relations department for the Detroit Public Schools until her retirement in 1985 and as director of the Human Rights Department for the city of Detroit from 1986 to 1987. Ref.: 8 (320); 144

DeROO, ALTA, of Paw Paw; one of the first two women chosen for combat training as a U.S. Navy pilot, in 1993. An Ensign, she began flying an F-14 combat jet in 1994. Ref.: 57 (Jun. 7, 1993, 1B)

DeROO, RUTH, of Flint; first place winner of the World Outboard Racing Championship, held at Bay City on October 9, 1932. She was the only woman among several world outboard racing champions from Flint to compete in the race. Ref.: 30 (246)

****

"Since 8,000,000 American women are employed in gainful occupation, every principle of justice known to a republic demands that these 8,000,000 toilers be enfranchised in order that they may be able to obtain and enforce legislation for their own protection."

Anna Howard Shaw of Big Rapids

****

DeYOUNG, LISA, of Ann Arbor; founder of the non-profit organization Food Gatherers, Michigan's first food rescue program, at Ann Arbor in 1988. Beginning with just a few volunteers, DeYoung collected 500 pounds of restaurant leftovers and fresh produce from several donors to deliver to some Washtenaw County shelters and charitable agencies. By 1995, there were seven full-time workers and 200 volunteers who collect a ton of perishable food from 150 donors each day, for delivery to 71 agencies that feed the hungry. Ref.: 22 (Jun. 6, 1995, 7D)

DHAENE, MARGARET, of Lansing; one of the first group of women assigned to a U. S. Navy combatant ship, in 1994. Lt. Dhaene was assigned to aircraft carrier USS Dwight D. Eisenhower. Women have served on non-combatant ships since 1978 and on combatant ships for short durations, but this was the first time in the Navy's history that women were fully integrated as crew members on board a combatant vessel. Ref.: 57 (Mar. 17, 1994, 1C)

DIETERLE, LORRAINE, of Rochester Hills; the first woman to be a U.S. Coast Guard photographer in the 3d Naval District in New York City, in the 1940s. A 1944 graduate of Detroit Southeastern High School and already an accomplished photographer, Dieterle joined the SPARS, the women's reserve corps of the U.S. Coast Guard, in June of 1944 at the time of D-Day. After convincing her superiors to let her into the photography unit, she became one of the Coast Guard's first female photographers and trained Coast Guard men who then went into the war zones as combat photographers. As a Photographers Mate, Third Class, she was the first and only woman in New York City's Third Naval District, where she processed the incoming battle film and sent the photos to mazagines, newspapers, motion picture agencies and the National Archives. Many of the men she had trained were killed in action. After the war, she continued as a photographer in civilian life. In 994 Dieterle visited Normandy for the 50th anniversary of D-Day, to see the places that she had known only through countless photographs of battle scenes and where many of the men she had trained were killed. She has also been Michigan chair for fund-raising and locating Michigan women veterans for the Women in Military Service Memorial in Washington, D.C. Ref.: 22 (May 15, 1994, 1A, 12A); 84 (May 28-Jun. 10, 1995, 8, 14)

DIX, EULABEE (1878-1961), of Grand Rapids; first Michigan woman to gain national and international recognition as a painter of miniatures, c. 1900. Born in Illinois, she studied at the St. Louis School of Fine Arts and in New York, London, and Paris. She was already a well-known painter in Grand Rapids when she went to New York in 1898. Dix specialized in miniature portraits, which were exhibited at galleries and museums throughout the United States and Europe. Her many famous friends and patrons included Mark Twain, whom she painted in 1908. She received many awards for her work. Ref.: 37 (88)

DIXSON, JOYCE, of Saginaw; first woman to earn a bachelor's degree from the University of Michigan while in prison, in 1991. Dixson was sentenced to prison in August of 1976 for killing her abusive partner. After 17 years of appeals and letter-writing campaigns, her conviction was reduced from first- to second-degree murder and she was released in 1993. During her prison stay, when she discovered that men prisoners were offered educational opportunities denied to women prisoners, she and other women sought the same rights. Through the help of some lawyers, a lawsuit was filed against the Michigan Department of Corrections (Glover v. Johnson) and a federal court ruled in favor of the women. Eventually community college classes and a four-year program were started for women prisoners. In addition to a bachelor's degree, Dixson earned a paralegal degree, which enabled her to help many women prisoners through her work in prison legal services. After her release, she began a master's program in social work at the University of Michigan. Ref.: 1 (Jan. 1994, 5-6)

DOAN, DONALDA, see **COLLAMER BAUMAN, ROSELLA E.**

DOCKERAY, MARY JANE, of Grand Rapids; founder of the Blandford Nature Center and its first Curator of Natural Science, in 1964. A Grand Rapids native, she received a degree in geology from Michigan State University in 1949 and joined the Grand Rapids Public Museum as a nature lecturer to city school children. Dockeray led the development of the Blandford Nature Center's original ten acre site into a much larger complex featuring several

buildings, a working farm, and programs for all age groups.
Ref.: 136; 183

DOLBEE, DORA B. (dates not known), of Muskegon; possibly the
first woman to practice dentistry in Muskegon, by or before 1908.
Dolbee arrived in Muskegon in 1902. Six years later she
purchased the business and dental offices of Dr. Frederick Osius
on First Street. It was reported that "with years of experience to
warrant her taking over the extensive work of the offices," she
would "carry out all guarantees of the former owner."
Ref.: 118 (Dec. 19, 1908, 3)

DOLLINGER, GENORA ALBRO JOHNSON (1913-1995), of Flint;
founder of the UAW Women's Auxiliary and the Women's Emergency
Brigade in the 1937 sitdown strikes in support of union organizing
at General Motors Corporation in Flint. Born in Kalamazoo,
Dollinger grew up in Flint. Attracted to Socialism when she was 16,
Dollinger was a candidate of the Socialist Workers Party for the U.S.
Senate in 1952. After the UAW-CIO was recognized by General
Motors Corporation, she organized and served as secretary of Local
12, WPA and Unemployed Union, UAW-CIO. Blacklisted in Flint,
she found work at the Briggs Manufacturing Company in Detroit,
where she became chief steward of UAW Local 212 for an all
women's department. Because of her UAW organizing activity, she
was badly beaten with a lead pipe while she was sleeping in her
Detroit home. A U.S. Senate investigating committee later revealed
that the Mafia, hired by corporate leaders, was responsible for the
beating of Dollinger and other union organizers, as well as the
shootings of UAW leaders Walter and Victor Reuther. The role of
Dollinger and other women in the struggle to unionize the
automotive industry is recorded in two documentary films, "With
Babies and Banners" and "The Great Sitdown Strike." Dollinger
served as State Development Director for the Michigan ACLU from
1960 to 1966. She also served on the executive board of the Flint
NAACP and as chair of Detroit Women for Peace, participating in
demonstrations against the Vietnam War. She was inducted into
the Michigan Women's Hall of Fame in 1994. Ref.: 184

DOMINIC, WAUNETTA McCLELLAN (1921-1981), of Petoskey;
co-founder of the Northern Michigan Ottawa Association, in 1948.
Dominic, with her husband Robert and father, Levi McClellan,
founded the NMOA to secure for the non-reservation Ottawa and
Chippewa peoples of Michigan the settlement of claims for lands
ceded to the federal government in the Treaties of 1821 and 1836.
These lands later became the major portion of the state of Michigan.
Dominic succeeded her husband as president of the 7,000 member
Association in 1976, remaining its head until her death. In 1948
the Dominics initiated land claims suits for Michigan Indians which
awarded $13 million to members of the Ottawa and Chippewa
tribes. As a member of the Grand River Band of Ottawas, Waunetta
Dominic led the push for payment of $1.8 million on land claims for

2,800 Ottawa and Pottawatomie tribe members in 1979. She
advocated a stiff interpretation of Indian ancestry definition for
eligibility of government benefits, fought for federal recognition for
non-reservation Indians, and sought a just and peaceful solution to
the fishing controversy. A member of the Christian Life Center of
Petoskey and the Crooked Tree Arts Council, Dominic was named
Michiganian of the Year by the Detroit News in 1978. Ref.: 184

DOWD, LUCY LOCKWOOD STOUT (1835-1910), of Northville;
founder in 1892 of the Northville Circle of Friends, which became
the Northville Woman's Club in 1893; first president of the
Northville Woman's Club. Born in New York, she came to
Northville before 1848 with her mother and brother. Following her
marriage to William Stout in 1854, the couple lived in Northville
until sometime after 1870, when they moved to Philadelphia. After
William's death, Lucy returned to Northville with her three children
and wrote for the local newspaper, The Northville Record. In the
1870s she moved her family to Detroit, where she edited a suffrage
and temperance paper, Truth for the People. Returning to
Northville, she again wrote for the local newspaper, as well as for
other publications. In the 1890s she remarried and moved to
Texas, returning again to Northville after her second husband's
death in 1910. Her obituary described her as "an enthusiastic
pioneer in the women's movement and an early advocate for
franchise rights for women." Ref.: 200

****

*"Apr. 2. This morning we went to the polls in the Ninth Ward and
voted. Mr. Smith, Mr. Stebbins, Mr. Elder, Linnie and myself went
first. The carriage returned and took Ma, Mrs. Stebbens* [**Catharine
Stebbins**]*, Mrs. Starring and Millie. After Ma had deposited her
vote she presented Mr. Hill a beautiful boquet [sic] which was
placed on the table near the ballot box."*

From the 1871 diary of **Sarah M. Gardner**, 12-year-old daughter of
Nannette B. Gardner of Detroit, a widow who in 1871 claimed her
right to vote on the basis that she had no husband to represent her.

****

DRAGGOO, SANDRA L., of Laingsburg; first woman to be the
Executive Director of the Capital Area Transportation Authority,
serving from 1985 to the present. She has also served as State
President of the Michigan Public Transit Association, from 1988 to
1991. Ref.: 218

DRESSLER, MARIE (LELIA KOERBER) (c. 1870-1934), of Saginaw;
first Michigan woman to become a world-famous actress on stage
and screen; first Michigan woman to win an Academy Award, as the
best actress of 1931. Born in Canada, young Lelia moved with her
parents to Saginaw in 1883. She probably made her first stage
appearance at Bordwell's Opera House in Saginaw. Taking the
name of Marie Dressler, she joined a touring opera company,
performing in numerous small opera houses and learning the art of

acting that would take her to both Broadway and Hollywood. During her years with touring road shows, she answered to the nickname of "Sag" (for Saginaw). Throughout her long career on the stage and in films, she appeared in many theatrical productions in the United States and Europe, gaining a reputation as the "Queen of Comedy" and co-starring with such well-known actors and actresses as Wallace Beery, Lillian Russell, Greta Garbo, and Lillian Gish. In 1916 she made her silent film debut in "Tillie's Punctured Romance," a Max Sennet farce with Charlie Chaplin and Mabel Norman and the first of many movies in which she had leading roles. She received the Academy Award as "best actress" in 1931 for her portrayal of Min in "Min and Bill" with Wallace Beery. At the age of 65, she enjoyed a successful film comeback, as Martha in "Anna Christie." Dressler was much admired for her humor and kindness, as well as for her acting ability. Her host of friends included United States presidents, the Prince of Wales, and many other famous people, in addition to countless lesser-known persons. Ref.: 85 (82-84)

DUGGAN, ANNIE, see **COWLEY, MRS. B. P.**

DURFEE, FLORENCE A. NELSON MAYER (1899-1992), of Chelsea; first woman to be on the Chelsea School Board, from 1945 to 1950, serving as treasurer from 1948 to 1949. Born in Houghton-Hancock, she moved to Chelsea in 1930. A graduate of Ypsilanti Normal Teachers College (now Eastern Michigan University) and the University of Michigan, she taught at Chelsea High School from 1937 to 1939. She was a member of the Washtenaw County Library Board and the Chelsea PTA and was active in the Girl Scouts and Boy Scouts. Ref.: 4 (May 15, 1992, C5)

DYE, MARIE (1891-1974), of East Lansing; first woman on the faculty of Michigan Agricultural College (Michigan State University) to hold a Ph.D., in 1922. A native of Chicago, Dye earned her degrees in nutrition at the University of Chicago, where she also taught. She joined the Home Economics School at Michigan Agricultural College in 1922 and was named Dean in 1929, a position she held for 25 years. During her tenure she began a Ph.D. program in Home Economics and greatly expanded the Home Extension program. She served as president of the Michigan Home Economics Association, Omicron Nu (home economics honor society), and American Home Economics Association. During World War II she served on the Consumer Committee and as chair of the Nutrition Committee of the Michigan Council of Defense. Ref.: 57 (Jan. 1, 1956, 44; Apr. 29, 1956); 184

EDMUNDS, NATHALIE ELLIOTT, of Ypsilanti; founder of the Ypsilanti Historic District, 1970-1978; founder of the Ypsilanti Heritage Festival in 1978. When a proposed master plan threatened the demolition of Ypsilanti's historic buildings in 1970, she ran for and was elected to the Ypsilanti City Council, where she worked for passage of Ypsilanti's Historic District in 1978. To save the historic GAR building, home of the Women's Relief Corps, she re-established the WRC chapter and declared herself president. A native of Ypsilanti, Edmunds graduated from the University of Michigan in 1949. She has served as vice president of the Historical Society of Michigan and on the board of the Ypsilanti Historical Society. Among her awards are the Distinguished Service Award from the Ypsilanti Chamber of Commerce, the Zonta Founders Award for Outstanding Community Service, a Person of the Year Award from the Ypsilanti Press, and the first Pioneer Award from the Ypsilanti Visitors and Convention Bureau. Ref.: 4 (Aug. 16, 1995, 23); 146

EDUT, OPHIRA, of Ann Arbor; co-founder in 1992, with **Tali Edut** and **Dyann Logwood**, of HUES (Hear Us Emerging Sisters), a bi-yearly multi-cultural publication by, for and about the advancement of women. The three women, who were students at the University of Michigan when they founded HUES, have since graduated. Beginning as a southeast Michigan publication, HUES had reached a nationwide distribution of 40,000 and was also being distributed in London by 1995. Ref.: 4 (May 24, 1995, D1); 147

EDUT, TALI, see **EDUT, OPHIRA**

EGGLESTON, ELLA C. MILLS HECOX (1873-1948), of Hastings; first woman to be a probate judge in Michigan, appointed by Gov. Albert E. Sleeper, on November 14, 1919. Born in Barry County, she graduated from Nashville High School in 1892 and taught in rural schools before her first marriage. In 1902 she was appointed as Register of Probate for her father, Probate Judge James B. Mills, and served in that position for four judges before her own appointment as Judge of the Probate Court. She presided over the Probate Court for 13 years, retiring in 1931. Eggleston was also appointed by the United States Department of the Interior to act as agent for pension claimants in the area. In addition, she served as president of the Ladies Aid Society of Hastings. Ref.: 97

EVANGELISTA, STELLA, of Bloomfield Hills; first Asian-American appointed to the Michigan State Board of Medicine. A physician, she came to the United States from the Philippines in 1968 with her husband, Dr. Jose Evangelista. In recognition of their contributions to Filipino professional and ethnic groups, they were inducted into the International Institute of Metropolitan Detroit's International Heritage Hall of Fame in 1990. Ref.: 22 (May 4, 1990, 4B)

EVANS, EVA L., of Lansing; international president of Alpha Kappa Alpha Sorority, the nation's first sorority for African American women, founded in 1908 at Howard University in Washington, D.C.; founder of the Lansing Association of Black Organizations; founder of the "Be a Star" Children's Performing Arts Program; first African American to be in charge of the Lansing School District. She was named international president of the sorority in 1994, after four years as vice president and 28 years as a member of Delta Tau

Omega Chapter in Lansing. Evans, who has a Ph.D. from Michigan State University, spent 30 years in the Lansing School District, as an elementary school teacher, assistant principal, associate superintendent for personnel and for curriculum, and deputy superintendent for instruction, before her retirement in 1995. She has served as chair of the Michigan Civil Rights Commission, chair of the MSU Alumni Association, commissioner of the Lansing Board of Water and Light, resource consultant for both the U.S. and Michigan Departments of Education, and chair of the 1995 Capital Area United Way. Evans has been honored with the Diana Award for outstanding leadership in education, the NAACP educator of the year award, the Lansing Regional Chamber of Commerce's ATHENA Award and the Black Caucus Foundation of Michigan Community Service Award. Ref.: 57 (Jul. 17, 1994, 3B; May 14, 1995, 1B); 90 (Winter 1995, 44); 150

****

"Apr. 14. Mrs. Susan B. Anthony stopped here last night on her way to St. Clair and is coming back tomorrow.
"Apr. 16. Mrs. Anthony came back yesterday and will remain here until tomorrow. She said that she could not rest contented until she had slept under the roof of the house of the first that had voted under the 14th and 15th Amendments."

From the 1871 diary of **Sarah M. Gardner**, 12-year-old daughter of **Nannette B. Gardner** of Detroit, a widow who in 1871 claimed her right to vote on the basis that she had no husband to represent her.

****

FAITH (formerly **NAOMI WILLIAMS**), of Detroit; founder of Shepherd House, a shelter, school and chapel for the homeless, in 1992. By 1993 Shepherd House was serving 40 families in its 44 units, helping them get an education and find employment. A former Detroit school teacher with degrees in education and religious studies, Faith gave up her teaching position and graduate studies in 1980 when she felt led to take homeless people into her own home. She legally changed her name in 1983. She came to Detroit from Louisiana as a young woman, put herself through school by working, then married and had three children. She says that as she recovered from her husband's death in 1971, God told her she would get "a new beginning." At Shepherd House she has many responsibilities, including tutoring, taking residents to doctor's appointments, helping them get into college and find jobs, teaching classes on self-esteem, and finding the funds to maintain the shelter and its programs. Ref.: 25 (June 13, 1993, 1A, 12A)

FARQUHARSON, RHODA PAMELA (1882-1972), of Detroit; first woman to be an intern at Grace Hospital in Detroit; first woman to be a physician for the Detroit Juvenile Court from 1910-1916, the Detroit House of Correction in 1918, and the House of Good Shepherd (now Vista Maria School); first woman to be a member of the Federal Parole Board; co-founder of the Detroit Business and

Professional Women's Club. Born in Ontario, she grew up in
Detroit and Cheboygan. After attending Detroit's Central High
School, she graduated from the University of Michigan in 1905 and
received her medical degree from the university's Homeopathic
College in 1907. She was an instructor in the prenatal clinic at
Wayne State University Medical School and served for many years
on the staff at Women's Hospital. The oldest practicing woman
physician in Michigan until her retirement in 1970, she still made
house calls to friends and longtime patients during the 1960s. She
served on the boards of the Redford Boys Clubs and Brightmoor
Community Center, was a lifelong Quaker, and a member of the
Order of the Eastern Star. Ref.: 25 (Feb. 24, 1972); 204 (Box 2)

FARRAND, HELEN WHEATON (1824-1891), of Port Huron; founder
of the Ladies' Library Association of Port Huron, in 1866. Its
members, who met every Saturday for reading, writing and
discussion, also sponsored lectures, international spelling bees,
concerts and plays. Still in existence, the LLA is the fourth oldest
continuous women's federated organization of its kind in the nation.
Ref.: 197

FAY, MAUREEN, of the Detroit area; first woman to be president of a
Jesuit university, as president of the University of Detroit Mercy in
1990. The University was formed through the merger of the
University of Detroit and Mercy College. A Dominican nun, Fay
began teaching English and speech in 1961 at St. Paul High School
in Grosse Pointe. As the University president, her goals include
helping the city of Detroit to rebuild, by utilizing the expertise of the
School of Architecture and developing programs to increase the
number of minorities in health and engineering fields. In 1994 the
School of Nursing launched a federally funded program to teach
minority students from disadvantaged backgrounds. Ref.: 57
(Jan. 4, 1994, 3B)

FELDNER, MARY BAPTIST, see **McCORD, MARY IGNATIUS**

FERGUSON, JOAN, of Portland; founder of Great Lakes Sailing for
Women, in 1989. A science teacher with a captain's license from
the Coast Guard, Ferguson saw the need for sailing classes geared
to women, whose sailing experience is often limited to work in the
galley or cleaning the boat. She and colleague **Marcia Boynton** of
Traverse City use 31-foot Allmand sailboats on three- or five-day
training runs on Lake Michigan, between Charlevoix and Mackinac
Island, from June until September. Instruction covers various
aspects of sailing, including navigation, handling the sails, and
making proper knots. Ref.: 22 (Aug. 31, 1993, 6F)

FERRIER, ORPHA RAY LUMSDEN (1895-1985), of Dearborn; first
woman elected to the Dearborn Board of Education, in 1947; first
woman elected president of the board, in 1951; co-founder of the
Dearborn YWCA. Born and educated in Ontario, she taught school
before marrying Donald Ferrier and moving to Michigan. She and

her husband settled in Dearborn, where she was active in various organizations, serving as president of the League of Women Voters, vice president of the Michigan School Board Association, on the Advisory Board for Michigan State Normal College (now Eastern Michigan University) and the boards of the Dearborn YWCA and the Mental Health Society of Michigan. In her late 60s she earned M.Ed. and Educational Specialist degrees in Psychological Testing and taught adult education classes for several years before retiring in 1969. Ref.: 169

FERRY, AMANDA WHITE, see **WHITE, MARY A.**

FINATRI, SUELLEN, of Roscommon; quite possibly the first woman to ride horseback from St. Ignace to Anchorage, Alaska, a 5,000-mile trip. She started out February 1, 1995, on her horse Nakota, accompanied by her dog Cheyenne and pack horse Savona, camping out or staying in National Guard Armories along the way. Fighting through blizzards in Canada and Alaska, she reached Anchorage by December of 1995. Finatri, who managed a Roscommon restaurant, has also been an interstate truck driver and has lived in Flint, Sault Ste. Marie, and Sugar Island. Ref.: 22 (Mar. 1, 1995, 1D; Mar. 3, 1995, 6C; Apr. 19, 1995, 1D)

FISHER, MARY, formerly of the Detroit area; founder of the Families with AIDS Network. Infected with the HIV virus by her ex-husband, she established the non-profit organization to educate the public, provide support to AIDS care givers, and promote research on a cure for the disease. In 1992 she spoke at the Republican National Convention, stressing understanding of AIDS and compassion for its victims, and now travels throughout the country with the same message. A book of her speeches, Sleep With the Angels: A Mother Challenges AIDS, was published in 1993. She was appointed by President George Bush to the National Commission on AIDS and in 1993 she received an honorary doctorate degree in the humanities from Michigan State University for her contributions to public awareness of the disease. Fisher, an artist and the mother of two sons, now lives in Bethesda, Maryland. In 1995 an exhibit of her collages and sculpture based on an AIDS theme was removed from the U.S. Senate Office Building after senators objected to its centerpiece, a gilded coffin. The exhibit, entitled "Messages," was reinstalled in the nearby United Brotherhood of Carpenters and Joiners of America headquarters. Ref.: 4 (Sept. 29, 1993; Nov. 30, 1994, F1-2); 25 (Apr. 11, 1993, 5R; Dec. 12, 1993, 2C); 57 (Dec. 12, 1993, 1B; Sept. 26, 1995, 8A); 91 (Nov. 24, 1993, 2)

FORD, CAROLINE L. (1815-1904), of Hillsdale; first schoolteacher in Hillsdale, in 1838; first art instructor at Hillsdale College, in 1855. The first school, a private school for neighborhood children, was housed in a log building. In 1841 she taught in the first public school in Hillsdale, a one-story frame building. In 1848 she moved her classes to a stone building on the courthouse square and was named "Lady Principal" of the Union School. In 1855, she became an art instructor at Hillsdale College, teaching painting, composition and penmanship.   In 1865 she moved to Louisville, Kentucky, to become City Missionary to the Freedmen's Bureau. She later returned to Hillsdale, where she remained until the end of her life. Ref.: 123

FORHAN, ELIZABETH (1891-1968), of Benton Harbor; first woman to be a U.S. Commissioner, in 1933; first woman attorney to try a case in Berrien circuit court; first woman to be a municipal judge in Benton Harbor, in 1959. She was the second woman to practice law in Berrien County, the first having been **Dora B. Whitney** of Benton Harbor. (See **Whitney, Dora B**. in Michigan Women: Firsts and Founders, Vol. I.) Forhan received her first legal training as secretary to Justice of the Peace Harry Plummer, whom she succeeded after his death in 1923, serving until 1932. In 1931 she became a full-fledged lawyer by passing the state bar examination. She later qualified to practice before the Michigan Supreme and U.S. District courts. As an appointed U.S. Commissioner from 1933 until the mid-1960s, she presided over the arraignment of federal prisoners. Appointed municipal judge in 1959, she was elected twice to that position. Ref.: 152

****
"Failure is Impossible."
Susan B. Anthony
****

FOSTER, EUNICE F., of East Lansing; the first woman hired as an assistant professor in Michigan State University's Crop and Soil Sciences Department, in 1992. Now a professor, Foster has received national recognition for leading research on innovative ways of teaching. Ref.: 57 (May 6, 1994, 7D)

FREY, MARY CAROLINE, of Grand Rapids; founder of the Greater Grand Rapids Women's History Council in 1988; founder and president of the Nokomis Foundation in Grand Rapids, in 1991. The Council seeks to discover and preserve the history and contributions of women in the Grand Rapids area. One of its major projects is a biennial celebration of women's achievements called Legacy. The Nokomis Foundation, named for an Odawa word denoting the traditional passing of wisdom from grandmothers to younger women, encourages change in the lives of women and girls by funding organizations that provide opportunities for women and girls. Some of its grants have gone to Women in Skilled Trades (a pre-apprenticeship training program), an educational video about Planned Parenthood of West Michigan, the Michigan Women's Leadership Project at the University of Michigan's Center for the Education of Women, and the Women Matter! Project, which brings women together to identify issues and a plan for action. The Foundation also conducts a Technical Assistance Workshop Series, for agencies to learn about grant-writing, fund-raising and strategic planning. A native of Grand Rapids with bachelor's and master's degrees in education, Frey taught for many years before establishing her own foundation in 1991. Her realization that programs for women and girls receive less than 5 percent of the money awarded by state foundations led her to concentrate on encouraging systematic change in women's and girl's lives. Ref.: 84 (Feb. 19-Mar. 4, 1995, 10); 158

FRON, MARY, of Niles; co-founder of ROCKING (Raising Our Children's Kids: An Intergenerational Network of Grandparenting), in 1992. ROCKING is a network of support groups for people who are raising their grandchildren, as a result of their own children's inability or unwillingness to care for their offspring. Studies have shown that more than half of those raising grandchildren are 55 or older, and one quarter are 65 or older. ROCKING receives hundreds of calls and letters each week from grandparents who are coping with financial, legal, and emotional problems. Fron and her husband Tom have adopted and are raising their grandson Nathan. Ref.: 4 (March 9, 1994, B1)

GAINES, LOUISA (dates not known), of Grand Rapids; co-founder of "The Study Class" (later called the Grand Rapids Study Club), in 1901. Founded to provide an opportunity to study current issues, the organization held its first meeting at Gaines' home. The oldest African American women's civic club in Grand Rapids, its motto is "Rowing, not drifting." Ref.: 98

GALL, ELIZABETH BABCOCK (1931-1993), of Ann Arbor; co-founder and leader of the first Michigan chapter of the La Leche League in the early 1960s. Born in Markville, Minnesota, she received a bachelor's degree in nursing education and public health nursing from the University of Minnesota in 1955 and a master's degree in journalism from the University of Michigan in 1971. Certified as a pediatric nurse practitioner, she served 10 years as preceptor for graduate students in the U-M's Pediatric Nurse Practitioner Program, 13 years in joint pediatric practice with her husband, pediatrician John C. Gall, and four years as breast-feeding consultant for the continuing education department of the Ann Arbor Public Schools. She also directed local seminars and workshops on the health of mothers, children and families, and, with her husband, co-authored a book, Elegant Parenting: Strategies for the Twenty-First Century. At the time of her death, she was completing a textbook, The Way of Breastfeeding: A Casebook for Consultants. In her memory, the Washtenaw County chapter of the Michigan Association for Infant Mental Health has established the Beth Gall Award to be given to professionals for excellence in clinical infant care. Ref.: 4 (Feb. 23, 1993, C3)

GARRATY, ANNE (dates not known), of Presque Isle; first woman to be a lighthouse keeper at the Presque Isle Range Light on Lake Huron, from 1903 to 1926, after replacing her husband, Patrick Garraty, as keeper. Ref.: 18 (164)

GARZA, LILA, formerly of the Detroit area; founder of the Michigan Hispanic Chamber of Commerce, in 1989. Born in Mexico, she graduated from high school in Michigan and received a bachelor's degree in business administration from Northwood Institute in 1977. In 1986, after several years in purchasing at Ford Motor Company, she began her own successful air freight transportation and forwarding company, Airex International Freight Service, which she closed after her major contractors reduced fast-track shipping. In the 1990s she undertook other new business ventures that also proved successful. Garza, who has served on the boards of both the Michigan Hispanic Chamber of Commerce and the United States Hispanic Chamber of Commerce, was awarded the 1990 Hispanic Business Woman of the Year award for Region IV in Michigan, as well as an award from the National Chamber of Commerce. Ref.: 95 (176)

GAUCHEY, NANCY, of Marquette; founder of Voices for Youth, an agency to help rural runaway teens, in 1992. A former police-woman from Detroit, Gauchey began the agency when she found many homeless teens living in the woods and abandoned buildings of the Marquette area. During 1994 more than 300 young people younger than 21 were aided by Voices for Youth, which is affiliated with Lutheran Social Services of Upper Michigan and Wisconsin. Ref.: 23 (Sept. 11, 1994, 6-17)

GEARHART, FERN E. BRIGGS (1914-1995), of Charlotte; co-founder of the Michigan Maple Sugar Association; only woman to be elected to the MMSA Board; only woman to be a Michigan delegate to the International Maple Syrup Institute and alternate delegate to the North American Maple Syrup Council. Born in Vermontville, Gearhart began working in the syrup industry in 1930. She and her husband started their own maple syrup business in 1952. After her husband's death in 1967, she continued to operate the business, the largest home-owned, home-tapped maple syrup production in Michigan. Gearhart worked closely with the Michigan State University Agriculture Department to study environmental hazards as they relate to the maple syrup industry. She initiated the position of the MMSA Maple Syrup Queen and was chair of the selection process for many years. Known for her marketing skills in the syrup industry, she lectured on the state, national and international levels. In 1960 she was chosen Michigan Mother of the Year and in 1985 she was named Honored Citizen at the Vermontville Syrup Festival, with which she was associated for 55 years. She also served as president of the Eaton County Federation of Women's Clubs and the Charlotte Women's Club. Ref.: 57 (Sept. 29, 1995, 2B)

GEHA, SUZANNE, of Grand Rapids; one of the first two women hired as news anchor/reporters on the Western Michigan University campus radio station, in 1971; first woman to anchor prime time news in West Michigan, as the evening news co-anchor for WOOD-

TV in Grand Rapids, in 1976. Geha says that she was influenced in her choice of career by the example of her aunt, veteran journalist **Helen Thomas**, who is White House Bureau Chief for United Press International. (See **Thomas, Helen** in Michigan Women: Firsts and Founders, Vol. I.) Ref.: 84 (Nov. 11-Dec. 19, 1994, 10); 155

GENDZWILL, JOYCE A., of Iron River; first woman to be a trained physician in the Iron River area, in 1952. Ref.: 34 (368)

GENTILE, JUDY KAY TAYLOR (1946-1993), of DeWitt; first wheelchair-user admitted as a freshman to Michigan State University; founder and first president of the MSU Handicapper Student Organization; co-founder and first director of the Office of Programs for Handicapper Students at MSU in 1973; founder of the Lansing Committee on Handicappers. Born in Lansing, Gentile had polio at the age of eight, leaving her a quadriplegic. In spite of physical obstacles, she graduated from MSU and became a national advocate on behalf of handicappers. She was a member of the President's Committee on Employment of the Handicapped, the National Association of the Physically Handicapped, and the MSU 4-H Handicapper Mainstreaming Developmental Committee. She served as National Director of the Handicapper Advocacy Alliance and as president of the Michigan Association of Handicappers in Higher Education. Gentile was the author of published articles and poetry, as well as a book of poetry illustrated with her graphic art. Among her awards are the Governor's Citation as the Most Outstanding Handicapper Citizen in 1969, the Governor's Citation from the Michigan Commission on Handicapper Concerns and the Michigan Rehabilitation Association in 1974, "Handicapper Professional Woman of the Year" by PILOT International in 1976, and a university-wide award for outstanding leadership and support of Affirmative Action/Equal Opportunity and for Diversity and Excellence at MSU in 1990. Ref.: 22 (Apr. 30, 1993, 4B); 57 (Apr. 30, 1993, 2B)

****

"Neither Delay Nor Rest."
Motto of the Michigan Equal Suffrage Association

****

GERBER, DOROTHY SCOTT (1903-1988), of Fremont; originator of the idea of producing canned strained baby foods to add to the adult product line of the family's Fremont Canning Company, in 1927. After she urged her husband to produce strained baby foods, the idea was researched and sample products were developed for mothers to test. The convenient, nutritional foods, introduced commercially in 1928, were a marketing success. Gerber herself promoted the new baby foods with personal appearances across the country. A flood of letters from parents led to her national newspaper column, "Bringing Up Baby: Hints by

Mrs. Dan Gerber, Mother of Five." By 1929 the company was the largest baby food supplier in the country and in 1941 its name was changed to Gerber Products Company. Gerber gave her art collection to the Grand Rapids Art Museum, where a gallery is named in her honor. Ref.: 214

GERUS, KATHLEEN, of Sterling Heights; founder of the Women's Outreach Network. Infected with the HIV virus through her late husband, a hemophiliac who received the virus through blood transfusions, Gerus founded the Network to support women, both "affected and infected," in the hemophiliac community. She has chaired the National Hemophilia Foundation, serves on the board of the National Association of People with AIDS, is a safe-sex educator at the Midwest AIDS Prevention Project in Detroit and a speaker for the Michigan Medical Society. Ref.: 25 (Mar. 5, 1995, 5C)

GHOUGOIAN, JOAN, of Detroit; first woman to command the homicide division of the Detroit Police Department, in 1995; perhaps the only woman in the U. S. to head a major city homicide division. Holding the rank of Inspector, she oversees a 70-person staff that includes eight women. A Detroit native, Ghougoian began with the DPL in 1974, working as a patrol officer and sex crimes investigator before joining the homicide division in 1988. She graduated from Wayne State University in 1991 with degrees in sociology and criminal justice. Ref.: 22 (Sept. 9, 1995, 1A-2A)

GIBSON, JO ANN, of Detroit; founder of Excel Network (now called Affirm), the Detroit chapter of the National Association for Female Executives (NAFE), in 1989, and its first director until 1994; founder of Women's History Presentations in 1991. The largest businesswomen's professional organization in the country, NAFE is dedicated to the advancement of women in the workplace through education and networking. The Excel Network provides an environment where women in all occupations can come together for support, education, networking and communication. After 26 years as supervisor in the customer service department at Bendix Corporation and DynaPath Systems, Gibson founded her own business, Matters & More, in 1991, to provide temporary office assistance, on-site customer service training and support to small businesses and professionals. She also presents programs on women's history to schools, organizations, businesses and through radio. Her other memberships include the National Association of Women Business Owners (NAWBO), NAACP, and Strive Network. Ref.: 22 (Mar. 1, 1994, 1E); 156

GIESE, ELIZABETH HOMER, of Lansing; first State Director of the national model, Project on Equal Education Rights (PEER), and the author of the NOW Legal Defense and Education Fund's 1980 PEER report on sex equity in Michigan schools, the first statewide grassroots effort to ensure compliance with Title IX and the first such state study in the nation; as chair of the NOW Education Task Force, the initiator of a law suit by the NOW Legal and Defense

Education Fund and the Michigan ACLU against the Detroit Public Schools to stop a nationwide movement to establish all-male academies, in violation of Title IX; founder in 1994 of the Women's Book Project, to increase the number of books and educational materials about women's history and women in public school libraries. Giese holds a B.A. in Education from the University of Michigan and an M.A. in Occupational Administration from Ferris State University. She has been Education Director of the Michigan Women's Historical Center and Hall of Fame since 1987. Formerly she served as consultant with the Michigan Department of Labor's Bureau of Employment Training, State Director of PEER for NOW, consultant with the Michigan Department of Education, and as a preschool and elementary school teacher. She has been chair of the NOW Education Task Force since 1989, a convening member of Michigan ERAmerica since 1976, and a member of the Michigan Women's Assembly since 1982. She has also served on many boards, including those of Livingston County Voice for Choice and and Livingston County Womanfest. Her memberships include the Democratic Women's Caucus, Michigan BPW, Michigan LWV, NOW, MWSA, NWSA, NCSEE, and the Women's Conference of Concerns. Giese received the Women In Communication's Vanguard Award and the Detroit City Council's Spirit of Detroit Award in 1980, the Michigan Women's Hall of Fame Lucinda Stone Award in 1983, and NOW Leadership Awards in 1982, 1984, 1992, and 1995. Ref.: 157

GLOVER, SARA, of Grand Rapids; first African American licensed practical nurse in Grand Rapids, in the early 1950s; charter member of the Grand Rapids Urban League Guild; founding member of the XYZ (Extra Years of Zest) Senior Citizens Center, for which she located the building that serves as its headquarters. Born in Alabama, Glover moved to Grand Rapids in 1922. After holding a series of different jobs, she enrolled in the Grand Rapids Junior College School of Practical Nursing in 1950. She is also a member of the Grand Rapids Civic Club and the NAACP, and is active in the Messiah Baptist Church. In 1988 she was honored for her long service to the XYZ Senior Citizens Center. Ref.: 41 (Sept. 14, 1988, C8); 136

GOEBEL, JANE, see **ATKIN, KAREN HALLER**

GOETSCH, ALMA, see **WINCKLER, KATHRINE**

GOGGIN, FLORA, see **COLLAMER BAUMAN, ROSELLA E.**

GOODALE HITCHCOCK, HELEN R. (dates not known), of Traverse City; first schoolteacher in Traverse City, from 1853 to 1854. She taught school in an abandoned log building previously used as a stable. She later married Thomas A. Hitchcock. Ref.: 116 (36)

GOODWIN, DELLA MAE McGRAW, of Detroit; founder of the Associate Degree Nursing Program at Wayne County Community College in 1972; first woman and first African American elected as board president of the Comprehensive Health Planning Council of Southeastern Michigan (CHPC-SEM), a federal regulatory body that oversees a seven-county region, in 1979; founder and chair of the National Center for the Advancement of Blacks in the Health professions (NCABHP). The nursing program eliminates barriers that formerly screened out non-traditional students, making it possible for minority women of low income, family responsibilities, and minimal employment opportunities to become registered nurses. By the time of her retirement in 1986, more than 2400 nurses had graduated from the program. In 1982 the Michigan Legislature adopted a resolution to recognize her contributions to the state as president of CHPC-SEM. She was the first nurse to receive the Bertha Lee Culp Human Rights Award from the Michigan Nurses' Association in 1985, for her contribution to increased numbers of minorities in nursing. Ref.: 184

GORRECHT, FREIDA (1917-1994), of Detroit; founder and president of Citizens for Better Care (a statewide organization monitoring nursing homes), of the National Citizens Coalition for Nursing Home Reform, and of the National Institute on Senior Centers, now part of the National Council on Aging. A native of Pennsylvania, she earned a degree in education at West Chester State College, then worked in settlement houses in New Orleans and Milwaukee before moving to Detroit. She directed the Walter Reuther Retired Workers Centers from 1964 until her retirement in 1981, then served six years as president of the Legal Aid and Defenders Association of Detroit. Gorrecht was also executive director of the East Grand Boulevard Senior Center and a member of the Michigan Society of Gerontology. She was named Michigan Social Worker of the year in 1979, received the Michigan Senior Power Day Heritage Award in 1980, and in 1992, while chair of the Detroit Commission on Aging, was named a Distinguished Warrior by the Detroit Urban League for her contributions to better care for older adults. Ref.: 22 (Mar. 18, 1992, 4A); 25 (Aug. 7, 1994, 2C)

****

"Grand Rapids is noted for its furniture factories,
and after equal suffrage is granted it will supply
plenty of material for the President's cabinet."

Josephine Ahnefeldt Goss, 1899

****

GOSS, JOSEPHINE AHNEFELDT (1859-1938), of Grand Rapids; founder of the first open-air school in Michigan; first Grand Rapids educator to use motion pictures and radio in school work; founder of the first summer playground on school grounds in Grand Rapids. Born in Ontario, she moved in 1865 to Muskegon, where she began teaching in 1876. After teaching in the Elk Rapids schools, she returned to Muskegon as a principal from 1882 to 1887, when she went to Grand Rapids to serve as principal in various schools until 1891, the year she married. As principal of the Jefferson Street school, Goss started the first open-air schoolroom in the state, with the financial help of **Florence Hills Waters**. She then became principal of the Grand Rapids Normal Training School. As a member of the Board of Education from 1896 to 1907, she started the first summer playground. She also advocated manual training. She later served as principal of the Central and Sigsbee schools, before retiring in 1931. Goss was also active in the Woman Suffrage Movement. Rev.: 41 (Nov. 21, 1938); 136; 183

GOULD, JOSEPHINE WHITE (1845-1923), of Owosso; co-founder of the Owosso Literary Society in 1876; founder of the private Oakside School at Owosso in 1883; co-founder of the Current Topic Club at Owosso in 1894; co-founder of the Shiawassee Chapter, Daughters of the American Revolution, in 1907. Active in the Owosso Women's Club, she was twice elected president of the Michigan State Federation of Women's Clubs, serving from 1902 to 1904. A native of Massachusetts, she arrived in Michigan in 1870 and taught school in Corunna and Owosso before her marriage to Lucius Gould in 1875. Her Oakside School prepared many young people for entrance into universities and military academies. Ref.: 49 (196)

GRAUNSTADT, CHERYL, of Westland; founder of CHECK (Concerned for the Health and Environment of Our Kids), an environmental activist organization, in 1991. After learning that the Livonia school her children attended had been built in 1965 over a landfill, she led public pressure to close the school and transfer the students to another nearby school. The landfill site, contaminated with lead, mercury, arsenic and DDT, is considered one of Michigan's worst. Graunstadt's extensive research on landfill dangers and CHECK'S political activism to force regulation has brought national awareness of landfill problems. As a result of the group's work, state legislation establishing guidelines about building schools near landfills went into effect in 1993. CHECK has received a national environmental award from consumer advocate Ralph Nader. Ref.: 25 (May 2, 1993, 3C, 8C)

GRAVES, ANN E. LAPHAM (1822-1894), of Battle Creek; co-founder of the Battle Creek Ladies' Library, in 1864, which became the Ladies' Literary and Art Club in the mid-1870s, and was renamed the Woman's Club in 1892; co-founder of the Battle Creek Woman's League in 1895; co-founder and first president of the Battle Creek Equal Suffrage Association, in 1874; first woman elected to the new Battle Creek School Board in 1874 and chosen as its first president. At the State Suffrage Association meeting in Lansing, she was named a vice president of the Third District, Calhoun County. Born and educated in Erie County, New York, she came to Battle Creek in 1846 and opened Miss Lapham's Select School. She was married in 1851 to Benjamin Graves, who later became a Michigan Supreme Court Justice. For 26 years, she was president of the Woman's Club, which still exists. Throughout her life in Battle Creek, she was a staunch supporter of the Woman Suffrage Movement. It is highly probable that she was a friend of **Sojourner Truth**, since her son Henry is known to have played with Truth's grandson, Billy Boyd. Ref.: 106 (Feb. 1995, 8-11)

GREEN, MARY E. (1844-1910) of Charlotte; said to be the first woman physician in the U.S. to be admitted to any medical association, with her election to the New York Medical Society c. 1870. Born near Machias, New York, she came to Michigan with her family in the 1850s, settling in Barry County. During her school years, she did housework for a family in exchange for her board and enough money to pay for school. At age 14, she passed a "teacher's examination" and began teaching school. Later she attended Hastings Public School and Battle Creek High School, followed by study at Olivet College and Oberlin College. In 1865 she entered the New York Medical College for Women and did clinical work at Bellevue Hospital. The following year, after marrying Alonzo Green, she entered the Woman's Medical College in Philadelphia, graduating in 1868. She began her medical practice in New York, where she was Visiting Physician to the Midnight Mission, the Five Points Mission, the Prison Home for Women and Dr. Blackwell's Infirmary. She was the first to advocate separate prison wagons for men and women prisoners. In a poor tenement district, she organized a free Western Dispensary for Women and Children, which was so successful it received city and state aid. When she decided to enter the medical society, she was advised by Drs. Emily and Elizabeth Blackwell that she could never succeed and would only retard the progress of women. Despite much opposition, she was finally elected. In 1873 she moved to Charlotte, where she continued her practice, specializing in diet and sanitation, and became a member of the State Medical Society, which twice elected her as its delegate to the American Medical Association. During the Cuban War, she was asked to establish a diet kitchen for typhoid patients at Fort Thomas in Kentucky. Green, who was also a painter and woodcarver, carved a handsome stair rail in her home, which today serves as the Burkhead-Green Funeral Home. Ref.: 101 (235-238); 119; 176

GREENWOOD, MABEL S. (dates not known), of Detroit; foreman of the first all-woman jury in Michigan, in Judge Bolton's Detroit court on March 19, 1919. The other women on the jury were **Lelah McCauley, Emily M. Birmingham, Winifred G. Burdick, May Hayes**, and **Aulga Sutterly**. Greenwood was an officer and the other women were members of the Detroit Women Citizens' League. The case involved a damage suit brought against an "autoist, who was charged with negligently colliding with the plaintiff's wagon." The jury's verdict was not recorded. Greenwood was also active in the Woman Suffrage Movement. Ref.: 132

GRIFFIN, JEAN, see **COLLAMER BAUMAN, ROSELLA E.**

GRIFFITH, ROBERTA A. (1870-1941), of Grand Rapids; first blind person to attend Western Reserve University in Cleveland; co-founder of the American Association of Workers for the Blind in 1905; compiler of the first Braille dictionary, a six-volume work, c. 1905; co-founder and first executive secretary of the Association for the Blind and Sight Conservation (now called Vision Enrichment Services) in 1913. Born in Philadelphia, she lost her sight as a small child. After attending schools for the blind in Michigan and Ohio, she entered Western Reserve University on a scholarship, supple-mented by her work as a writer and music teacher, and graduated with honors. In 1900 she moved to Grand Rapids to be near her mother, continuing to work as a writer and real estate agent. The American Association of Workers for the Blind developed out of the first national meeting of superintendents of schools for the blind, who came to Grand Rapids at Griffith's invitation. As the only executive secretary until her death of the Association for the Blind and Sight Conservation, she led the fight for state legislation providing for compulsory use of nitrate of silver as an antiseptic in the eyes of infants, thus saving the sight of many newborns. She also created Braille classes in public schools, trained Braille teachers, and sponsored a Braille club for former Michigan School for the Blind students. Griffith was inducted into the Michigan Women's Hall of Fame in 1993. Ref.: 184

****

"If the women of Michigan do all they plan to do,
there will be no need of equal suffrage after November 5,
for the women will all be dead."

Caroline Bartlett Crane of Kalamazoo, speaking of the
Suffrage campaign conducted by Michigan women in 1912

****

GRIMES, LUCIA ISABELLE VOORHEES (1877-1978), of Detroit; originator of a political strategy used during the Michigan Suffrage Campaigns of 1912 and 1913; co-founder of the Wayne County Equal Suffrage League; co-founder of the Michigan branch of the Congressional Union, later called the National Woman's Party; founder of the Wayne County Republican Women's Club in 1919; first chair of the Legislative Council of Michigan Women; leader in the Detroit Women's Citizens League and officer in the Michigan Equal Suffrage Association. As chair of the Michigan branch of the National Woman's Party, Grimes developed a card index filing system to record the attitude of every Michigan legislator toward suffrage for women. The system was so successful that Alice Paul invited her to Washington, D.C., to institute a similar filing system recording opinions of members of the U.S. Congress. In 1916 Grimes and her 5-year-old daughter **Emily** went to Washington, where she set up her card file system at the headquarters of the National Woman's Party. Armed with information about each Congressman's opinions, history and interests, the women were able to target and bring pressure on those opposed to equal

suffrage. As legislative chair of the Michigan Federation of
Women's Clubs, Grimes led the fight that culminated in Michigan
becoming the second state to ratify the Suffrage Amendment. In
1968, at the age of 90, she recorded her experiences in a book,
A History of the Suffrage Movement as Related to Michigan and
Detroit, recalling that it took five weeks to complete the Congressional card file, later called the "pressure system." Born in Illinois,
Grimes earned degrees in education from the University of
Michigan in 1902 and 1905, taught in one-room schools before her
marriage, and later at Cass Tech High School in Detroit from 1929
until 1948. She also served as vice president and purchasing
agent for the Grimes Molding Machine Company that she and her
husband founded in Detroit. In 1968 she was honored by the
Michigan Federation of Republican Women for her 50 years of
leadership. Two days before her 97th birthday in 1974, she made
a speech on behalf of the Equal Rights Amendment at a Women's
Equality Day rally in Detroit. She received the National President's
Award from the Daughters of Founders and Patriots of America in
1976 and in her 100th year she was honored by the University of
Michigan with its Outstanding Achievement Award for her work as a
teacher, business executive, and women's rights advocate. She was
also a member of the Hypatia Club and OES. Grimes was inducted
into the Michigan Women's Hall of Fame in 1995. Ref.: 160

GRISWOLD, MRS. JOHN (dates and first name not known), of Eagle
River; first woman to be lighthouse keeper of the Eagle River
Lighthouse, from December of 1858 to February of 1859, following
the death of her husband, the previous keeper. Ref.: 88 (39); 170

GUBBINS, ROBERTA M., of Ann Arbor; first woman to be on a men's
varsity rifle team in the Big Ten, as a member of the University of
Michigan Men's Varsity Rifle Team in the mid-1950s. A junior from
Birmingham, she was on the winning U-M team in the Western
Conference rifle meet in 1956, placing seventh among all
competitors. After the meet, the coaches of the Western Conference
Rifle Association voted to bar women from competing in future
meets, in spite of support from her coach and team members.
Gubbins, who learned to shoot from her father, had already won
more than 100 medals and cups in rifle competition and had been
on the U-M team two years. After graduating from U-M and the
University of Cincinnati, she taught school in Ohio before receiving
a law degree from the Detroit College of Law in 1987. Now an
attorney in Ann Arbor, she has served as chief assistant prosecutor
for Antrim County. Her memberships include the LWV and the
Women Lawyers of Michigan. Ref.: 4 (Jun. 6, 1956; 25 (Jun. 6,
1956); 73 (May 27, 1956); 162

HAINES, BLANCHE MOORE (1865-1944), of Three Rivers; first
woman to be a member of the Three Rivers Board of Education, from
1899 to 1902. Born in Delaware, she moved west with her parents
to Nebraska, graduated from Illinois schools, received her medical

degree in 1886 from Woman's Hospital Medical College of Chicago
(later named the Woman's Medical School of Northwestern Univer-
sity), and interned at Women's and Children's Hospital in Chicago.
After her marriage in 1890 to Dr. Thomas J. Haines, the couple
began their medical practice at Three Rivers, where she was the
City Health Officer from 1897 to 1898. She served as president of
both the St. Joseph County and Third and Fourth District Equal
Suffrage Associations, and on the board of the Michigan Equal
Suffrage Association and the executive council of the National
Woman Suffrage Association. She was elected as medical examiner
for the Ladies of the Maccabees at Port Huron, serving from 1920 to
1922, when she was appointed to organize and direct the Bureau of
Child Hygiene and Public Health Nursing in the Michigan
Department of Health. In 1925 she was appointed as a director in
the Maternity and Infancy Division of the Children's Bureau of the
U. S. Dept. of Labor in Washington, D.C. She was a member of the
American Public Health Association, American Women's Medical
Association, AMA, AAUW, DAR, Michigan Daughters of Colonial
Wars, and Three Rivers Woman's Club. Ref.: 204

HAMER, SYLVIA J. COLE (1900-1993), of Ann Arbor; founder in
1954 of the Ann Arbor Civic Ballet, the first regional civic ballet
company in Michigan, serving as its director until her retirement.
A native of Peck, Michigan, Hamer was a professional dancer before
founding the Sylvia Studio of Dance in 1932. She was a Fellow of
the Imperial Society of Teachers of Dance of England and a charter
member of the Cecchetti Council of America, an organization to
improve the quality of instruction of dance teachers. **Lee Ann King**,
her granddaughter, now directs the Sylvia Studio of Dance.
Ref.: 4 (Dec. 13, 1993, C4); 173

HAMILTON, ALICE (1869-1970); first woman to teach at Harvard
University, as Assistant Professor of Industrial Medicine; one of the
first persons in the nation to be concerned about the effects of
industrial pollution on human lives and the first to diagnose lead
poisoning and the ill-effects of using lead paint. Born in Fort
Wayne, Indiana, she graduated from the University of Michigan
Medical School in 1893, interned at the New England Hospital for
Women and Children, and then studied at the Universities of
Leipzig and Munich in Germany. Her sister **Edith Hamilton**, who
became a well-known translator of Greek classics and the head of
Bryn Mawr preparatory school for girls, studied the classics at the
two universities at the same time. After further study at John
Hopkins, in 1898 Alice joined Jane Addams at Hull House, the
Chicago settlement house, staying until 1919. She taught at the
Woman's Medical College of Northwestern University during the day
and spent nights and weekends working among the poor in the
slum around Hull House. In 1910 she began her lifelong study of
occupational disease by traveling across the country, visiting
factories and mines to discover the effects of industrial pollution on
workers' health. Her industrial investigations led to some of the

first workers' compensation laws. She attended both the First International Congress of Women, held in 1915 in The Hague, and the Second International Congress of Women, held at Zurich in 1919. Returning to the United States, she was hired to teach at Harvard, where she was asked never to use the Harvard Club nor to demand her quota of football tickets, and, athough she was invited to march in commencement academic processions, her invitation always warned that "under no circumstances may a woman sit on the platform." Beginning in 1879, Alice, Edith, and their sister **Norah Hamilton**, an artist who studied with James McNeill Whistler and illustrated Jane Addams' autobiographies, spent many summers at Mackinac Island in the three cottages built by their family, visiting the island as late as 1960. In 1995 a United States stamp bearing Alice Hamilton's image was issued to honor her contributions to industrial medicine and world peace. Ref.: 57 (Jul. 16, 1995, 1C); 64 (May 21-17, 1994, 18); 68 (89-94)

****

"When woman gets her rights, man will be right."

Sojourner Truth of Battle Creek

****

HAMILTON, RENA LOUISA TOMPKINS (1873-1943), of Battle Creek; co-founder of the Sturgis Woman's Club; co-founder of the garden club movement in Michigan and first president of the Garden Club of Battle Creek. Born in Coldwater, she moved with her family to Sturgis, where she married Burritt Hamilton in 1894. After moving to Battle Creek, she joined the Woman Suffrage League, serving as president from 1913 to 1915. She became president of the Michigan State Federation of Women's Clubs in 1919. Fond of roses, she grew 300 varieties in her rose garden and organized the Rose Study Club. She was also active in the DAR, the YWCA, the Battle Creek Woman's Club, the Michigan Women's Press Association, and the National Women's Committee for the National Cathedral. Ref.: 49 (197); 77 (Sept. 1914, 7)

HAMPTON, CHRISTINE, see **TILLEY, BARBARA**

HARBOR, GLADYS, see **THE MARVELETTES**

HARRISON, MRS. DONALD E. (dates and first name not known), of Sault Ste. Marie; first woman to be the lighthouse keeper at the St. Mary's River Light, from 1902 to 1904. Ref.: 18 (164)

HASKINS, CAROL L., of suburban Detroit; first woman in Michigan to be designated a Certified Executive Chef by the American Culinary Federation Educational Institute, in 1982. Of the 2,230 executive chefs certified by the institute from 1977 until 1993, only 56 had been women. Haskins has been an executive chef at many of southeast Michigan's finest restaurants and has helped to train hundreds of chefs throughout the Detroit area during her 35 years of food preparation. With no formal training, she learned the art of cooking by working in the family restaurant in southwest Detroit. She helped to introduce Continental Cuisine in the 1970s, Nouvelle Cuisine in the 1980s, and healthier cooking and eating in the 1990s. As a person with insulin-dependent diabetes, she learned to adjust her own diet and has incorporated many of those changes into her professional cooking. Ref.: 17 (Autumn 1993, 2+)

HAWKINS, PAULA, of Richland; first Michigan angler in the 16-year history of the Bass'N Gal tournament trail to qualify to fish in the circuit's world championship, the Classic; founder of Lady Bass Anglers of West Michigan, a women's bass club; first woman to fish in Michigan's BASS Federation circuit. Hawkins finished second in the Bass'N Gal Classic, held in October, 1992, at Mark Twain Lake in Missouri. Ref.: 4 (Sept. 5, 1992, C1-C2; Sept. 4, 1993)

HAWLEY, ROSE DAMARIS HORNE (1889-1991), of Ludington; founder in 1951 and first director of the Mason County Museum (renamed the Rose Hawley Museum in 1970) in Ludington. Born in Auburn, she studied at the Bay City Business College before her marriage to Guy Hawley in 1910. She was the club editor for the Ludington Daily News and a writer for the Mason County Enterprise and Grand Rapids Herald. She also published three books, two written in her nineties. She began the Museum by collecting artifacts and documents from Mason County's past and headed the drive to preserve the county's first courthouse in Buttersville, leading to the creation of White Pine Village, a living history museum. She was active in the Mason County Red Cross, the Young Women's Club, and the Mason County Garden Club and was honored by the City of Ludington, the Mason County Historical Society, and the Ludington Optimists Club. Ref.: 62 (Nov. 11, 1989, 1-2); 206

HAYES, JENNIE (dates not known), of Lansing; first woman to enlist as a Civil War nurse in the 1st Michigan Regiment of Volunteers, organized in 1861. Ref.: 83 (17-18)

HAYES, MAY, see **GREENWOOD, MABEL S.**

HEATH, LENORA COOPER (1875-1964), of Hastings; first woman elected to the Hastings School Board, serving from 1922 to 1932. Born in Charlotte, she moved as a child to Hastings, where she married and worked as a bookkeeper. During World War I she headed the Loyalty League, an organization to raise funds for the war effort. Ref.: 97

HEMMINGSEN, CHRISTINE (d. 1884), of Negaunee; founder of the national Danish Sisterhood of America (Danske Sostersamfund) in 1883. Its goals were to promote friendship and the Danish heritage, to work for the betterment of this country, and to aid its members, including the giving of funeral benefits. The first lodge was named for its founder, Christine Lodge No. 1. Hemmingsen's husband was a member of the Danish Brotherhood, which officiated at the opening and served in the Supreme Offices for several years. The next lodges were organized in Iowa, Illinois and Wisconsin. The Sisterhood's first convention was held at Chicago in 1887. Spurred by the influx of Danish immigrants, 84 lodges had been formed by 1904, including two in Detroit and Royal Oak. In 1910, for the first time, women were elected to all of the offices at the national convention in Iowa. Membership is restricted to women of Danish birth, descent, or heritage, or of Danish lineage by marriage or relationship. Ref.: 29 (256-257)

HENDRICKS, JENNIE MARIA BURNETT (1889-1989), of Traverse City; founder and first president of the PTA in Kalkaska. Known as "Jennie B," she was born in Vermont, where she graduated from high school, taught in a one-room school for a year, and earned a registered nurse's certificate. In 1914 she married a physician and they moved to Traverse City, where she became active in the Grand Traverse County Equal Suffrage Association, marching and passing out literature on street corners. After the 19th Amendment became law, she proudly voted in the 1920 election and in every subsequent election during her long life. She was also active in the Traverse City PTA, WCTU, and her church. Ref.: 113 (Dec. 9, 1990, 1D-2D)

HENDRIE, KATHLEEN McGRAW, see **REYNEAU, BETSY GRAVES** and **ALDINGER, ELLA HOUGH**

HERING, BARBARA C., formerly of Lansing; founder and president of Mid-Michigan ALMACA (Association of Labor-Management Administrators and Consultants on Alcoholism); founder and president of the Capitol Area Chapter, Coalition of Labor Union Women (CLUW). A switching equipment technician for Michigan Bell Telephone Company in Lansing, Hering has served as Labor Representative to the Joint Employee Counseling Program of the Communications Workers of America (CWA), Local 4040, and Michigan Bell Telephone Company. In 1977 she organized and chaired Local 4040 CWA's Community Services Committee and in 1983 she organized the first statewide ALMACA conference. She has served on the Ingham-Eaton County Substance Abuse Advisory Council, the Capitol Area Substance Abuse Commission, the Council Against Domestic Assault, the committee for the Michigan Historical Museum exhibit on Michigan women and the labor movement, and the committee to establish the Michigan Women's Historical Center and Hall of Fame. She has acted in local theater productions with the Lansing Civic Theater and Lansing Community College. In 1982 she received a YWCA Diana Award honoring her work to enhance union and community life for women. Ref.: 184

HETH, CYNTHIA H. (c. 1908-1991), of Grand Rapids; founder and first director of the Eastern Orthopedic School in 1923 and the Indian Trails Camp for children with disabilities in 1953; founder and first director of the Special Education division of the Grand Rapids Public Schools, 1940s-1950s; founder of programs for special needs children in the Kent County school systems, 1940s-1950s. A native of Grand Rapids, Heth graduated from Eastern Michigan University. She taught and served as a principal in Grand Rapids schools, including 23 years as principal of the combined Eastern Elementary and Eastern Orthopedic School and Mary Free Bed School for handicapped children. In 1960 she was named Woman of the Year by the Association for Childhood Education and in 1964 she received the Distinguished Service Award from Rotary International for her work with disabled children. Ref.: 136; 183

****

"It is not less chivalry women seek, but more justice;
and power always commands respect."

Clara B. Arthur, of Detroit

****

HILDING, ELSIE (1890-1981), of Grand Rapids; winner of the first Women's City Golf Championship at Grand Rapids, in 1921. She won six more women's city championships, in addition to the state amateur title in 1923, west Michigan amateur titles and the Florida women's west coast golf championship, before retiring from tournament play in 1939. She was a member of the Michigan Women's Golf Association and the Women's City Golf Association, which holds an annual Elsie Hilding Day golf tournament and presents the Elsie Hilding Trophy in her honor. On her 90th birthday, she played in the Michigan Senior Women's Golf Tournament at the Dearborn Country Club. Ref.: 41 (Jun. 15, 1969; Aug. 29, 1970); 186

HILL, HARRIET, of Grand Rapids; first African American woman to join the Grand Rapids Police Department, in 1955; first woman detective in the Grand Rapids Police Department, in 1977; first woman officer to retire from the Grand Rapids Police Department, in 1981. First employed as a clerk-typist in the Identification Bureau, Hill originally planned to work no more than 3 years, but the work of the female officers in the Juvenile Division inspired her to become an officer. Specializing in investigating family-related crimes, Hill taught numerous police recruit classes in dealing with domestic violence and child abuse and neglect. Ref.: 41 (May 19, 1968; Jan. 7, 1977; Sept. 30, 1981, 4C); 136; 183

HILLARY EARHART, NOREEN E., of Grand Rapids; one of the first two women, with **KAY E. WHITFIELD McENTEE** of Pontiac, to become Michigan State Police Troopers, on May 26, 1967. A Grand Rapids native, Hillary earned a sociology degree from Marymount College in Kansas and became a Kent County social worker. Whitfield earned a degree in police administration in 1964 from Michigan State University, joined the Kalamazoo Police Department and became a detective. Ref.: 25 (May 28, 1957); 57 (May 27, 1957); 159

HILLIARD, WENDY, formerly of Detroit; first African American member of the U.S. Rhythmic Gymnastics team; first African American woman elected as president of the Women's Sports Foundation, 1994. A 1978 Cass Tech High School graduate, Hilliard studied Russian and physical education at Wayne State University before graduating from New York University with a degree in broadcast journalism. She often faced racial discrimination as a nine-time member of the national team and, as president of the WSF, has focused on removing such barriers, as well as on Title IX issues, health and fitness. Now living in New York City, she is director of amateur sports for the NYC Sports Commission, is a TV analyst for rhythmic and artistic gymnastics, and performs with a traveling dance/gymnastics company called "Antigravity." Ref.: 22 (Oct. 17, 1994, C2)

HINE, DARLENE CLARK, of East Lansing; editor of the first major history of African American women, Black Women in America, a two-volume encyclopedia, in 1993. A graduate of Roosevelt University in Chicago and Kent State University, Hine has been the John A. Hannah Professor of History at Michigan State University since 1987. While teaching at Purdue University in 1980, she researched and wrote the history of black women in Indiana, aided by a grant from the National Endowment for the Humanities. Realizing that very little recognition had been given to the achievements of black women in America, she expanded her research to include women throughout the country, helped by associate editors Elsa Barkley Brown of the University of Michigan and Rosalyn Terborg-Penn of Morgan State University in Baltimore, as well as 400 scholars and graduate students throughout the country. The resulting encyclopedia includes more than 800 entries, 641 individual biographies and 163 essays. Ref.: 22 (Jan. 16, 1994, 1C, 3C); 25 (Feb. 6, 1993, 1C-2C); 57 (May 25, 1993, 1E); 92 (Spring 1993, 4)

HINSDALE, MARY LOUISE, see **VAN HOESEN, GRACE AMES**

HOGUE, GWENDOLYN, see **LOVE, JOSEPHINE HERRALD**

HOGUE, MICKI KING, formerly of Pontiac; first woman to coach and teach at the U.S. Air Force Academy, 1973 to 1977, 1983 to 1989; first woman to coach a male diver to an NCAA championship; first woman inducted into the University of Michigan Hall of Honor; co-founder of the Women's Sports Foundation. A 1966 graduate of the University of Michigan, Hogue won a gold medal in springboard diving at the 1972 Olympics in Munich. She holds nine U.S. national diving titles and four Canadian titles, was named Diver of the Year in 1965, 1969, and 1972, and NCAA Division II Coach of the year three times. She served for 26 years in the U.S. Air Force. In 1989 she became commander of the Air Force ROTC program at the University of Kentucky, where she also advises the swimming team. She has also served as an Olympic representative and as president of U.S. Diving Inc., the national governing body of

Olympic diving. She was elected to the International Swimming Hall of Fame in 1978, the Women's Sports Hall of Fame in 1983, and the State of Michigan Sports Hall of Fame in 1993. Ref.: 4 (Nov. 7, 1991, B1, B7; May 13, 1993, B8); 66 (118)

HOLLISTER, JUSTINA MERRICK, see **VAN HOESEN, GRACE AMES**

HOMMEL, FLORA SUHD, of Detroit; founder of the Childbirth Without Pain Education Association, to teach the psychoprophylactic Lamaze Method of painless childbirth. After studying in Paris with Dr. Fernand Lamaze, the method's originator, she came back to Detroit in 1953 to enroll at Wayne State University, from which she graduated with a BS degree in Nursing in 1958. Meanwhile she started teaching Lamaze classes to expectant parents. The organization she founded has had over 18,000 students, trained hundreds of instructors, and inspired the formation of many similar organizations across the country. She was elected to the National Board of the International Childbirth Education Association, serving from 1964 to 1968. She has been an activist for women's equality, including Women's Strike for Peace and Women's Conference of Concerns. As a civil rights worker, she was with the Michigan Friends of the South during the 1950s and 1960s. She has also been active in anti-war movements, is a member of the U.S. Peace Council, New Jewish Agenda, and the National Board of the Gray Panthers, has served on the Detroit and the State of Michigan Health Commissions, and is involved with UHCAN (Universal Health Care Action Network) and MichUHCAN to achieve universal single payer health care. She was inducted into the Michigan Women's Hall of Fame in 1994. Ref.: 25 (Apr. 9, 1989); 26 (Aug. 2, 1971); 84 (Jan. 8-21, 1995, 7); 184

HOOD, DENISE PAGE, of Detroit; first African American woman elected as president of the Detroit Bar Association, in 1993. Since 1983 she had been on the board of the association, organized in 1836. A graduate of Columbia University Law School, she was elected to the Wayne County Circuit Court bench in 1992. Ref.: 22 (May 13, 1993, B1)

HOROWITZ, JUNE, of Grand Rapids; first woman to be president of the International Brotherhood of Magicians (IBM), 1987-1988. Horowitz, a retired teacher of music and math in the Grand Rapids public schools, is from a family of magicians, including her father, husband, sons, sister, brother and grandchildren. Ref.: 63 (5)

HOUHANISIN, MARY, of Brighton; first woman to be a drum major for Michigan State University's Marching Band in the band's 125-year history. A junior majoring in business administration and pre-law, she performed officially as drum major for the first time during the 1995 season's opening game on September 9, 1995. Women musicians were not allowed in the band until 1972's Title IX was enacted. Ref.: 57 (Sept. 5, 1995, 1B)

HOUSTON, FANNIE KANTER HUBBARD (1870-1950), of Port Huron; first woman to serve as clerk of St. Clair County, appointed in 1938, elected in 1939, serving until 1943. Born in St. Clair County, she grew up in Detroit, where she attended school. Four years after her 1898 marriage to Smith Houston in Ogdensburg, New York, the couple returned to Port Huron, where he became an invalid and she worked to support their family. In 1920 she was appointed deputy county clerk, a post she held until her appointment as county clerk. She was a member of the DAR, the Zonta Club, and the P.E.O. Sisterhood. Ref.: 141

****

"Equal Suffrage is the Birthright of Women"
Popular slogan used on Suffrage posters and banners

****

HUBBARD, MERRY HENDERSON GREEN (1910-1993), of Detroit; co-founder and first president of Eta Phi Beta business and professional sorority in 1942. Born in Youngstown, Ohio, she moved to Chicago and worked as a radio announcer before relocating to Detroit, where she graduated from the Lewis College of Business and became a legal secretary. (See **Lewis, Violet Temple** in Michigan Women: Firsts and Founders, Vol. I.) Hubbard was a childless widow of 43 when she married her second husband and became the stepmother of 13 children, ages 6 to 25. She was also an elder, deacon and president of the Women's Association at St. John's Presbyterian Church. Ref.: 22 (Sept. 2, 1993, 4B)

HUMPHRIES, BECKY, of Lowell; first woman to be a district wildlife biologist for the Michigan Department of Natural Resources, in 1986. One of just 13 district biologists in the state, she oversees a staff of biologists in the eight counties of the Grand Rapids district. Raised in Oakland County, she graduated from Michigan State University in 1977. Previously she worked in the real estate division and the land and water division of the DNR. Ref.: 4 (Dec. 18, 1993, C5)

HUNT, DIANN MARIE ROBINSON (1944-1994), of Redford Township; founder and director of New Outlook Inc., a nonprofit organization to find homes for mentally impaired people outside of institutions. Hunt was a special education teacher at Plymouth Center when deinstitutionalization forced its residents to find homes in the community. In 1980 she started New Outlook to help them relocate in suitable homes. A Detroit native and graduate of Eastern Michigan University, she also coached Livonia softball teams and was cheerleader director for the Livonia Junior Football League. She served on the boards of the Michigan Residential Care Association, American Association of Mental Retardation, Adult Retarded Citizens of Redford and Livonia, and the Jewish Association of Retarded Citizens. Ref.: 22 (Jul. 13, 1994, 4B)

HWALECK, MELANIE, see **TILLEY, BARBARA**

INGALLS, BLANCHE (dates not known), of Chesaning; first woman to be marshal of Chesaning, appointed in 1914 "in a moment of levity" by the village council, which soon regretted it. When Ingalls, who took her appointment seriously, presented her bill for sixteen days at $2 a day, the aldermen said it would have to be reduced, inasmuch as the former marshal, a man, had acted as street commissioner and dog warden. "So have I," replied Ingalls, "There haven't been any dogs to ward, but I hired a man to shovel off the walks and clean the catch basins of snow and ice. I paid him with my own money." Ingalls, described as "one of the most ardent suffragists in Saginaw County," helped garner a majority of votes in Chesaning for the 19th Amendment. Ref.: 77 (Apr. 1914, 9)

JACKSON, GAIL GEORGE of Saginaw; first woman to be Chief of the Saginaw Chippewa Indian Tribe in Mt. Pleasant, elected in 1993. Jackson, who grew up in her grandmother's home on the Chippewa reservation, held many positions on the reservation before deciding to run for tribal council, after she lost her first husband and a son in 1990. She was remarried in 1992, to Bernard Jackson. As chief, she has established a one-time $3,000 payment to be given to Tribal elders when they reach the age of 50 and required mandatory drug-testing for all employees, including herself, to demonstrate her commitment to a drug-free community. The highly successful Soaring Eagle Casino, which opened in 1993 and is managed by the tribe itself, is the first casino in Michigan to give profits back to its members in quarterly, per capita payments. Not surprisingly, many new people are claiming to be rightful members of the tribe, although membership enrollment has been closed since 1987. Jackson faces such problems with equanimity, buoyed by her strong religious faith and family support.
Ref.: 56 (Mar. 1995, 20-23)

JACKSON, NELL CECILIA (1929-1988), formerly of East Lansing; first African American head track coach of an Olympic team, as coach of the U.S. women's track team at the 1956 Olympic games in Melbourne, Australia; first woman to serve on the board of directors of the U.S. Olympic Committee; first woman to be an assistant athletic director at Michigan State University. Born in Georgia, she grew up in Tuskegee, Alabama, where she graduated from Tuskegee Institute (now Tuskegee University) in 1951. She was a member of the 1948 U.S. Olympic team and the 1951 Pan American team and for many years held the American record in the 200-meter event. After receiving a master's degree from Springfield College in 1953 and a Ph.D. from the University of Iowa in 1962, she taught physical education and coached track at the Tuskegee Institute, Illinois State University, the University of Illinois, and MSU, where she was Assistant Director of Athletics in charge of Women's Programs in 1973. At the time of her death, she was professor and director of intercollegiate athletics and physical education at the State University of New York at Binghamton. She was the author of many articles on track and the textbook, <u>Track and Field for Girls</u>

and Women. She was also head women's track coach at the 1972 Olympic games in Munich, manager of the U.S. women's track team at the Pan-American games in 1987, and conducted many track workshops throughout the country. She served as vice president and secretary of The Athletic Congress, and was active in the National Association for Girls and Women in Sports (NAGWS) and the National Collegiate Athletic Association. She was inducted into the Black Athletes Hall of Fame, won the NAGWS Honor Award twice, received the Outstanding Alumni Award from Tuskegee Institute, and a presidential citation from the NAGWS. Ref.: 8 (625-626; 57 (Mar. 20, 1992, 10S)

JACOBS-BOND, CARRIE (1862-1947) of Iron River; first Michigan woman to achieve national fame as a composer of popular music, in the early 1900s. Born in Janesville, Wisconsin, she married Frank L. Bond in 1889 and moved to Iron River, where her husband died in 1895. With her young son she moved to Chicago, to find employment and a publisher for the songs she had written. Her first published book of songs included "I Love You Truly" and "Just a Wearyin' for You," two songs that enjoyed great popularity. In 1901 she started her own publishing company, the Bond Shop, and began to give recitals of her own music, gradually gaining recognition. After her move to California in 1910, the great popularity of her song, "A Perfect Day," brought financial security and lasting fame. Throughout the years she maintained contact with her friends in Iron River, where the Carrie Jacobs-Bond Musicale honors her memory. During a visit in 1938, she recalled her time in Iron River as the "happiest years of my life." The Carrie Jacobs-Bond Room in the Iron County Museum at nearby Caspian was set up by the Iron County Historical and Museum Society, which also moved her Iron River home to Caspian to preserve as a historical site. Ref.: 7

JAMES, MARIE and LUCILLE (dates not known), of Calumet; the first two women in Calumet to register to vote, in 1918 after Michigan women won that right. They were graduates of Northern Michigan University and active in the Woman Suffrage Movement. Ref.: 47; 193

JASINSKI, LUCILLE (1920-1993), Royal Oak; founder of the Concert Under the Stars by the Detroit Symphony Orchestra; founder of the Polish-American hootenanies at Wayne State University. She received her teaching certificate from Central Michigan University in 1942. After serving in the Army Signal Corps during World War II, she taught school for several years before earning her master's degree in education from Wayne State University and another master's degree in library science from Rutgers University. Born in Detroit's Poletown area, she was active in the Polish community and a member of the Kosciuszko Foundation, Polish National Alliance, Polish Aid Society of Michigan

and Friends of Polish Art. In teaching history and the social
sciences, she also taught her students about the harmful effects of
ethnic jokes about people of Polish origin. Ref.: 25 (Apr. 4, 1993)

JEFFERS, CORA DOOLITTLE (1871-1949), of Painesdale; the first
woman to register to vote in Adams Township, Houghton County, in
1918 after Michigan women won that right. Born in North Adams,
Hillsdale County, she graduated from Michigan State Normal
College (now Eastern Michigan University) in 1891 and was a high
school principal at Sault Ste. Marie before her marriage in 1894 to
Frederick A. Jeffers, superintendent of schools at Atlantic Mine in
Houghton County. After serving for 14 years as principal of the
Atlantic Mine High School, she became principal of the Painesdale
High School, where she stayed for 41 years. At the age of 75, she
was still teaching mathematics, history, choral singing, physical
education, aeronautics and swimming, which she had learned in
her 60s when a swimming pool was installed. She was the author
of a book on folk dances and rhythmic exercises, published by the
Michigan State Department of Education. In 1912 she and her
husband were both active in the suffrage movement, speaking at
rallies across the Upper Peninsula. When she became president of
the Upper Peninsula Education Association in 1914, she invited
Charlotte Perkins Gilman, a national suffrage leader, to address the
convention in Marquette on "Votes for Women." Cora Jeffers was
awarded an honorary doctorate posthumously by Northern Michigan
University and the name of Painsdale High School was changed to
Jeffers High School in honor of Cora and Fred Jeffers. Ref.: 142;
192; 215
****

Question: "If woman has the ballot, would she not sell her vote for a
new bonnet?

Anna Howard Shaw: "Perhaps she might, who knows. A new
bonnet is a fine thing and most women would hanker after it.
But a good bonnet costs more than a glass of whiskey, and that,
they say, is the market price of male votes nowadays."
****

JENNISON, MRS. G. B., see **REYNEAU, BETSY GRAVES** and
ALDINGER, ELLA HOUGH

JEROME FOX, MARY RUTH (1903-1951), of St. Clair; one of the
first three women (with **Marjorie A. Ross** of Detroit and **Lois
Manning** of Lansing) to wear knickers on the streets of Albion, in
1922. The outrageous behavior of the three Albion co-eds caused
the dean of women to issue an edict forbidding women students to
wear knickers, in or out of school. A photograph and article in the
Detroit News was captioned, "Three Knickered Co-eds Bring Down
Albion's Wrath." Ref.: 25 (Apr. 7, 1922)

JOHNSON, JEANE A. CONLIN, of Jackson; first girl to be a page in
the Michigan State Legislature, as Messenger to the Speaker of the

House of Representatives from 1949 to 1950. At the time, she was
a 12-year-old eighth-grade student. A graduate of Adrian College,
she later served as field representative for U.S. Rep. Carl Purcell
and U.S. Rep. James Dunn and as executive vice president of the
Greater Jackson Chamber of Commerce. Johnson is a member of
the Jackson BPW. Ref.: 167

**JOHNSTON, SUSAN (Ozhawguscodaywaquay, "Green Meadow
Woman")** (1776-1843), of Sault Ste. Marie; the first Native
American woman within the Michigan territory to facilitate a treaty
between her people and the U.S. Government, the 1820 Treaty of
Cession between the Ojibwa people and the United States
government, providing land for the founding of Fort Brady at Sault
Ste. Marie. Born and raised in the Chequamegon area, near
present-day LaPointe, Wisconsin, she was the daughter and
granddaughter of powerful Ojibwa chiefs. After marrying Irish fur
trader John Johnston in 1792, she was baptized into the Christian
faith as Susan. She and her husband became prominent pioneer
settlers at Sault Ste. Marie. The mother of four sons and four
daughters, she traded furs, farmed, fished, made maple sugar, and
entertained dignitaries such as Michigan Territorial Governor Lewis
Cass, who arrived in 1820 to negotiate with the Ojibwas for land.
When violence threatened, she assembled the chiefs and convinced
them that the matter should be settled peaceably. The successful
signing of the treaty was credited to Cass, who later acknowledged
Johnston's pivotal role in averting bloodshed. Her daughter Jane
married Henry Rowe Schoolcraft, the U.S. Government Indian agent
and Ojibwa scholar for whom Schoolcraft County is named. The
native legends that Schoolcraft recorded were based in part on
Susan Johnston's Ojibwa tales and inspired the epic poem, "Songs
of Hiawatha," by Henry Wadsworth Longfellow. Ref. 22 (Jun. 29,
1992, 1B, 3B); 57 (Mar. 4, 1993, 1C)

JONES, IRMA THEODA ANDREWS (1845-1923), of Lansing; co-
founder of the Lansing Woman's Club and the Unity Club. Born in
Victory, New York, she moved with her family in 1849 to Rockford,
Illinois, where she was educated at a female seminary and briefly
taught school. After moving to Lansing, she married Nelson B.
Jones and wrote for various newspapers about women's clubs, the
WCTU, and the Lansing Industrial Aid Society. She was a member
of the Michigan Women's Press Association, president in 1896 of
the Michigan State Federation of Women's Clubs (for which she
wrote the history of its first 25 years), and a founder of Pilgrim
Congregational Church in Lansing. Ref. 49 (198)

JONES, MINA C. (dates not known), of Iron River; co-founder and
first president of the Twentieth Century Club in Iron River, in
1912. During the next decades, the study club helped to improve
the community by raising funds for a free library in the new city
hall, developing city parks, assisting the poor, establishing a
college scholarship, and opening a Youth Center. Ref.: 34 (270)

JOSAITIS, ELEANOR M., of Detroit; co-founder (with Rev. William T. Cunningham) of FOCUS: Hope, a Detroit civil and human rights organization, in 1968. Founded after the 1967 riots in Detroit, the organization's goal has been to "build a just society with black and white people working together." Josaitis works with government agencies and local officials, solicits funds, and gives speeches, implementing FOCUS: Hope's mission of "intelligent and practical action to overcome racism, poverty and injustice." Ref.: 4 (Mar. 3, 1993, D8); 22 (Mar. 15, 1992, 4H)

JURNEY, DOROTHY MISENER, of Detroit; first woman to be assistant city editor and later acting city editor of the Washington Daily News, 1944 to 1946; first woman to be a board member of the Associated Press Managing Editors (APME) association, in 1972; founder of the Women's Network, an executive placement agency for women journalists with management aptitude, in 1975; founder of the New Directions for News Program at the University of Missouri School of Journalism, in 1987. Born in Michigan City, Indiana, she attended Western College for Women in Wayne, Pennsylvania, and earned a journalism degree from Northwestern University in 1930. She was a reporter for the Michigan City News and News Dispatch and the Gary, Indiana, Post Tribune, and was women's editor for the Miami News, Miami Herald and Detroit Free Press. She was also assistant managing editor of the Detroit Free Press and the Philadelphia Inquirer. As chair of the nominations committee of the American Society of Newspaper Editors, she was chosen as one of two women to accompany the Society's delegation to the People's Republic of China in 1975. She has served as one of two women members of the APME Regents, an organization of retired newspaper people. Ref.: 103 (233-234)

KALLEN, JACKIE, of West Bloomfield; the world's first and only woman to be a big-time boxing manager. The owner of Redford's Galaxy Gym, she has managed 12 boxers since starting in 1988. She was a journalist who covered celebrities before becoming a boxing publicist in 1978. Ref.: 22 (Dec. 13, 1994, 1D)

KARLSTROM, SIGNE, of Detroit; founder and first president of the Jenny Lind Club, organized to arrange concerts and preserve Swedish cultural tradition; founder and first Executive Secretary of the Detroit Swedish Council, in 1963; first Swedish-American woman to receive the Golden Plaque, given to her in 1980 as the Swedish-American of the Year by the Vasa Order of America in Stockholm, at ceremonies in Stockholm. Born in Gothenburg, she first came to the United States in the 1920s and married a Swedish-American, Gunnar Karlstrom, in 1928. As president of the Woman's Association for the Detroit Symphony Orchestra, she led its fund campaign to restore the solvency of the orchestra and to sponsor free concerts at the Masonic Temple for school children. She worked with the War Production Board in Washington during World War II, while assistant secretary-treasurer of the Swedish

Gage Company of America. She was secretary of the board of the
Detroit Grand Opera Association, instructor in Swedish at Wayne
State University and Oakland University, Resident Director for
Alpha Phi sorority at the University of Michigan, and Resident
Director at the Cranbrook Institute of Arts. She also served as a
board member of the Swedish Council of America. Her other
activities and memberships included the American Red Cross,
Michigan Federation of Music Clubs, Altrusa Club, Cranbrook
Music Guild, and the Michigan Assembly for Ombudsmen. In
1975, she received the Royal Order of Vasa, Knight, presented on
behalf of King Carl XVI Gustaf of Sweden. Ref.: 111 (221-232)

****

*"For the Safety of the Nation/To Women Give the Vote
For the Hand that Rocks the Cradle/Will Never Rock the Boat."*

1915 Suffrage Banner

****

KEATING, MARTHA ADALAIDE COOK (1848-1942), of Muskegon;
co-founder of the Muskegon Woman's Club in 1890; founder of the
Woman's Club Parliamentary Class, later called the Martha A.
Keating Parliamentary Class, in 1904. A graduate of Hillsdale
College, she was twice president of the Muskegon Woman's Club
and its parliamentarian until her death, and was president of the
Michigan State Federation of Women's Clubs from 1898 to 1900.
She was also active in the Woman Suffrage Movement. Ref.: 49
198-199)

KECK, CHRISTINE M., see **VAN HOESEN, GRACE AMES**

KELLY, DELTA M. HUTCHINSON (1911-1993), of Oakland
Township; co-founder and first president of the Oakland Township
Historical Society. Born in Owosso, she graduated from Central
State Teachers College in 1934 and taught for 14 years at Baldwin
School in Goodison, where she organized the Baldwin School Environmental Student Council and its Nature Study Area. One of the
first members of the Oakland Township Open Spaces Committee,
she helped map and preserve the Paint Creek Wetlands. She was
the author of a booklet, Heritage in Oakland Township, about
historic homes in the area, and wrote a township history column for
the local newspaper. In addition, she taught chair caning for 20
years with the Rochester Community Education Program and served
as Girl Scout and Brownie leader. Among her memberships were
the Oakland Audubon Club, the Rochester Women's Club and the
Paint Creek Methodist Church. Ref.: 25 (Dec. 5, 1993, 6C)

KENNEDY, JESSIE MARIE CARTER (c. 1919-1992), of Detroit; first
African American high school principal in Detroit, at Northwestern
High School; first African American woman to be a regional
superintendent; first director of the Detroit Center for Professional
Growth and Development at Wayne State University, where she
designed a national prototype for in-service training of educators;

first superintendent of Area G in the Detroit Public School system, in 1982, responsible for all senior high schools, vocational-technical centers and adult educational programs. Kennedy held bachelor's, master's, and doctoral degrees in Education from Wayne State University. Her community activity included the Children's Center of Wayne County, New Detroit, Greater Wayne Chapter of the Links, City of Detroit Elected Officials Compensation Committee, and the successful Detroit Public Library millage election. She was a member of Alpha Kappa Alpha Sorority and many professional organizations, was the author of articles for professional journals, produced two record albums of African fables for children, and co-authored a textbook on public education. She also established a scholarship at Northwestern High School for prospective teachers in her mother's name, Sallie Turner Carter. In 1982 she spent six weeks in Zimbabwe as the director of a group of Fulbright-Hays grant recipients. Ref.: 22 (Oct. 23, 1992, 4B)

KETCHAM, EMILY BURTON (1838-1907), of Grand Rapids; founder of the Susan B. Anthony Club, a Grand Rapids branch of the Michigan Equal Suffrage Association, in 1892. She became active in the Woman Suffrage Movement in 1873 and developed lasting friendships with Elizabeth Cady Stanton and Susan B. Anthony. Ketcham served as president of the MESA and on the executive board of the National American Woman Suffrage Association, which she persuaded to hold its 1899 convention in Grand Rapids. Ref.: 15 (98-99, 126); 136; 183

KILLGORE WERTMAN, SARAH (b. 1843); first woman to study law at the University of Michigan; first woman to graduate from the U-M Law School; first woman to practice law in Michigan, in 1871. Born in Indiana, she graduated from Ladoga Seminary in 1862, taught school for a time, then attended law school in Chicago during 1869. In 1875 she married Jackson S. Wertman, an Indianapolis attorney. Because Indiana statutes restricted the Bar to "Male citizens of good moral character," they moved to Ashland, Ohio, in 1878. After passing the Ohio Bar exam in 1893, she practiced law in that state. Ref.: 70 (Jun. 1984, 448)

KING, ROSALIE GRANDELIS, of Caspian; first woman to be a city manager in the Upper Peninsula, as City Manager of Caspian, 1979 to the present. Born in Hurley, Wisconsin, King moved to Caspian in 1967. As city manager, she has obtained and administered grants totalling more than $7 million. Among her many activities, she is a member of the Carrie Jacobs-Bond Singers. King received the Woman of the Year Award for Iron County in 1980 from the Northern Michigan University Women's Center. Ref.: 128

KINGSFORD, MINNIE FLAHERTY (b. 1865), of Iron Mountain; co-founder and first president of the Iron Mountain Women's Club, in 1912. She taught school after coming to Iron Mountain in 1880. Ref.: 128

KLAUSSEN, DORIS DEXTER DAVIS, of Battle Creek; co-founder and executive board member of Goodwill Industries in Battle Creek, in 1953; founder of the Child Guidance Clinic in Battle Creek; founder of the Council for Exceptional Children Chapter in Calhoun County, serving twice as state president; co-founder of the United Cerebral Palsy Chapter in Calhoun County. She was principal for 25 years of the Ann J. Kellogg School, one of the first schools in the United States to mainstream the handicapped with other children and a national model for other schools. The Doris Klaussen Developmental Center, built in 1976, serves mentally and physically handicapped persons of Calhoun County. In 1980 she received the Distinguished Service Award from the United Cerebral Palsy Association of Michigan. Ref.: 184

KNAPP, RUTH MARGARET (1892-1977), of Hillsdale and Northville; founder of ten community libraries in Hillsdale County; co-founder of the Northville Historical Society. After graduating from Hillsdale High School in 1912, she trained at Harper Hospital's Farrand School of Nursing, then served for 18 months as a Red Cross nurse in France during World War I. She was appointed city and school nurse in Hillsdale, where she created a hot lunch program for needy children. In 1938 she graduated from Hillsdale College and served as Hillsdale County librarian until 1948. She then became school nurse and health instructor in the Northville Public Schools, retiring in 1957. During her retirement, she started a blood bank, taught home nursing, and was active in the DAR, American Legion, American Red Cross, Northville BPW, Northville Women's Club, Northville Historical Society, and Delta Kappa Gamma. She was named the 1973 Outstanding Woman of Northville by the Northville Jaycettes. Ref.: 123

KNOX, DOROTHY D., of Detroit; first woman to be a commander in the Detroit Police Department, in charge of the Community Services Division in 1986. Born in Mississippi, she grew up in Louisiana and moved with her family to Detroit in 1953. After joining the force in 1969, she earned a degree in criminal justice from Wayne State University in 1975 and worked her way up through the ranks, becoming head of the Community Services Division, where she oversaw 57 mini-stations, drug prevention programs, crime analysis and public information. Following her retirement from the DPD in 1995, Knox joined the Wayne County prosecutor's office as chief investigator. Ref.: 22 (Mar. 14, 1993, 1J); 117 (Summer 1995, 25)

KOSTIELNEY, MONICA, of Lansing; first woman to be elected president of the National Association of State Catholic Conference Directors, serving from 1990 to 1992. In 1994 she was named president and CEO of the Michigan Catholic Conference, the public policy voice of the Catholic Church in Michigan. Kostielney, a nun who has been with the MCC since 1972, was formerly executive vice president for public affairs. Ref.: 57 (Sept. 17, 1994, 7D)

KRONE, JULIE, formerly of Eau Claire; first woman jockey to compete in a Breeders' Cup race, in 1988; the only jockey to win six races in one day, at the Meadowlands, on September 16, 1989; first woman jockey to win titles at major race tracks; first woman jockey to ride in the Belmont Stakes, in 1991 and 1992; first woman jockey to win a Triple Crown event, riding Colonial Affair in the 125th Belmont Stakes, in June 1993; first woman to win five races in one day, at Saratoga on August 20, 1993; first woman jockey to surpass the $50 million mark in career earnings. When she won her 1,205th race in 1988, she became the woman jockey with the most wins ever. By 1994 she had won more than 2,700 races. At Saratoga, her horse fell in one race and she was trampled by another horse, shattering her ankle and causing other injuries. After undergoing two operations and recuperating for nine months, she again rode in the Belmont in May of 1994. Growing up in Eau Claire, Krone was fascinated by race horses at an early age and rode her pony around her own private track. When she was 14, she watched the Belmont on TV and announced that she wanted to be a jockey. She rode her first race in January of 1981 and won her first race the next month. In 1993 she and basketball player Sheryl Swoopes were chosen as Sportswomen of the Year by the Women's Sports Foundation. On August 26, 1995, Krone rode in six races at the Saratoga Race Course before her evening wedding to Matthew Muzikar. Ref.: 22 (Jun. 7, 1993, 3D; Oct. 5, 1993, 2E; May 26, 1994, 1C, 10C); 25 (Jun. 6, 1993, 1E, 3E; Jul. 12, 1993, 1D, 4D); 57 (Aug. 28, 1995, 10B)

****

"Resolved, That it is the duty of the women of this country to secure to themselves their sacred right to the elective franchise."

Ninth Resolution of the Woman's Rights Convention
Seneca Falls, New York, July 29, 1848

****

LAMBERTS, EVANGELINE, of Grand Rapids; first woman to become an elected city official in Grand Rapids, with her election as the 2nd Ward City Commissioner in 1961, serving until 1965. She was an active member of the LWV and had led a successful annexation drive. During her tenure, Lamberts promoted taxation reform and the restructuring of county government. She also was an ex-officio member of the county Board of Supervisors. Ref.: 136; 183

LATHROP, MARION BERTSCH GRAY, of Grand Rapids; first professionally-trained medical social worker at Butterworth Hospital in Grand Rapids, in 1939. After earning a degree in medical social work from the University of Michigan in 1935, she worked for two years among the Mexican and Indian peoples in Tucson, Arizona. Following further study at the New York School of Social Work, she joined Butterworth Hospital as a medical social worker, handling cases in the Mental Health Clinic and the Crippled Children's Clinic. She has been president of the East

Grand Rapids PTA Council and Women's City Club, on the board of the Grand Rapids Symphony, and active in the Community Chest, Kent County Mental Health Association, and Association for Blind and Sight Conservation. Ref.: 41 (Oct. 7, 1993, C5); 172; 175

LEAVEY, KATHLEEN, of Detroit; first woman to be the director of a major wastewater operation, as assistant director at the Detroit Wastewater and Sewerage Department, in 1992. Detroit's treatment plant is the largest in the country, possibly in the world. Born in New York, she grew up in Detroit, where she taught social studies before graduating from Wayne State University Law School in 1980. She joined the water department as assistant corporation counsel in 1985 and was appointed manager of the office of program management assistance in 1989. In her present position, she monitors the waste of more than 600 industries that discharge into the Detroit sewerage system. Ref.: 22 (Apr. 25, 1993, 3H)

LEE, GERTRUDE, see **BRUNSON, ROSE T.**

LEGGETT, ELIZABETH SEAMAN (d. c. 1900), of Detroit; first person in Detroit to advocate the making of Belle Isle into a public park. Born in New York City, she was the daughter of Dr. Valentine Seaman, who had introduced vaccination into the U.S. and narrowly escaped mob violence when it was learned that he had vaccinated his little daughter. After her marriage, she moved in 1850 to Detroit, where she raised a family of 11 children. An ardent abolitionist and suffragist, she was associated with Susan B. Anthony, Lucretia Mott, **Laura Smith Haviland**, **Sojourner Truth**, and other women working for these causes. (See **Haviland, Laura Smith** in Michigan Women: Firsts and Founders, Vol. I.) She was also a friend and correspondent of Walt Whitman, Louisa M. Alcott, and other literary figures. Keenly aware of her civic duties, Leggett secured passage of a bill in the Michigan State Legislature requiring merchants to provide seats behind the counters for their clerks and led a successful drive for public drinking fountains. She urged other women to form organizations that would work for better government and civic improvements. Ref.: 77 (Jun. 1915, 11)

LEMANSKI, LENORE JENSEN, of Carrollton; first place winner of the National Women's Smallbore Rifle Championship, in 1959, 1960, and 1963. A member of the Dewar International Rifle Team, she competed in the iron sight matches of the National Championship and fired in postal competition with participants from five other countries. Ref.: 93 (151)

LEONARD, VIOLA (1898-1967), of Iron River; founder in 1923 of the Cloverland Band, the first all-girl band in the Upper Peninsula. Born in Commonwealth, Wisconsin, she came to Iron River with her family in 1908, graduated from Iron River High School in 1917 and taught music in the James School from 1918 to 1919. Ref.: 34 (411-412)

LESNIESKI, FRANCES L. (1915-1995), of Lansing; pioneer in the community and national credit union movement, founding 11 credit unions, beginning in 1948; first woman to serve on the Thrift Institutions Advisory Council of the Board of Governors of the Federal Reserve Board; first president of the World Computer Credit Union Association. She served as manager, general manager and president of Michigan State University Federal Credit Union from 1957 until her retirement in 1988. During her tenure the MSU credit union grew to 10 times its original size. She also served as the director of the Credit Union National Association, as a charter member of the National Credit Union Society's Michi-Gami Council and the Electronic Transaction Exchange Corporation, and on the boards of the National Credit Union Executives Society, the Education Credit Union Council, and the National Association of Retired Credit Union People. She was a charter member of the Zonta Club in East Lansing, worked actively to support the Council of Domestic Assault, and helped the inner-city community organize financial cooperatives. Lesnieski was recognized with a Diana Award from the YWCA for community leadership. Ref.: 57 (Sept. 6, 1995, 2B; Supplement, Oct. 19, 1995, 2)

LEVINE, ELLA, see **SANDERS, MRS. JOSEPH**

LEWIS, EMILY, see **CAMPBELL EAGLESFIELD, CARINA BULKLEY**

LINDQUIST ARNDT, LILLY (1877-1965), of Detroit; first woman to be president of the American Association of the Teachers of French; first woman to be president of the National Federation of Modern Language Teachers. Born in Stockholm, Sweden, she lived with her family in England, France and Germany while still young, learning the languages of all three countries. After her family came to the United States to live, she was educated at Smith College, began teaching at Ypsilanti High School, then moved to Detroit, where she continued to teach. During her years with the Detroit schools, she developed a course of language study for the inter-mediate grades and wrote general language textbooks. For her textbooks in French, she received the French Palmes Academiques, carrying the title of Officier d'Academie. After retiring in 1974, she married and moved to Lima, Peru. In recognition of her contributions to the teaching of modern foreign languages, the National Federation of Modern Language Teachers awarded her its first Achievement Award in 1958. She was also a member of Delta Kappa Gamma, a national honorary society for educators. Ref.: 29 (142-145)

LIPCZYNSKI, VALERIA GLOWCZYNSKA (1846-1930), of Grand Rapids; co-founder of St. Mary's Church in the 1870s, St. Adalbert Church in 1881, and St. Isidore Church in 1897; co-founder in 1871 of the Wiarus Society, the first Polish organization in Western Michigan; co-founder in 1878 of the Polish National Society, which in 1883 joined with the Polish National Alliance; co-founder of the first Polish ball in Grand Rapids, as well as the first Polish parade in 1883; co-founder in 1886 of the Polish Dramatic Circle, with which she performed; founder of the Society of Polish Ladies, which in 1899 became the first women's organization admitted to the Polish National Alliance; first woman to be a delegate to the PNA National Convention, in 1901; first woman elected to the PNA board of directors, as vice censor (councilor) in 1905; founder and first president of the PNA Women's Division in 1906; first woman to serve on the PNA supervisory council, in 1907 as commissioner-at-large for the United States, a position she held until her election in 1918 as honorary commissioner for all states. Born in Prussian Poland, Lipczynski came to Grand Rapids in 1869 with her husband in search of freedom and opportunity. In the 1870s she was the Grand Rapids correspondent for several national Polish newspapers, in which she wrote about the opportunities available for new settlers. The Lipczynskis sponsored forty other Polish immigrant families to come to Grand Rapids, and helped them find housing and employment. When this service grew too great to do alone, she trained a corps of young people to help the immigrants get settled. She served also as a social worker, tutor, translator, midwife, nurse, intermediary with local officials, and as godmother to numerous children born to the newcomers. Her contributions to Polonia in Grand Rapids earned her the title of "Queen of the Poles." An advocate of women's rights, she persuaded the PNA to give women equal rights and privileges in the organization. In 1923 she received a gold medal for her services to the PNA at the Women's Division Convention, where she spoke on women's struggle for equality. In 1927 she was presented with the Polish Golden Service Cross for her assistance to immigrants, her work with the PNA, and her services during World War I. Ref.: 43 (1-12)

****

"To My Valentine: Love me, Love my Vote."
Valentine Message, c. 1912-1917

****

LITOGOT ANTAYA, CAROLINE AMEDIA TAYLOR (1845-1903), of Grosse Ile; first woman to tend the lighthouse at the Mama Juda Light at the north end of Grosse Ile, from 1874 to 1885 after the death of her husband, Barney Litogot, the previous keeper. She later married Adolph Antaya. Caroline Litogot's sister-in-law was Mary Ford, wife of William Ford and mother of Henry Ford I. She was also the great-grandmother of **Lynda Litogot Trinklein.** (See **Trinklein, Lynda Litogot.**) Ref.: 18 (163); 161; 196

LIUZZO, VIOLA GREGG (1925-1965), of Detroit; first white woman to be murdered as a civil rights worker, in 1965. While driving black civil rights marchers between Selma and Montgomery in Alabama, she was shot by a group of white men. Four Ku Klux Klan members were arrested, acquitted of murder, but found guilty of violating Liuzzo's civil rights and sentenced to prison. Her death, the third in the voter registration drive, was used by President

Lyndon Johnson to hasten passage of the voting rights bill. The
mother of five children, Liuzzo was studying sociology at Wayne
State University at the time of her death. In 1983 she was honored
posthumously as a Distinguished Warrior by the Detroit Urban
League for her contributions to civil rights. Ref.: 22 (Mar. 26,
1965, 1A; Mar. 17, 1993, 1B); 107 (81-102)

LOGWOOD, DYANN, see **EDUT, OPHIRA**

LONGSTREET, MARTHA (1870-1953), of Saginaw; co-founder of
the Council for Social Agencies in Saginaw, the Saginaw YWCA, a
home for girls, a home for the aged, and the First Ward Community
Center. Born in Erie, Pennsylvania, she moved with her family to
Unionville, Michigan, while still young. After graduation from the
University of Illinois Medical School in 1904, she opened a practice
in Saginaw, serving for ten years as a general practitioner and for
35 years as a pediatrician. She was the only staff doctor at
Saginaw's Children's Hospital and was on the consulting staffs at
St. Luke's, St. Mary's, and Saginaw General Hospitals. Always
ready to make house calls when necessary, she never billed
patients who were unable to pay. Instead, she sent them packages
of food and clothing. She was also active in the Zonta Club, the
DAR, the AAUW, and her church. Named "Michigan's Most
Outstanding Woman" in 1938 and made a life member of the
Michigan Medical Society in 1949, Longstreet was inducted into the
Michigan Women's Hall of Fame in 1984. Ref.: 184

LOVE, JOSEPHINE HERRALD, of Detroit; co-founder in 1969, with
Gwendolyn Hogue, of Your Heritage House, a fine arts museum in
Detroit for children, featuring classes in visual and performing arts
as well as exhibits of art. Born in Atlanta, Georgia, she earned a
bachelor's degree from Spelman College and a master's degree in
musicology from Radcliffe College, and has studied music at the
Juilliard School in New York and the Mozarteum Academy in
Salzburg, Austria. Before settling in Detroit, she performed as a
concert pianist throughout the United States. In 1993 she was
honored by the Detroit Urban League as a Distinguished Warrior for
her contributions to the community. Ref.: 22 (Mar. 17, 1993, 1B)

LUCAS, TERESA (1856-1944), of Calumet; founder and first
president of the first Croatian women's lodge in America;
co-founder of a Croatian church in Calumet. A native of Croatia,
she came to the United States with three small sons in 1883 to join
her husband, a miner in the Keweenaw Peninsula. By taking in
other miners as boarders and working long hours, the Lucases were
eventually able to buy a large house in Calumet, where they opened
a tavern, operating it with the help of their 11 sons, as well as many
nieces brought from Croatia. Well-known as a healer, Lucas also
provided medical treatment to sick and injured miners. Over the
years she brought about 80 Croatian girls to work in the tavern
until they married and then served as godmother to more than 300
of their children. Ref.: 35 (75-77)

MacPHERSON, IDA GROUT RUST (1869-1946), of Bay City; founder and first president of the Saginaw County League of Women Voters; co-founder and president of the Saginaw Art Club; co-founder of the Free Kindergarten Association. An ardent supporter of equal rights, she was active in the struggle to gain votes for women. After the 19th Amendment was passed, she founded the county LWV, became a state and national LWV leader and worked for American approval of the World Court of International Relations and for entry into the League of Nations after World War I. She represented American women's organizations at the League of Nations sessions in Geneva and at the International Congress of Women in Berlin. She also pushed for adoption of the child labor amendment to the Constitution. MacPherson served on the board of directors of the YWCA, the Home for the Aged, and the Saginaw General Hospital, and was a major benefactor of these and other organizations, including the Children's Home, Rollins College in Florida, California Institute of Technology and Scripps College in California. She was one of three Michigan women listed on a National Honor Roll tablet, dedicated in 1930 by the National League of Women Voters. Ref.: 121 (102-104)

MAGOON, JOHANNA MEIJER (1916-1994), of Ypsilanti; first manager and clerk of the first Meijer Store in 1934; co-founder of community concerts and a new hospital at Greenville. A native of Greenville, Magoon edited her high school newspaper and worked in her parents' dairy business before and after her graduation as class valedictorian. In 1934 she started the first Meijer store in a vacant building owned by her father. When the business was well launched, she enrolled at the University of Michigan, supporting herself by scholarships and by working for her room and board. During her vacations, she continued to work at the store. After graduating in 1939, she taught at Mt. Pleasant High School for three years while also working on her master's degree. In 1942, at her father's request, she gave up her teaching position and the completion of her master's degree to manage a second Meijer Store in Cedar Springs for four years. During the 1940s she also gave violin concerts in the Grand Rapids area. Following her marriage to Donald Magoon in 1946, she opened the third Meijer store in Ionia, continued to work in the stores until the birth of her first child, then worked part-time in the stores until 1960, when the Magoons moved to Ypsilanti after a Meijer family disagreement resulted in her disinheritance. Over the years she was active in the PTA, the Civil Rights movement, the American Diabetes Association, the P.E.O., Planned Parenthood, and the First Congregational United Church of Christ of Ypsilanti. One of her activities was a trip to Chicago to take part in a protest against an arms bazaar which sold weapons world-wide. Ref.: 4 (Nov. 21, 1994, D2); 65; 115 (Aug. 2, 1994, 1A)

MAJORS, INA, see **BRUNSON, ROSE T.**

MANDERFIELD, ANGELA, of Atlantic Mine; first 14-year old girl to win the 42-mile Gwinn-to-Munising Classic sled dog marathon, in January of 1995. Although she was two years below the minimum age rule, the race directors agreed to let her compete if her father competed as the next starting sled. Starting 12th in a field of 15, she mushed her six-dog team to victory. At her family's 14-acre spread in Houghton County, she helps to train sled dogs, giving special attention to her own team. Ref.: 22 (Mar. 20, 1995, 10C)

MANNING, LOIS, see **JEROME FOX, MARY RUTH**

MARSH, ANN, of Royal Oak; first place winner in the National Women's Foil event at the United States Fencing Association's Second North American Circuit, at Louisville, Kentucky, in 1992. She began fencing as a student at Roeper High School in a program sponsored by the Fencing Academy of Michigan and was a student at Columbia University when she won the gold medal. Ref.: 24 (Feb. 1993, 24)

****

"Men their rights and nothing more;
women their rights and nothing less.

Susan B. Anthony

****

MARTIN, DEBRA L., of Flint; first woman admitted to the Graduate School of Public Administration at Harvard University; first woman to be a member of the national council of the American Society for Public Administration (ASAP). During 1990-1991, as the national president of Women in Public Administration (a section of the ASAP), she negotiated an agreement with Cleveland State University to house the WPA national archives and establish a Women's Hall of Fame. She also marketed the organization's gender-free language guide, Say the Right Thing. Martin, the coordinator of prevention and public information services for Genesee County Community Mental Health, received the Julia Henderson Award from Women in Public Administration in 1992 for her contributions to the field. Ref.: 6 (Jun. 19, 1992)

MARTIN, HELEN (1889-1973), of Lansing; co-founder of the Department of Natural Resources RAM Center, a conservation school for teachers at Higgins Lake. She worked for the Geological Survey Division, Department of Conservation (now the Department of Natural Resources) from 1917 to 1923 as an economic geologist, editor and director of the Land Economic Survey. From 1934 to 1958 she worked as the compiler of geologic maps, lecturer and research geologist, compiling the centennial geological map of Michigan in 1936 and the surface formation map of Michigan in 1955, both still in use. Among her books are They Need Not Vanish, Ne-Saw-Je-Won (story of the Great Lakes) and Rocks and Minerals of Michigan. For six years after her retirement in 1958, she served as national Conservation Chair of the National Council of State Garden Clubs. She was also president of the Lansing-East Lansing Chapter of the AAUW. Martin was inducted into the Michigan Women's Hall of Fame in 1988. Ref.: 184

THE MARVELETTES, of Inkster; a singing group of young women from Inkster High School who recorded the first national No. 1 vocal group hit song for Motown Record Corporation, their debut single, "Please Mr. Postman," which reached the top spot in 1961. The original members of the group were **Gladys Harbor**, **Wanda Young**, **Katherine Anderson** and **Georgeanna Tillman**. As a trio by the mid-1960s, the Marvelettes had other hits, including "Don't Mess With Bill," "Playboy," and "I'll Keep Holding On." (**Mary Wells** also recorded Motown Record's first solo hit song in 1961. See Michigan Women: Firsts and Founders, Vol. I.) Ref.: 71 (Jan. 25-31, 1995); 187

MARVIN, KATE (dates not known); first woman to keep the Squaw Point Lighthouse on Little Bay de Noc near Gladstone, from 1897 to 1904, replacing her husband who had kept it for just six months before his death. Ref.: 18 (107)

MARX, JEAN, of Bloomfield Hills; founder in 1991 of Animal Crafters, an organization that makes and sells handcrafted items to fund spaying and neutering operations for pets. Concerned about the high animal birth rate and the large number of animals that are euthanized each year, Marx and other members patrol Pontiac streets weekly looking for stray dogs and giving them shelter and medical treatment. They also provide pet supplies, information, and spay/neutering services free to owners. Since its beginning, the organization has paid for hundreds of operations that will reduce the number of animals needing to be destroyed. Marx publishes and distributes posters that publicize the services offered by the group, which meets monthly at her home to work on their craft projects. Their handcrafts are sold primarily through bazaars at schools and shopping malls in the Detroit area. Ref.: 24 (Apr. 1994, 31)

MASSINGILL, ALBERTA R., of Grand Rapids; first woman to head a city department in Grand Rapids, as the Director of the Grand Rapids Public Library, in 1971 after the library had become a city department. A native of Missouri, she earned degrees from Park College, the University of Denver and the University of Michigan. In 1941 she joined the staff of the Grand Rapids Public Library, where she served in various capacities before becoming Associate Director in 1962, Acting Director in 1971 and Director in 1972, a position she held until her retirement in 1979. Her 1954 article, "Remedial Reading and the Public Library," brought national recognition to the summer program she developed with local teachers to aid children with reading difficulties. She is a past president of Zonta and was named Woman of the Year by the Grand Rapids BPW in 1968. Ref.: 136; 183

MAWBY, KATIE, of Rockford; first place winner of the U.S. Disabled Snow Ski Championship, in 1988, winning in slalom, giant slalom, and downhill competitions; first place winner of the U.S. National Disabled Water Ski Championship in 1989, winning in slalom and trick skiing competitions. Ref.: 184

McCAULEY, LELAH, see **GREENWOOD, MABEL S.**

McCLENDON, MARY UPSHAW, of Detroit; founder of the Household Workers Organization in 1969, to upgrade private household workers' skills and wages, and to obtain Federal legislation providing protection for all household workers in America. She received a Labor Award from the Detroit Committee for Human Rights in 1972 and a Sojourner Truth Award from Women and the Law in 1974. Ref.: 184

McCORD, MARY IGNATIUS (dates not known), of Grand Rapids; co-founder, with **Mary Anthony McMullen** and **Mary Baptist Feldner**, of St. Mary's Hospital at Grand Rapids in 1893. Members of the Sisters of Mercy religious order, they had previously begun a hospital at Big Rapids for sick and injured lumbermen. The Grand Rapids hospital was named in honor of Mary McNamara, in whose home it was established. The original hospital was greatly enlarged over the years and a modern facility now stands on the site. Ref.: 12 (23)

McFALL, NANCY, of rural Charlotte; first woman to complete the Lansing Board of Water and Light's apprentice program for maintenance mechanics, in 1990. A graduate of Okemos High School, she joined the utility company in 1986 as a power plant operator. By 1992 she was a turbine mechanic at the Erickson power plant in Delta Township. Ref.: 57 (Oct. 16, 1992, 5B)

McGEE, SUSAN G. S., of Washtenaw County; executive director of the first publicly-funded domestic violence shelter in the country, the SAFE House in Ann Arbor, in 1995; co-founder in 1986 of the Coalition to End Legalized Rape, which worked to eliminate the marital rape exemption in the criminal sexual conduct statute; founder of the annual vigil in honor of battered women who have been killed, 1985 to 1991. A successful millage and bond proposal vote in 1992 provided the new facility for SAFE House, which had been housed in an inadequate and deteriorating structure. SAFE House is one of few buildings ever constructed specifically for a domestic violence shelter and one of a growing number to create a public presence by revealing its location. McGee, a graduate of the University of Michigan and George Washington University, has been head of The Domestic Violence Project, Inc./SAFE House since 1987. She previously was executive director of the Child Abuse and Neglect Council in Jackson. Her many publications on domestic violence include <u>Fighting for Justice for Battered Women: A Law and Advocacy Manual</u> (1991, with **Amy Coha** and **Kathleen Hagenian**), <u>Survivor's</u>

Handbook (1991), and Counselors' Dos and Don'ts: A Guide to
Counseling the Battered Woman (1982). McGee was the recipient
of the first annual Feminist Achievement Award in 1986 from the
Washtenaw County NOW, the 1987 Outstanding Service Award
from the Child Abuse and Neglect Council of Jackson County and
the 1995 Liberty Bell Award from the Washtenaw County Bar
Association. Ref.: 181

McGUIRE, ANNIE (dates not known), of Pentwater; first woman to
keep the Pentwater Lighthouse at Pentwater on Lake Michigan, in
1877. Ref.: 18 (164)

McLELLAND, LILLEY, see **COWLEY, MRS. B. P.**

McMULLAN, MARY ANTHONY, see **McCORD, MARY IGNATIUS**

****

*"I share no fears of the degradation of women by the ballot.
I believe rather that it will elevate men. I believe the tone of our
politics will be higher; that our caucuses will be jealously guarded
and our conventions more orderly and decorous."*

U.S. Senator Thomas W. Palmer of Michigan
First speech on Woman Suffrage before Congress, Feb. 6, 1885

****

McPHERSON, JOANNE, of East Lansing; founder of Safe Place, the
first on-campus domestic violence shelter in the country, at
Michigan State University in 1994. McPherson, who grew up in
Washington, D.C., came to East Lansing with her husband, MSU
President M. Peter McPherson, in 1993. Concerned about campus
domestic violence, she formed the MSU Domestic Violence Steering
Committee to explore ways of alleviating the problem. Coordinated
with the Council Against Domestic Assault in Lansing, Safe Place
serves students, faculty and staff, providing safety and aid to
victims of domestic violence or threatened violence, as well as
counseling to their abusers. Since its inception, the shelter has
received national attention. Ref.: 54 (Feb. 1995, 16-19); 56 (Jan.
1995, 16-17); 57 (Jan. 21, 1995, 4B); 90 (Summer 1994, 1)

MERRILL CARPENTER, MARY J. C. (dates not known), of East
Lansing; first full time librarian at Michigan Agricultural College,
appointed in 1883. When her first husband died, she became a
student at MAC and was the second woman to graduate in 1881.
(For the first woman to graduate, see **Coryell, Eva Diane**) As the
first librarian, Merrill greatly enlarged the collection by doubling
the annual book allotment that each professor could request and
she also expanded the library hours. In 1888 she remarried and
moved to Denver, Colorado. Ref.: 102

MERTZ, MARTHA MAYHOOD, of Okemos; founder in 1982 of the
ATHENA Award Program honoring outstanding business and
professional women (and now men) for their achievements,

community service and assistance to others, especially women, in gaining leadership skills. The owner of a real estate company, Mertz conceived of the idea to honor women for their business and professional achievements, community service, and encouragement of other women. First created through the Chamber of Commerce in Lansing, the ATHENA Award Program became national in 1985, with the formation of the National ATHENA Society, a national network of chambers of commerce, local sponsors, ATHENA recipients and friends, working together to expand leadership opportunities for women. Since then the award has been given to more than 1600 women and men by chambers of commerce in hundreds of cities nationwide, as well as in other countries such as Russia, where in 1994 Moscow became the first city outside of the United States to present the ATHENA award. ATHENA State Awards are presented to companies and institutions recognized for their professional accomplishments, community service and initiatives to provide leadership roles for women. The program has been sponsored by General Motors' Oldsmobile Division since 1985 and by First of America Bank Corporation since 1993. In 1994 the non-profit ATHENA Foundation held its first national conference in Washington, D.C., when the first ATHENA National Award was presented. The sculpted bronze ATHENA Award, named for the Greek goddess of wisdom and patron of the arts and crafts, was designed by Michigan native **Linda Ackley**, a Michigan State University graduate, who hand casts each award in her Tampa, Florida, foundry. Mertz, a native of Minnesota, has degrees from the College of St. Catherine in St. Paul and from Michigan State University. She serves on many boards of directors, including the Zonta Club of East Lansing, is president of the National ATHENA Foundation and received the Lansing Regional Chamber of Commerce ATHENA Award in 1986. Ref.: 57 (Jan. 20, 1993, 2D; Apr. 10, 1994, 5C; Jun. 3, 1994, 9A); 182

METER, ETHELYN (dates not known), of Benton Harbor; first woman to be a post adjutant in the American Legion, Department of Michigan, in 1919 and 1920 at Benton Harbor Post No. 105. As there was no vice-commander of the post during those years, she served as second in command. She was later employed by the Department headquarters. Ref.: 114 (268)

MICKLOW, PATRICIA LENORE JOHNSON, of Marquette; first woman elected as a judge in Marquette County and first woman to serve as a district judge in the Upper Peninsula since the 1970 establishment of the 96th District Court, with her election in 1986. She was also the first woman to work in the county prosecutor's office, serving since 1976 as a trial lawyer in the criminal division, chief civil counsel for the Marquette County Board of Commissioners, and first woman to be an assistant prosecuting attorney. Born in Ironwood, she spent her early years in Bessemer until her family moved to Marquette, where she attended high school. After marrying and having a family, she earned a B.A. in history and an

M.A. in English literature at Northern Michigan University, followed by a law degree from the University of Michigan. Her 1974 legal study, co-authored with another woman law student, dealt with the failure of the justice system to respond to the problem of domestic violence and inspired the 1975 opening in Ann Arbor of the first spouse abuse shelter in the country. She also co-chaired a legislative advisory committee on the legal reform of spouse abuse, which led to Michigan laws addressing the problem. In 1982 she was appointed by Gov. William Milliken to serve on the state's Domestic Violence and Treatment Board. Ref.: 86 (Mar. 11, 1982; Nov. 8, 1986; Dec. 30, 1986); 193

MILFORD, BETH WHARTON (1908-1992), of Ypsilanti; first woman elected president of the Ypsilanti Board of Education, in 1965; first woman appointed to serve on the Tax Review Board for the City of Ypsilanti. Born in Bradford, Pennsylvania, she received bachelor's and master's degrees in economics from the University of Michigan. After teaching at Bradford High School, and Pennsylvania State College, she became head of the Economics Department at St. Mary's College of Notre Dame in South Bend, Indiana, in 1938, then joined Michigan State Normal College (now Eastern Michigan University) to organize the business department. She later taught at Lincoln High School from 1963 until 1974, when she was appointed to the Board of Regents of Eastern Michigan University. She also served on the Ypsilanti Board of Education, Family Agency Board, Huron Valley Child Guidance Board, Community Chest (as chair), Ypsilanti Area School Planning Committee, Michigan Association for Retarded Children, Cancer Society Fund Drive (as chair), and Human Relations Commission, and was a member of the BPW and the Ypsilanti Republican Women's Club. In 1956, as president of the Auxiliary to the Michigan State Medical Society, she received the top national award for raising the most money of any state for scholarships for nurses and medical students. She was honored in 1985 by the Ypsilanti Area Chamber of Commerce for her community leadership and in 1988 she received an Honorary Doctorate from Eastern Michigan University in recognition of her achievements. Ref.: 4 (Aug. 10, 1992, C4); 114 (Jun. 25, 1968, 1; Aug. 8, 1992, 3A)

MILFORD, EDNA C. McNEELY (1898-1993), of Detroit; co-founder and first president of the Michigan Women Realtors in 1946, serving until 1957. A graduate of the Detroit Conservatory of Music and Wayne State University, she was a concert pianist and taught music, orchestra and drama in the Detroit schools for 30 years. Ref.: 4 (Aug. 15, 1993, F4)

MILLER, CANDICE SNIDER, of Harrison Township, Macomb County; first woman elected as Michigan Secretary of State, in 1994. Born in St. Clair Shores, she is an alumna of Macomb County Community College and Northwood Institute. She was elected a Harrison Township Trustee in 1979 and was the first woman (and youngest person) to be Harrison Township Supervisor, serving from 1980 to 1992, when she became the first woman elected as Macomb County Treasurer. As Secretary of State, Miller is Michigan's chief motor vehicle administrator, chief historian and chief elections official. She is second in line of succession to the governor, acting in that capacity whenever both the governor and lieutenant governor are out of the state. Ref.: 57 (Oct. 30, 1994); 84 (Oct. 16-30, 1994, 2); 185

MILLER, LINDA, of the Detroit area; first woman to be a plant manager for the Ford Motor Company, in 1993 at the Dearborn Engine and Fuel Tank plant in the Rouge Manufacturing Complex. Previously she had been assistant manager of a Ford engine plant in Cleveland, Ohio. Born in Missouri, she earned math degrees from Northeast Missouri State College and the University of Kansas and briefly taught math in junior high school before becoming a quality control analyst in Ford's Engine Division in 1973. Since then she has been the first woman in almost every job she has held at Ford. Ref.: 22 (Business Monday, Nov. 8, 1993, 4F)

****

"There are so many things a woman can do/And the men approve of them all the way through/When demanding the ballot they say to us "nay"/But surely we're going to get it some day!"

From a poem by **Cora B. Metz** of Oxford

****

MILLS, FLORENCE GERTRUDE BALCH (1851-1935), of Kalamazoo; co-founder in 1904 of the Women's Civic Improvement League, with **Caroline Bartlett Crane** (see Michigan Women: Firsts and Founders, Vol. I.); co-founder of the Kalamazoo League of Women Voters; co-founder of the Kalamazoo County Federation of Women's Clubs. Born in Barry County, Mills was educated in Kalamazoo, began teaching at age 16 and was married in 1874. She served as president of the Ladies' Library Association, the Michigan State Federation of Women's Clubs, and the Kalamazoo Board of Education, and was active in the Woman Suffrage Movement and The People's Church, where Crane was pastor. Ref.: 49 (200)

MILONAS, MARIA VASOULIDIS (1905-1992), of Grosse Pointe; founder of Greek language and culture classes for Detroit area children, begun in the 1970s by the Detroit Hellenic Education Committee, which she headed. Born in Greece, she came to Detroit in 1929 and became active in the Greek-American community, including the Greek American Progressive Association chapters of Detroit and Grosse Pointe. Ref.: 22 (Nov. 3, 1992, 4B)

MONROE, MRS. WILLIAM M. (first name and dates not known), of Muskegon; first woman to keep the lighthouse at Muskegon on Lake Michigan, from 1862 to 1871 after the death of her husband, the previous keeper. Ref.: 18 (164)

MOORE, JULIA A. DAVIS (1847-1920), of Manton; first Michigan woman to achieve national notoriety for her sentimental poetry, in the 1870s; inspiration for the founding of the annual Julia A. Moore Poetry Festival at the Flint Public Library. Known as the "Sweet Singer of Michigan," Moore produced many mournful and morbid poems, most of them based on deaths in her Kent County community near Rockford. Because of her torturous poetic style, however, her published verses were often regarded as humorous rather than sad. Critics called her Sentimental Song Book of 1876 a "mile post in the history of bad poetry." One poem read, in part: "Railroads now from every way/Run through the city, Grand Rapids/The largest town in west Michigan/Is the city of Grand Rapids." The popularity of her usually maudlin poems led to public appearances in Grand Rapids and other nearby towns, where she read from her own works. Mark Twain, who admired her unintentional humor, is said to have modeled the Huckleberry Finn character Emmeline Grangerford after Moore. In 1882 Moore and her husband moved to Manton. The Julia A. Moore Poetry Festival, an annual competition for the best (or worst) bad poetry in the Julia Moore tradition, brings contestants from many states, including her own descendents. Her great-great-great-granddaughter presents the "Julia" award to the worst poet. Ref.: 22 (Jun. 13, 1993, 4); 76 (Jul.-Aug. 1995, 10)

MOORE, MARILYN, of Ypsilanti; first woman to be promoted to sergeant in the Ypsilanti Police Department, in 1986, and the first to be promoted to lieutenant, in 1991. When she retired in 1994 after 21 years with the department, she was the highest-ranking African American woman on the force. Moore, who has a master's degree in Criminal Justice, worked as a clerk-dispatcher for the Pontiac Police Department for six years before serving as an undercover narcotics officer during her first six years at Ypsilanti. Ref.: 4 (Jul. 6, 1994, B1)

MOORE, WILLIE HOBBS (1934-1994), of Ann Arbor; first African American woman to receive a doctorate in physics at the University of Michigan, in 1972. A native of Atlantic City, New Jersey, she earned bachelor's and master's degrees from the University of Michigan in 1958 and 1961. After receiving her Ph.D., she taught physics at U-M before joining Ford Motor Company in 1977 as an engineer in the assembly division. During the 1980s she wrote a widely circulated pamphlet promoting the emphasis on quality advocated by Genichi Taguchi, a Japanese engineering professor and consultant. She also stressed the importance of quality when tutoring young people in math and science during her spare time. She was a member of Links, Inc., a community service organization of African American women, Delta Sigma Theta Sorority, and Bethel AME Church. In 1991 Ebony magazine named her as one of the 100 "most promising black women in corporate America." Ref.: 4 (Mar. 15, 1994, C3); 22 (Mar. 17, 1994, 2B)

MORRISON, WEALTHY M. (1822-1903), of Grand Rapids; co-founder of the Female Union Charitable Association (later called the United Benevolent Association), in 1848. The association, among the first to aid the sick and needy in Grand Rapids, opened the first of several homes for orphans in the 1850s and in 1886 opened a hospital, which became Blodgett Hospital in 1916. Wealthy Avenue in Grand Rapids was named for Morrison. She was also a member of the Ladies' Literary Club. Ref.: 12 (22); 41 (Jun. 3, 1903, 6)

MULDOWNEY, SHIRLEY, of Mt. Clemens; first woman to drive in the National Hot Rod Association races in 1975; first woman to win an NHRA drag racing championship, at the Spring Nationals in 1976; in 1977 she became the World Top Fuel Champion and by 1983 had been the NHRA World Champion a record three times; first woman to be inducted into the Michigan Motor Sports Hall of Fame. Muldowney began racing professionally in 1959. Despite a 1973 engine fire and a 1984 crash that left her with serious injuries requiring many operations and extensive physical therapy, she has continued racing and is ranked among the top ten drag racers. Her career was documented in a 1983 film, "Heart Like a Wheel." Ref.: 22 (Jul. 1, 1995, 2B); 57 (Nov. 18, 1992, 2F)

MUNGER, EDITH GOTTS (1865-1945), of Hart; first woman elected to the Hart School Board, serving ten years, six years as president. Munger was a teacher in Whitehall and Muskegon before going to Chicago for nurse's training. She moved to Hart after her marriage in 1895. Known as the "Bird Woman" because of her avid interest in birds, she joined the Michigan Audubon Society in 1907 and in 1913 became president, serving for 21 years. During her presidency, the robin was selected as the state bird, the Society sponsored educational programs and lobbied for legislation to ban the sale and purchase of egret plumes, to educate children in humane treatment of wildlife, and to designate all state parks as bird sanctuaries. Munger spoke about birds to children and service clubs throughout Michigan. She served as president of the Oceana County Equal Suffrage Association from 1917 to 1918. In the 1920s she led a movement to save the sand dunes along Lake Michigan from exploitation by mining companies supplying the glass industry. She was also active in the Wild Flower Preservation Society, the LWV, the Hart Ladies' Literary Club, and the birth control movement. Ref.: 60 (18-24); 77 (Mar. 1917, 7)

MUNSELL, SUSAN GRIMES, of Howell; first woman elected to the Michigan Legislature from Livingston County, elected to the House of Representatives in 1986. A graduate of Michigan State University in 1973 and the University of Michigan in 1979, she has served on the House Standing Committees of Conservation and Environment, Human Services and Children, Labor and Taxation, as well as the Michigan Association of Certified Public Accountants' Committee on State and Local Taxation and the House Republican Policy Committee. She was Republican Whip from 1988 to 1992.

Among her other activities are the LWV of Livingston County, Huron Valley Girl Scout Council and the Women's Resource Center of Livingston County. Ref.: 188

MURTLAND, CLEO (1875-1965), of Ann Arbor; teacher in the Manhattan Trade School for Girls in New York City, the first school of its kind in the United States; founder and director of the Trade School for Girls at Worcester, Massachusetts in 1911 and the Simila School (a trade school for girls) at Philadelphia in 1917; first woman appointed to an academic position at the University of Michigan, as associate professor of Vocational Education in 1919; first woman to be an Emeritus Professor at the University of Michigan, in 1943 after her retirement. Ref.: 198

NEALE, VICTORIA, see **TILLEY, BARBARA**

****

"WORKING WOMEN need the ballot to regulate conditions under which they work. Do WORKING MEN think they can protect themselves without the right to vote?"

Michigan Equal Suffrage Association

****

NEMETH, VALLA SALTZGIVER, of Lansing; co-founder in 1974 of the Coalition of Labor Union Women (CLUW), at national, state, and local levels; first woman to receive the Olga Madar Award from CLUW (See **Madar, Olga** in Michigan Women: Firsts and Founders, Vol. I.); first labor woman to receive the Diana Award from the Lansing YWCA, in 1975; co-founder of the Lansing chapters of the National Women's Political Caucus and NOW. A native of Kentucky, Nemeth moved to Lansing in 1935, and worked for 33 years at Fisher Body of Lansing, where she became an active member UAW Local 602, serving as chair of the Election Committee and Women's Committee, first woman member of the Fair Practices Committee, and 12-year member of the UAW's Greater Lansing Community Action Program Council. She has also been a member of the Ingham County Women's Commission, Lansing YWCA board member, chair of Tri-County Human Services, and delegate to the National Women's Political Caucus Conference in 1973 and White House Conference on Aging and Families in 1981. Ref.: 184

NESTOR, AGNES (1880-1948), of Grand Rapids; co-founder of the International Glove Workers Union (IGWR) in 1902; founder and first President of Operators Local #1 of the IGWR, in 1902. The IGWR was formed when Nestor and Elizabeth Christman led women workers out of the American Federation of Labor to begin their own union. She was a member of the executive board of the IGWU from 1906 to 1948, serving as vice president from 1903 to 1906, president from 1913 to 1915, vice president from 1915 to 1938, and director of research and education from 1938 to 1948. She was also a member of the executive board of the National Women's Trade Union League in 1907 and served as president of the

Chicago chapter from 1913 until her death. Nestor was awarded an honorary doctorate by Loyola University in 1929. Ref.: 103 (308)

NEUENFELT, LILA M. (1902-1981), of Dearborn; first woman to be a circuit court judge in Michigan, serving on the Wayne County Circuit Court, from 1941 until her retirement in 1966. A graduate of the University of Detroit Law School in 1922, she had to wait for six months until her 21st birthday before she could become a member of the State Bar. She was then the youngest woman attorney practicing in the United States. She became Michigan's youngest justice of the peace with her election in 1924 to that position in Dearborn. She served as president of the Women Lawyers Association of Michigan. Ref.: 25 (Apr. 8, 1941, 5B); 70 (Jun. 1984, 448)

NICHOLS, JUDY, of Highland; first Program Director of the Michigan Sheriff's Association Victim/Witness Assistance Network and the first person in the country to hold such a position for a law enforcement association, in 1986; founder of the Oakland County chapter for Parents of Murdered Children in 1986; co-founder of the Michigan Crisis Response Association in 1987. Nichols has been active in the fight for the rights of crime victims since her son was murdered in 1983. She helped to pass Michigan's Crime Victims Rights Act (Public Act 87 of 1985), requiring law enforcement agencies to provide crime victims with information on emergency services, compensation and prosecution rights at the scene of the crime. As Program Director of the MSA Victim/Witness Assistance Network, she was responsible for the development, implementation and direction of the network's statewide training programs conducted for law enforcement and criminal justice agencies and community service providers. In 1988 Nichols and the MSA Network were recognized for private sector initiative by President Ronald Reagan at ceremonies in Washington. Her other honors include the Crime Victim's Rights Outstanding Advocate Award presented at the second annual Crime Victim's Rights Awareness Vigil held at Lansing in 1993. She has also been president of the Michigan Victim Alliance, state coordinator for Parents of Murdered Children, and a certified instructor on domestic violence for the Michigan Law Enforcement Training Council. Among her memberships are Mothers Against Drunk Driving and the Sexual Assault Information Network of Michigan. Ref.: 57 (May 7, 1993, 7C); 189

NIEDZIELSKI, ELEANORE CRAVES (1911-1981), of Bay City; founder (in 1975) and first director of the Bay City Ballet, a non-profit organization to promote dance as an integral part the life of the community. In 1929 Niedzielski founded the Craves Dancing School, which she served as director and instructor. Concerned for the special needs of physically disabled children, she also taught dancing to those with cerebral palsy and donated the proceeds of her dance recitals to the March of Dimes. Ref.: 121 (34)

NORIOT MILLER, MARJORIE MAY (1911-1990), of Gaylord; first girl to compete and win in horse racing at the Otsego County Fair, in 1920 at the age of nine. Ref.: 174

NURIEL, R. HEDY, of Huntington Woods; one of the first two social workers (with **Amy Coha**) to testify as an Expert Witness in court cases involving battered women, in 1985. By 1995 she had qualified as an Expert Witness on behalf of battered women in over 25 cases. A University of Michigan graduate, Nuriel is the executive director of HAVEN, Oakland County's violence, sexual assault and child abuse center. Located in Pontiac, HAVEN provides a shelter for battered women and their children and counseling for survivors, perpetrators and family members. Nuriel has also been executive director of the Michigan Coalition Against Domestic Violence (a statewide network of battered women shelters which operated the National Domestic Violence Hotline) and as vice chair of the National Coalition Against Domestic Violence. She is the co-author of Families of Abuse: The Connection Between Substance Abuse and Violence. Ref.: 190

OAKES, PAM, of Holt; first woman to be a firefighter in the Lansing Fire Department, in 1984, and first woman to become an engineer, driving and operating a fire rig at Lansing's Station 9 in 1993. Ref.: 57 (Jan. 7, 1993, 1B)

O'DONNELL, SARAH G. (dates not known), of Jackson; first President of the Federation of Clubs of Jackson, the first city in Michigan to unite its clubs, c. 1893. Ref.: 45 (10)

OMALLEY, MRS. CHARLES M. (first name and dates not known), of Bois Blanc Island; first woman lighthouse keeper at the Bois Blanc Light in Lake Huron, from 1854 to 1855. Ref.: 18 (163)

OREN, MARTHA CARLSON (dates not known), of Detroit; first woman in the Detroit area to receive a War Production Board Commendation, for her improved methods of checking valve seats on engines for World War II P.T. boats manufactured at the Packard Motor Car Company, in 1943. Oren received much recognition for her innovations, including a personal meeting with Eleanor Roosevelt, who was visiting the Packard plant. Ref.: 74 (Mar./Apr. 1992, 16)

OWEN, CHARLOTTE PLUMMER, of Ann Arbor; first and only director of the United States Marine Corps Women's Reserve Band, the official band of the women in the Marine Corps during World War II; only woman to have guest-conducted the U.S. Marine Band, in 1945 at Camp Lejeune and in 1993 at the Marine Barracks in Washington D.C., for the 50th anniversary of the founding of the U.S. Marine Corps Women's Reserve Band, organized in 1943 under the sponsorship of Col. William F. Santelmann, leader of the U. S. Marine Band. Holding the rank of Master Tech Sergeant, Owen led the 43-piece all-woman band on radio broadcasts, on U.S. tours to sell war bonds during World War II, and at theaters, dress parades, hospitals and rallies for Marines going overseas. The Women's Band, which also included a 15-piece dance band led by Owen on her clarinet, disbanded in 1945. A native of Oregon, Owen studied music at the University of Oregon and taught music in Oregon schools before joining the Marine Corps Women's Reserve. She has been the conductor of the 75-piece Ann Arbor Civic Band since 1986. She is active in Mu Phi Epsilon (professional society for musicians), has sponsored Tau Beta Sigma Chapter for the University of Michigan Bands, is a member of the Women Band Directors National Association and Rotary International, and has served on the board of directors of the Association of Concert Bands. Ref.: 115 (Jun. 3, 1995, A6); 192

PALM, MERRITT, see **RILEY, DAWN**

****

"Self development is a higher duty than self sacrifice and should be a woman's motto henceforward."

Elizabeth Cady Stanton

****

PALMER, ALICE FREEMAN (1855-1902); first woman to receive an honorary Ph.D. degree from the University of Michigan, in 1882. A graduate of the University of Michigan in 1876, she became a teacher and principal at Saginaw High School. In 1879, at the age of 24, she was appointed head of the history department at Wellesley College, where she was the youngest professor. She served as president of Wellesley from 1881 to 1887, the youngest president of the college. She was also a member of the Massachusetts Board of Education and a co-founder and early president of the Association of Collegiate Alumnae, which later became the AAUW. Ref.: 68 (73); 85 (18-20)

PAPA, EVA, of Cheboygan; first woman to be the lighthouse keeper of the Cheboygan Light on Lake Huron, at the entrance to the Cheboygan River, in 1869. Ref.: 18 (163)

PARKS, SUE, of Ypsilanti; first girl to compete with and against boys in a Michigan high school dual track meet, finishing fifth in the 880-yard run, on May 9, 1972, when she was 16 years old. Her race took place two weeks after a Federal court ruling permitted girls to compete in high school sports. Ref.: 115 (May 10, 1972, 1, 25)

PAUL, HELEN LONGYEAR (1885-1960), of Marquette; first woman to graduate from the Massachusetts Institute of Technology with a Bachelor of Science in Architecture, in 1909. With her husband, Lt. Carroll Paul of the U.S. Navy, she returned to Marquette in 1922 at the death of her father, J. M. Longyear, benefactor and first president of the Marquette County Historical Society, in which she also became very active. As a historic preservationist, she was influential in securing a new home for the Society, purchased and restored the oldest standing home in Marquette, the Burt House, prevented the Army Corps of Engineers from blasting rock from the Huron Islands for the Portage Entry Canal, and received permission to restore the Officers' Quarters at Fort Wilkins, the Beaumont House on Mackinac Island, and the Schoolcraft House in Sault Ste. Marie, primarily at her own expense. In 1960 she was honored by the American Association for State and Local History "for a lifetime of distinguished leadership in local history activities in Michigan's Upper Peninsula." Helen Paul was the sister of **Abby Beecher Longyear Roberts**. (See **Roberts, Abby Beecher Longyear** in Michigan Women: Firsts and Founders, Vol. I.) Ref.: 193

PAUL, SARAH (dates not known), of Middleville; first schoolteacher in Barry County, in 1835 at Middleville. Ref.: 97

PEARL, DOROTHY WAITE (1896-1991), of Eastport; President of the Michigan Red Arrow Division Unit 36 of the American Legion Auxiliary, in 1936; President of the Michigan American Legion Auxiliary, in 1940 and 1941; the first Michigan woman to be National President of the American Legion Auxiliary, in 1946 and 1947; recipient of the French Legion of Honor for her work with French war orphans in 1946; and founder of Girls' Nation and Girls' State in 1946. Each year some 500 eleventh grade girls assemble in each state to learn how their state government functions. At the end of each session, they choose two girls as "senators" to represent their state at Girls' Nation in Washington, D.C. Pearl was honored for her role as founder at the 40th Girls' Nation in 1986. She was also a past president of the Detroit Women's City Club, chair of the Antrim County Republican Committee, and was appointed director of the Women's Civil Defense by President Dwight D. Eisenhower, serving from 1948 to 1963. Ref.: 113 (Jun. 12, 1991)

****

"If the men will agree to take care of the bad men,
we will agree to take care of the bad women; and we will not have
half the task they will for there are not half as many."

Zerelda Wallace

****

PECK, ANNIE SMITH (1850-1935). An honors graduate of the University of Michigan in 1878 and 1881, majoring in classical studies, Peck taught school in several locations, including Saginaw, Michigan, where she was preceptress at the high school. She also taught Latin and elocution at Purdue University, was the first woman admitted to the American School of Classical Studies at Athens, Greece, in 1885, and lectured on classical archaeology at Smith College, before turning her attention to mountain climbing. After her ascent of Mt. Shasta in California and the Matterhorn in Switzerland, Peck was a sensation in America, where her climbing activity and apparel were derided as "unladylike." Undaunted, in 1897 she conquered Mexico's live volcano Popocatapetl and was the first woman in the Americas to climb a mountain over 18,000 feet, the 18,324 ft. Mt. Orizasba in Mexico. She had climbed 20 major mountains by 1900, the year she was the United States delegate to the International Congress of Alpinists in Paris. Peck was a founder of the American Alpine Club in 1902. Two years later, at age 54, she was the first person to conquer the 21,300 ft. Illampu peak of Mt. Sorata in Bolivia and in 1908 was the first person to climb the north peak of Mt. Huascaran in the Peruvian Andes, at an altitude of 21,812 feet, the highest altitude ever reached in the Western Hemisiphere until that time. This last feat brought Peck international acclaim. She was awarded a gold medal by the Peruvian government and the Silver Slipper Award by the Lima Geographical Society, which in 1927 named Mt. Huscaran's north peak "Cumbre Ana Peck" in her honor. In 1911, at age 61, she was the first person to climb Peru's 21,250 ft. Mt. Coropuna, where she drove in a pennant declaring "Votes for women." She was awarded the Chilean Order of Merit in 1930 on her 80th birthday. In 1933, at the age of 82, Peck climbed 5,380 ft. Mt. Madison in New Hampshire, her last ascent. Billed as the "Queen of the Climbers," Peck lectured and wrote books on South America, between climbing expeditions. Ref.: 68 (69-71); 103 (337-338)

PERKINS, DELLA FOOTE (c. 1849-1936), of Grand Rapids; founder of the first weekly reading group in Grand Rapids, "The Reviewers," in 1883; founder and first president of the Grand Rapids Art Association in 1910. Perkins led the drive to raise funds for the association's building and its permanent collection of paintings and was instrumental in establishing the association's Grand Rapids Art Gallery in 1924. She was also president of the Grand Rapids Federation of Women's Clubs and a member of the DAR and the Women's City Club. Ref.: 136; 183

PERRY, BELLE McARTHUR (1856-1925), of Charlotte; co-founder and first president of the Michigan Women's Press Association in 1890; co-founder of the Michigan State Federation of Women's Clubs in 1895; first woman to serve on the Charlotte School Board. Born in Brookfield, she graduated from Charlotte High School and taught school before her marriage in 1876. She also completed the four years' course of the Chautauqua Literary and Scientific Circle, receiving her diploma at Bay View. Perry and her husband George were owners and editors of the <u>Charlotte Tribune</u>. She founded and edited the <u>Interchange</u>, a publication of the Michigan Women's Press Association that later became the <u>Bulletin</u> of the Michigan State Federation of Women's Clubs. Perry also served as president of the State Women's Christian Temperance Union, the Michigan Equal Suffrage Association, the Charlotte Woman's Club, the Century Club, and the Michigan State Federation of Women's Clubs, and was the founder and first president of the Woman's Council at county fairs. Ref.: 49 (201); 176

PETTIBONE, DEBORAH, see **RILEY, DAWN**

PHOTOGRAPHS OF

THE WOMAN SUFFRAGE MOVEMENT

IN MICHIGAN

Nannette B. Gardner of Detroit, one of the first two women to vote in Michigan, in 1871. (Bentley Historical Library, University of Michigan)

Sojourner Truth (1797-1883) of Battle Creek, former slave and nationally-known speaker on behalf of Abolition and Women Suffrage. (Michigan Women's Historical Center & Hall of Fame)

Emily Grimes helping her mother, Lucia Grimes of Detroit, with the national Suffrage campaign in Washington, D.C., 1915. (Bentley Historical Library, University of Michigan)

Grace Kelley-Freehouse, Grand Rapids Suffragist, c. 1912. (Grand Rapids Public Library)

The Michigan Equal Suffrage Society tent at the Michigan State Fair, 1912. (The State Archives of Michigan)

Supporters of votes for women at a meeting held at the Ypsilanti fairgrounds. (Ypsilanti Historical Society)

Anna Howard Shaw of Big Rapids, president of the National
American Woman Suffrage Association, speaking on behalf
of votes for women.
(Michigan Women's Historical Center & Hall of Fame)

Anti-Suffrage activists at Marquette illustrate the dire effects of
extending the vote to women. (Marquette County Historical Society)

Michigan Grange women on Fraternal Day in Battle Creek, 1914.
(Roland Winter)

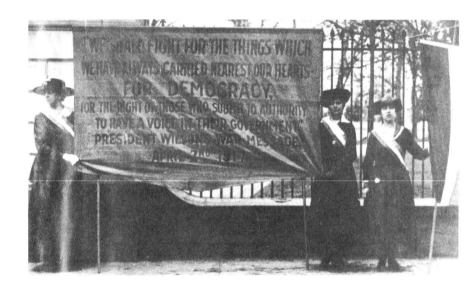

Michigan Suffragists picketing the White House in 1917.
L to R: Kathleen Hendrie, Betsy Reyneau and Ella Aldinger.
(Bentley Historical Library, University of Michigan)

Gov. Albert E. Sleeper signing a bill granting Michigan women the right to vote in presidential elections, May 8, 1917. Present were Mary M. Sleeper, Mrs. Wm. F. Bright, Nellie S. Clark, Mrs. G. Edgar Allen, Mrs. C. G. Parnell, Ella Aldinger, Belle Brotherton, Ida Chittenden, Mrs. F. B. Perkins, Mrs. Luther Burton, Mrs. Fitzpatrick, Mrs. Lockwood, Mrs. Hopkins, Jennie Carley, and Frances E. Burns. (The State Archives of Michigan)

Members of the Grand Rapids League of Women Voters at their first Election Day parade in 1924. (Grand Rapids Public Library)

Poster given to women who registered to vote after the Nineteenth Amendment was ratified in 1920. (The State Archives of Michigan)

THE PITY OF IT!

Broadside distributed by the Michigan Association of Men Opposed to the Further Extension of Suffrage. (Michigan Women's Historical Center & Hall of Fame)

PETTIBONE, KATHERINE, see **RILEY, DAWN**

PHILLIPS, LEONORA (dates not known), of Whitewater; quite possibly Michigan's first weather reporter, furnishing the first recorded monthly weather reports to the <u>Grand Traverse Herald</u>, beginning in December of 1858. Ref.: 116 (See entry for S. E. Wait)

PICCARD, JEANNETTE RIDLON (1895-1981); first woman to reach the stratosphere, by making a solo flight in a stratospheric balloon, launched from the Ford Airport in Dearborn in June of 1934. On October 23 of that year she piloted the 175-foot-high balloon to the women's altitude record of 57,559 feet, while her husband, Jean Piccard, studied cosmic rays from outer space; a monument to mark Piccard's achievement was placed on the grounds of Dearborn's William B. Stout Junior High School in 1965. In July of 1974, at the age of 79, she was the first of 11 women who were the first women ordained priests in the Episcopal Church, at a ceremony in Philadelphia. In 1976 she spent six weeks as a visiting priest in residence at the University of Michigan's Canterbury House. Ref.: 25 (Sept. 18, 1976, 3A)

****

"Our enemy is not men, or men as lawmakers, but conservatism, which is a ready cloak for the supression of progress. It represents tradition, prejudice, selfishness."

Clara B. Arthur of Detroit
President, Michigan Equal Suffrage Association, 1908

****

PICKETT, ROBERTA McGUIRE, of Detroit; co-founder of the Detroit chapter of the National Council of Negro Women and the first international chapter of Delta Sigma Theta Sorority; charter member and vice president of the Detroit Chapter of Top Ladies of Distinction. Pickett attended Fisk University and holds a doctorate in educational leadership from Wayne State University. As a recipient of a scholarship from the NAACP and the Detroit Round Table of Catholics, Protestants and Jews, she studied intercultural relations at Harvard University, where she developed a project for use in the schools. Pickett has been an elementary school teacher, principal, college instructor, and writer. She received the Spirit of Detroit Award in 1980. Ref.: 89 (248-251)

PIERCE, ELLA MATTHEWS, see **UHL, ALICE FOLLETT**

PILZNER-STOKES, HELEN L. (c. 1915-1993), of New Baltimore and Detroit; co-founder of the women's substance abuse program at the Salvation Army in the 1970s; founder of the Robinwood Clinic in Detroit for alcohol and cocaine abusers in 1975, operating it until 1988. A graduate of Mercy School of Nursing and Michigan State University, Pilzner-Stokes received the Lamplighter Award from the National Council on Alcoholism in 1981, for outstanding work in the field. Ref.: 22 (Jan. 15, 1993, B4)

POLLOCK, E. JILL, of Orchard Lake; first management woman in the auto industry to serve as a "main-table" bargainer, as a member of the Ford National Negotiating Committee during the 1982 Ford-UAW contract talks. In 1983, after twelve years with the Ford Motor Company's personnel department, she founded Arbor Consulting Group, a personnel management consulting service in Plymouth and in 1993 she launched Pollock Consulting Group in Detroit, specializing in human resources management. She served as co-chair of the Michigan delegation to the White House Small Business Conference in 1995 and as president of the National Association of Women Business Owners Greater Detroit Chapter. Pollock holds degrees in personnel management and business administration from Michigan State University and the University of Detroit. Ref.: 22 (Jun. 5, 1995, 3F); 194

PRATER, CONSTANCE C., of Detroit; first African American to be chief of the Detroit Free Press City-County Bureau, in 1990. Ref.: 22 (Feb. 2, 1994, 3D)

PRESTON, MRS. E. J. (first name and dates not known), of Detroit; first President of the Detroit Day Nursery and Kindergarten Association, which opened an early day care facility in 1883. Ref.: 20 (30)

PRIES, MRS. J. F. (first name and dates not known), of Detroit; bicyclist who was the first Detroit woman to appear in public wearing bloomers, in 1897 while biking on Belle Isle. Pries, a member of the Ladies of the Unique Cycle Club, became the first Detroit woman to qualify for the Century Bar Award of the League of American Wheelmen, after completing a 106-mile course with fifteen men cyclists. Ref.: 59 (97)

PROCHNOW, ELLA BAREIS (1896-1985), of Ann Arbor; first woman in Michigan (possibly the first in the country) to own and manage an automobile dealership, in 1930. After attending the University of Michigan, Prochnow taught school in Northfield Township. She took over her husband Walter's Ann Arbor Buick dealership when he died, leaving her with two small children. She managed the dealership for many years and was actively involved in the move from its downtown location to a new site on Washtenaw Avenue in 1964. Prochnow served for more than thirty years as treasurer of the Ann Arbor Auto Dealers Association. Ref.: 5 (Oct. 1994, 29-30)

PULTE, MARY JO, of Kalamazoo; founder of the Michigan Women's Foundation in 1986, and of the Lodge at Yarrow, a women's retreat and conference center in Augusta, Michigan, in 1993. Pulte donated $500,000 in stocks to launch the endowment of the foundation. Since 1987, more than sixty grants, totalling nearly $500,000, have been awarded to groups that help Michigan women develop leadership skills and economic self-sufficiency. Ref.: 23 (Jul. 4, 1993, 4); 57 (Dec. 13, 1994, 1B); 84 (Jan. 22-Feb. 4, 1995, 10-11)

PUTNAM, CAROLINE WILLARD WILLIAMS (1825-1919), of Grand Rapids; co-founder and first president of the Ladies' Literary Club of Grand Rapids in 1869. Born in Deerfield, Massachusetts, she moved to Grand Rapids in 1850 to head the girls' department at St. Mark's School, an institution that lasted until the Civil War. Her published works included poetry, an autobiography and historical articles, written when she was in her 80s. Ref.: 136; 183

RABBERS, JAN, of Vicksburg; founder and publisher of <u>Michigan Women's Times</u>, a twice-monthly newspaper focusing on women's issues, which began publication in September of 1994 and suspended publication in September of 1995. Ref.: 22 (Nov. 9, 1994, 1E)

RAGOTZY, BETTY EBERT (c. 1924-1995), of Augusta; co-founder, with her husband Jack, of the Augusta Barn Theatre in Augusta, in 1945. A California actress, Ragotzy came to Michigan to work with a Kalamazoo community theater where she met her future husband. At the professional theater that they established in an Augusta barn, she appeared in many plays and musicals. Several of the actors who started in the Augusta Barn Theater went on to appear in television and Broadway productions. Ref.: 57 (Mar. 21, 1995, 2D; May 30, 1995, 1D; Jun. 8, 1995, "What's On," 5)

RANN, BETTY J. WRIGHT (1919-1994), of Charlotte; first Michigan woman to become a large animal Doctor of Veterinary Medicine, after graduating with honors from Michigan State University's College of Veterinary Medicine in 1943. Ref.: 57 (Jul. 9, 1994, 2B)

RANUCCI, SHARON C. (1939-1989), of Detroit; first woman to serve as a mediator in Wayne County; first woman partner of her Detroit law firm (Garan, Lucow, Miller, Seward, Cooper & Becker) in 1981; first woman member of the Association of Defense Trial Counsel, where she served as treasurer; former president of the Women Lawyers Association of Michigan. In honor of Ranucci, who graduated from the University of Detroit in 1960 and Fordham University Law School in 1963, the University of Detroit Law School has established the Sharon Ranucci Scholarship Fund to award an annual scholarship to a senior U. of D. law student. Ref.: 22 (Feb. 24, 1989, 6A); 31 (Dec. 1989-Jan. 1990, 5)

RATHBUN-NEALY COLEMAN, MELISSA, of Newaygo; first woman to become a prisoner of war in the Persian Gulf War, in 1991. Then known as Rathbun-Nealy, she was a U.S. Army specialist with the 233rd Transportation Company when she and another soldier were captured while delivering supplies near the Kuwaiti border. Wounded in the arm by shrapnel, she was held in a Baghdad cell by her Iraqi captors from January 31 to March 4. Later she was one of five former prisoners of war to receive medals. She was discharged from the Army in 1993 after completing five years of service and then married another Gulf War veteran, Michael Coleman. Ref: 4 (Mar. 4, 1994, A7)

RAVEN MORSE, PAULINA ELONA (d. 1959), of East Lansing; first
home extension agent in Michigan, representing the College of
Home Economics of Michigan Agricultural College (now Michigan
State University), from 1915 to 1917. Born in New York State, she
came to Michigan with her family in 1877, earned a bachelor's
degree from the Women's Division of MAC in 1905, and became a
professor of home economics at the Normal and Industrial School in
Aberdeen, South Dakota. She was a charter member of the
American Home Economics Association in 1910. Returning to MAC,
she earned a master's degree in Home Economics in 1913 and
served two years as the state's first home extension agent until her
marriage in 1917. Ref.: 102

RAY, BERTHA (dates not known), of Lansing; the first woman in
Lansing to vote and in 1923 the first woman to be elected as city
clerk for Lansing, serving in that office for 27 years until her
retirement. Ray was the second Lansing woman elected to public
office after the passage of the 19th Amendment. (The first was
Frieda A. Schneider, elected as city treasurer in 1920. See
Michigan Women: Firsts and Founders, Vol. I.) Ray worked in her
father's print shop while attending Lansing Central High School. A
strong supporter of woman suffrage, she proudly wore a "Votes for
Women" button. Ref.: 104 (5)

****

*"If prayer and womanly influence are doing so much for God
by indirect methods, how shall it be when that electric force is
brought to bear through the battery of the ballot box?"*
Frances E. Willard

****

RECK, SUSAN L., of Howell; first woman to be a judge for
Livingston County, with her election as Probate Judge in 1988.
Among many other achievements, Reck has been a partner in the
law firm of Reck, Reck & Erwin, a law professor at Cooley Law
School and Michigan State University, a public school teacher,
president of the LWV of Livingston County, president of Big
Brothers/Big Sisters of Livingston County, and chair of the
Livingston County United Way Campaign. Ref.: 199

REESE, DELLA (DELOREESE) PATRICIA EARLY, formerly of
Detroit; first woman to host a syndicated TV talk show, "Della," in
1969 and 1970; one of few women to guest host the "Tonight Show."
At age 13, Reese began touring with Mahalia Jackson's gospel
troupe during summer vacations. While attending Wayne State
University, she formed her own group, the Meditation Singers. In
1953 she moved to New York City, where she became a vocalist
with the Erskine Hawkins Orchestra and recorded many hit songs,
including "Don't You Know" in 1959. Her other credits include
roles in the TV series, "Sanford and Son," "The Love Boat," "Chico
and the Man," and the films "Let's Rock" and "Psychic Killer."
Ref.: 25 (Mar. 2, 1970, 12A); 71 (Sept. 7, 1985)

REEVES, MARTHA, of Detroit; the first Motown recording artist to sue the famous label for back royalties, settling the lawsuit out of court in 1991. Reeves' singing group, Martha & the Vandellas, signed with Motown in 1962 and were part of the first Motown Revue tour. Their hit recording of "Heat Wave" the following year was followed by five years of hits, including the 1964 smash hit, "Dancing in the Street." When Motown left Detroit during the early 1970s, Reeves' career declined and personal problems mounted. After a religious experience in 1977, she became an accredited Baptist missionary who counsels those she calls "the lost ones." Reeves also founded her Stars on the Rise program, a talent showcase held at a Detroit nightclub where would-be entertainers can receive helpful advice about their performances. Martha & the Vandellas, who perform 42 weeks a year, were inducted into the Rock 'n' Roll Hall of Fame in January of 1995. Ref.: 22 (Jan. 10, 1995, 1D)

REYES, ANGIE, of Detroit; founder and director of the youth program of Latino Family Services, a southwest Detroit community outreach agency. Since founding the youth program in 1986 as a recreational and tutoring service, with herself as the only full-time staff member, Reyes has expanded it to include job training, computer training and social service programs for hundreds of young people who come each week to the center for the programs, field trips, tutoring, recreation, and help offered by Reyes and her 14-member staff. Ref.: 25 (Apr. 11, 1993, 6R)

REYNEAU, BETSY GRAVES (1888-1964), of Detroit; one of four Michigan women in the first picket line at the White House on January 10, 1917, protesting President Woodrow Wilson's anti-Suffrage stand; first Michigan woman to be arrested and only one to be sentenced on July 14, 1917, to 60 days' hard labor in Occoquan prison for picketing on behalf of Suffrage. The other Michigan women in the first picket line were **Ella Hough Aldinger** of Lansing, **Kathleen McGraw Hendrie** of Detroit and **Mrs. G. B. Jennison** of Bay City. Reyneau was a painter. Her portraits of notable African Americans hang in the National Portrait Gallery in Washington, D.C. Ref.: 22 (May 6, 1917); 160

REYNOLDS, NANETTE LEE, of East Lansing; first African American woman to be director of the Michigan Department of Civil Rights, in 1993. Reynolds, who holds a doctorate from the Harvard Graduate School of Education and degrees in education and political science from Southern Illinois University and Howard University, had been director of the Community Services Bureau of the Department of Civil Rights since 1987. Previously she had been the first executive director of the Federated Council of Domestic Violence Programs and had held academic and administrative positions at Brown University, Massachusetts Institute of Technology, and the University of Rochester. Ref.: 22 (Mar. 23, 1993, 4A); 56 (Jul. 1994, 56-59); 57 (Jun. 1, 1993, 1B, 3B); 82 (Fall 1993, 16)

RIESTERER, JEANNE, of Roseville; first woman to be mayor of the City of Roseville, elected in 1982 and serving until 1994. A retired school psychologist and reading consultant, Riesterer is also the mother of 11 children and the manager of Roseville's Sacred Heart Cemetery. Ref.: 24 (Oct. 1993, 54-55)

RILEY, DAWN, of Detroit; one of four Michigan women on the first all-women America's Cup sailing team in 1995. The 24-member crew of the America 3 also included **Merritt Palm** of Grosse Pointe Farms and sisters **Katherine** and **Deborah Pettibone** of Port Huron. A graduate of Michigan State University, Riley is one of only seven women who have sailed in the America's Cup race since 1851, having sailed in the Cup's 1992 Defender Trials but not the finals for that year. She also skippered an all-women's crew in the 1993-94 Whitbread Round the World race and ranks 28th in the world on the match-racing circuit, the highest place ever reached by a woman. Palm, who graduated from the University of Miami, is ranked among the top 10 U.S. sailors in the European Dinghy class. Katherine Pettibone, who is studying marine biology at the University of Miami, has raced in many regattas in Michigan and Florida. Deborah, a 1991 graduate of the University of Michigan, joined the America 3 crew when more women were added. In January of 1995 the America 3 won its first race of the Defender Trials but failed to survive the four-month series of races to select a defender of America's Cup against a foreign challenger. The controversial addition of a male coach in March of 1995 meant that the crew of America 3 was no longer an all-woman team. Ref.: 56 (May, 1995, 40-42); 84 (Oct. 2-16, 1994, 1-3)

RISEMAN, META ROSENBERG (1905-1994), of Detroit; founder and director of the Riseman Summer Camp in Dryden, where young people were taught about interracial and international issues while they learned about gardening and farm life, during the 1930s and 1940s. Born in Dusseldorf, Germany, she came to the United States at the age of five. After receiving a bachelor's degree from Smith College in 1924 and a master's degree in history from Columbia University, she moved to Detroit in 1927 and taught school in Eastpointe. When she returned to Detroit from Dryden in the 1950s, she taught Latin and social studies in the public schools before retiring in 1968. A firm believer in international cooperation, she served as national, state, and local president of the Women's International League for Peace and Freedom. She was also active in UNICEF and the Mayor's Interracial Committee in Detroit, and worked for fair housing and employment laws. Ref.: 22 (Mar. 2, 1994, 2B)

RITCHIE, CATHERINE CAMPBELL (b. 1894), of Harrisville; first woman elected to county office in Alcona County, with her election in 1922 as Register of Deeds. She served in office for 26 years. Ref.: 36 (35-36)

ROBBERT, JACOBA BEUKER (1864-1957), of Grand Rapids; co-founder in 1909 of the Christian Psychopathic Hospital Association to promote a mental hospital that would include spiritual guidance. The Christian Psychopathic Hospital (renamed the Pine Rest Christian Hospital in 1940) opened its doors in 1911. Robbert was active in organizing support groups of women (later known as the Pine Rest Circles) to spearhead fund drives, resulting in facility construction and the purchase of therapeutic equipment. Ref.: 13; 136; 183

ROBERTS, ESTELLE (dates not known), of Lapeer; first woman to be elected as Register of Deeds for Lapeer County, serving from 1927 to 1938. Ref.: 168

ROBINSON, GLENDA, of Marquette; first woman elected as Mayor of Marquette, in 1979. Ref.: 86 (Nov. 19, 1979)

****

"THE FARMER KNOWS! The farm that is run without a woman's help isn't much of a farm. A government that is run without a woman's help is a one-sided government."

From a Suffrage Flyer

****

ROBINSON, ROBERTA, of Kalamazoo; founder and director of The Mad Hatters, an educational theatrical troupe that promotes understanding of the disabled. The six member troupe was founded by Robinson in 1979 after a Kalamazoo County Mental Health Board survey revealed that many people were uncomfortable with those they perceived as being disabled. The Mad Hatters perform shows nationwide, have produced a film, "The Wish List," that has been shown over the Public Broadcasting System, and have begun a satellite troupe in Bermuda. Robinson has also launched a corporate training program to educate prospective employees and co-workers of people with disabilities. Ref.: 69 (Sept./Oct. 1990, 75)

RODGERS, LaJUNE (1917-1973), of Detroit; part of the dance team of Rodgers and Rodgers (with her husband, Earnest E. Rodgers, Sr.) which traveled the nightclub and black theater circuit during the 1930s and 1940s. Rodgers and Rodgers Talent Agency became Detroit's first black booking agents in about 1948, lining up many pre-Motown acts, including Gladys Knight and the Pips and the Four Tops. LaJune Rodgers wrote Berry Gordy's first contract. After her husband's death in 1955, she founded RAPA (Rodgers' Academy of Performing Arts) House, a popular "concert cafe" where Rodgers and her aunt served New Orleans style cuisine. She also operated the Gold Coast Ballroom from 1958 to 1960 and ran the original "Downtown Under the Stars" concert series in Grand Circus Park during the late 1950s and 1960s. Ref.: 22 (Sept. 7, 1990, 7C); 25 (Apr. 1, 1973)

ROSCOE, GLADYS PELHAM (c. 1894-1993), of Detroit; first African American music teacher in the Detroit Public Schools; founding member of Patrons of the Arts, which sponsored concerts featuring such artists as Marian Anderson, Paul Robeson and Leontyne Price from the 1940s to the 1960s. Roscoe was a member of the Original Willing Workers' Society, a black service organization founded in Detroit in 1887. Its first meeting was held at the home of her grandmother, **Mrs. Robert Pelham**. (See **Clark, Mrs.**, in Michigan Women: Firsts and Founders, Vol. I.) Roscoe was also known as a singer, pianist, organist and church choir director. A member of Chi Chapter, National Sorority of Phi Delta Kappa, she was named "Soror of the Year" in 1982 for her community activities and volunteer work. Ref.: 22 (May 6, 1993, 2B); 25 (Mar. 8, 1981, 14C); 71 (Jun. 19, 1982)

ROSS, MARJORIE A., see **JEROME FOX, MARY RUTH**

ROSS-LEE, BARBARA, formerly of Detroit and East Lansing; first African American woman to lead a medical school in the U.S, as dean of the Ohio University College of Osteopathic Medicine at Athens, Ohio, in 1993. A graduate of Michigan State University's College of Osteopathic Medicine, Ross-Lee taught family medicine at MSU from 1983 to 1993. She is the sister of singer **Diana Ross**. Ref.: 22 (Aug. 29, 1993, 12F); 99 (Dec. 6, 1993, 151)

ROTHER, HELENE, of Metamora; first woman to be an automotive designer, for General Motors Corporation in 1943. Rother, a French designer of jewelry and fashion accessories, fled Nazi-occupied France with her seven-year-old daughter Ina in 1942. After working briefly in New York, she came to Detroit to join the interior styling staff at General Motors for four years, then opened her own design studio in the Fisher Building. She specialized in designs for automotive interiors, furniture, and stained glass windows. Ref.: 25 (Mar. 6, 1949); 16 (Mar. 2, 1950); 200

ROURKE, CONSTANCE DAVIS (1852-1944), of Grand Rapids; first kindergarten teacher in the Grand Rapids public schools, in 1890 at the Second Avenue School (later called the Franklin School); founder of the Grand Rapids Kindergarten Training School in 1891, after attending the first kindergarten training class in the country, conducted by kindergarten pioneer Susan Blow at St. Louis in 1890. Rourke taught other Grand Rapids women the principles of the new educational system. She also conducted an "Americanization" program for immigrants. Born in Illinois, she attended DuQuoin College in that state. During the summers she studied pedagogy and classroom innovation under John Dewey at the University of Chicago. From 1892 to 1924, she served as principal of several Grand Rapids schools, where she developed programs to encourage children in creative self-expression, including her own special interest in art. She was the mother of **Constance Mayfield Rourke**. Ref.: 136; 183

ROURKE, CONSTANCE MAYFIELD (1885-1941), of Grand Rapids; first cultural historian to recognize the importance and origins of American culture, including both fine and folk art and the folk traditions; organizer of the National Folk Festival in St. Louis in 1934; co-founder, with Linda Butler, of the "Friends of American Art," associated with the Grand Rapids Art Gallery, in 1939. Within a year the Friends had sponsored two exhibitions of American art, one on fine art and the other on folk art. The exhibition of American fine art became a national model for similar exhibitions. Rourke graduated from Vassar College, where she taught for several years before returning to Grand Rapids in 1915. She was the author of seven books and more than 100 articles and reviews focusing on America's cultural resources. Her 1931 book, American Humor: A Study of the National Character, is still considered a classic. She was also the editor of the Federal Art Project's Index of American Design of 1937. She conducted "living research," by traveling throughout the country to find the rich contributions of various ethnic groups, farmers, miners, cowboys and women to American culture. Her work led to the American Studies movement in the mid-20th century. She was the daughter of **Constance Davis Rourke**. Ref.: 136; 183

ROUSE, ROSAMUND R. (c. 1882-1962), of Grand Rapids; first full-time salaried medical social work director at Blodgett Memorial Hospital, from 1926 until 1953; co-founder, twice president and in 1921 the executive secretary of the Mary Free Bed Guild, which established an endowment to fund a free hospital bed; promoted presentation of "All-Star Concerts" in 1912, to raise funds for the free bed program; co-founder of a vocational guidance school for physically-impaired children, 1923; co-founder of the Mary Free Bed Guild Children's Hospital and Orthopedic Center in 1930; co-founder of the Michigan Society of the National Society for Crippled Children and Adults, Inc.; and charter member of the National Association of Medical Social Work. In 1958 she received the Distinguished Service Award of the National Society for Crippled Children and Adults, for her contributions to the Mary Free Bed rehabilitation program. Ref.: 96; 136; 172; 183

RUSSELL, ELLEN P. WELLS ENGLAND (1832-1902), of Detroit; in 1896 the founder and first president of the General Alexander Macomb Chapter of the National Society of United States Daughters of 1812. A native of Vermont, she came to Detroit with her second husband, Alfred Russell. Ref.: 20 (144)

RUTH, MARION "BABE" WEYANT, of Lansing; the first aviator to be inducted into the Michigan Motor Sports Hall of Fame, in November 1992; Ruth earned her pilot's license in 1937 and was one of only five civilian women chosen to teach instrument flying to military pilots during World War II. She has taught hundreds of flying students during her nearly sixty years as an aviator and founded the Professional Aviation Instructors Association in Michigan.

Ruth has flown in the All Woman Transcontinental Air Races, as well as in other races. She is a member of the 99's (international organization of women pilots), the Silver Wings, Early Birds, and OX5 Aviation Pioneers. In 1975 Ruth received an Associate Degree in Science Aviation Flight Technology, magna cum laude, from Lansing Community College, where she taught flight and flight simulator. An avid aviation historian with an extensive collection of aviation memorabilia, Ruth served as historical chair for the 50th Anniversary of the Michigan Aeronautics Commission in 1979 and as president of Michigan Aviation Heritage. She was named "Pioneer Woman of the Year in Aviation" in 1980 by the OX5 Aviation Pioneers, was the second woman inducted into the Michigan Aviation Hall of Fame in 1988, honored by the Aircraft Owners and Pilots Association as a charter member in 1989, received the first Lansing Community College Distinguished Alumni Award in 1993, and was inducted into the OX5 Aviation Hall of Fame in 1995. Ref.: 55 (Fall/Winter 1993); 57 (May 7, 1994, 3B; Sept. 7, 1995, 2C); 184

****

"She's Good Enough to Be Your Baby's Mother,
and She's Good Enough to Vote With You"

Popular song, Lyrics by Alfred Bryan, Music by Herman Paley

****

RUTHERFORD, CLARA WALLS (1923-1994), of Detroit; first African American woman elected to the Detroit School Board, in 1972, serving until 1988. During her tenure she chaired the finance committee. She was also active in the Detroit Council of Organizations and the Trade Union Leadership Council, and served as president of the National Caucus of Black School Board Members and the Wayne County Association of School Boards, 1988 chair of the Federal Relations Network for the State of Michigan, and consultant for the National School Boards Association. Ref. 22 (Nov. 15, 1972; Jun. 22, 1994, B2); 71 (Jul. 30, 1988, 2B)

RUTSON, MRS. GEORGE, see **COWLEY, MRS. B. P.**

SAARINEN, LOJA (LOUISE) GESELLIUS (1879-1968), of Bloomfield Hills; founder in 1928 and first director (from 1928 to 1942) of the textile department at the Cranbrook Academy of Art. A native of Helsinki, Finland, Saarinen came to this country in 1923 with her husband, architect Eliel Saarinen, who was invited to teach architectural design at the University of Michigan. In 1925 they relocated from Ann Arbor to Cranbrook, the Bloomfield Hills country estate of newspaper publisher George Booth, where Eliel designed and developed the Cranbrook Academy of Art, as well as the Cranbrook Institute of Science and two schools for girls and boys. Loja, trained in sculpture, interior design, and textile design, originated and developed the textile department into a major component of the Academy. During her tenure as director, she executed many commissioned textiles, held eight one-woman exhibitions, took part in numerous other exhibitions throughout the country, and displayed her work at the World Exposition held at Paris in 1937. Ref.: 29 (78-81); 138

SAGATOO, MARY HENDERSON CABAY (1828-1914), of Saganing, Bay County; founder of the Saganing Indian Methodist Church in 1875. Born in Massachusetts, Sagatoo became a city missionary at Boston. After meeting Joseph Cabay, a young Indian chief attending Harvard College, she agreed to marry him and accompany him to Michigan as a missionary to his tribe, the Chippewa of Saganing. Although Joseph became seriously ill, they were married in 1863 and traveled to Michigan. Before Joseph's death the day after their arrival, he asked Mary to stay with his people and she agreed. Joseph's father adopted her into the tribe, giving her the name "Wah Sash Kah Moqua," meaning "there was darkness but your coming brings light." Two years later, Mary married Joseph's cousin Peter Sagatoo, chosen for her by her father-in-law and Peter's father, according to tribal custom. In the following years, Mary taught her adopted tribe the language, laws and Christian beliefs of the white people. She told of her life with the Chippewa of Bay County in the 1897 book, <u>Wah Sash Kah Moqua, or Thirty-Three Years Among the Indians</u>. Ref.: 121 (10)

SANDERS, MRS. JOSEPH (first name and dates not known), of Detroit; member of the first mixed male and female trial jury to sit in Michigan, on March 19, 1919, in Justice Lemkie's court at Detroit. The jury, consisting of three women and three men, also included **Ella Levine** and **Theresa Steffens**. Mrs. Sanders was chair of the courts committee of the Wayne County Equal Suffrage League. On the same day, the first all-woman jury in Michigan sat in Judge Bolton's court in Detroit, with **Mabel S. Greenwood** as foreman. Ref.: 132

SAREINI, SUZANNE, of Dearborn; founder of the Southeast Dearborn Ethnic Festival Committee in 1979; first Arab-American member of the Dearborn City Council, elected in 1989, re-elected in 1993 and appointed Council President Pro-Tem. The owner of Westminster Market and president of Global Business Systems in Dearborn, Sareini is also chair of the National Arab-American Republican Heritage Council and has served as president of the Arabian Village Development Corporation and on several boards, including the Michigan Republican Heritage (Nationalities) Groups, the Arab-American Institute in Washington, D.C., and the U.S. Office of Personnel Management's Meritorious Rank Review Board. She was appointed in 1994 to the Michigan Women's Commission. Ref.: 25 (Feb. 13, 1994, 1B); 82 (Summer 1994, 4, 15; Summer 1995, 11)

SAUCEDO-SMITH, IRENE, of East Lansing; first woman in the Michigan Soccer Hall of Fame; first woman to serve as president of the 42,000-member Michigan State Youth Soccer Association, in

1990; member of the state 1994 World Cup committee that brought the U.S. Cup game to the Pontiac Silver-dome in June 1993. Saucedo-Smith became involved with soccer when her two sons began to play in the 1970s. Since then she has been a soccer enthuasiast, coach, team manager, owner of a soccer store in East Lansing, and head of the state association, which doubled in size during her tenure as president. Ref.: 57 (May 27, 1993, 1C)

SAUNDERS, PATRICIA (TRICIA) McNAUGHTON, formerly of Ann Arbor; first girl to compete and win a medal in a federation wrestling tournament, as the only girl in the Ann Arbor Wrestling Warriors club at the Youth Invitational held in 1975 at Schoolcraft College in Westland; first place gold medal winner in the women's freestyle world wrestling championship held at Villeurbaine, France, in 1992, by winning the 110-pound world title; first place gold medal winner at the first international Klippan Cup tournament, held in Sweden in 1994; first woman to be inducted into the USA Wrestling Hall of Fame. At the Youth Invitational in 1975, young Tricia won seven of nine bouts to take third place in the eight-and-under age group's 50-pound division. When the Amateur Athletic Union (AAU) tried to bar her from the Eastern National AAU Junior Championships held at Eastern Michigan University in June of 1975 because she was a girl, a federal district court judge ruled that the nine-year-old should be allowed to compete, since the tax-supported institution could not support discrimination on the basis of sex. Saunders has served on the board of directors of USA Wrestling and as chair of the USA Women's Wrestling Committee. With a degree in bacteriology from the University of Wisconsin, she now lives in Phoenix, Arizona, where she is a microbiologist. Ref.: 3 (Jun. 20, 1975; Jun. 21, 1975; Nov. 25, 1992, D1, D5; Feb. 3, 1995, B1, B5)

SCHILERU, DACIE, of Detroit; first woman to compete in a National Collegiate Athletic Association event, in 1973. Born in Rumania, Schileru came to this country at the age of 18. As a student at Wayne State University in Detroit, she qualified for the diving competition in the college division swimming championships. Before 1973, NCAA competitions had been restricted to male participants. After Congress passed Title IX legislation in 1972, banning sex discrimination and guaranteeing access for women in sports, NCAA events were opened to women in 1973, the year Schileru participated. Ref.: 103 (394)

SCHILLER, ROSE KRAUSE (1900-1994), of Detroit; founder and honorary president of the Detroit League of the National Home for Jewish Children, located in Denver; founder and co-chair of the Program Planners Institute at the Jewish Community Center. Born in Chicago, Schiller grew up in Detroit, where she was active in several Jewish organizations, including the Jewish women's service organization Hadassah, serving as president of its Central States Region, chair of its Israel Bond and Ways and Means Committees,

and on its National Board and National Speakers' Bureau.
Ref.: 25 (May 22, 1994, 2C)

SCHMOCK, HELEN CLOUTIER, of Manistee; first woman to become
a member of the Quarter Century Wireless Association, in 1954.
An amateur radio operator for 66 years, she is the oldest practicing
operator in the United States and is known around the world as
W8GJX. Schmock became interested in amateur radio at the age of
20, while she was working as a beautician in Frankfort and living
above the Slyfield Radio School for the summer. After taking a
class, in which she was the only woman, she returned home to
Manistee, where she and her father built her first ham-radio
station. During World War II she was a member of the Civil Air
Patrol and served as an Army Air Force radio-code instructor. Her
experiences as a ham operator inspired her to write her first book
in 1951, Sim Barton, Girl Radio Operator. She has since written a
total of 19 books, including a book about Isle Royale, published by
Eerdmans Publishing Co., and a series of nine children's books
published by Central Michigan University, where she received
bachelor's and master's degrees in art in the 1970s. Her most
recent book is an autobiography entitled I Never Shot a Rabbit,
published in 1991. Ref.: 57 (Apr. 12, 1993, 3B); 202

****

*"Every year gives me greater faith in equal suffrage,
greater hope of its success, and a more earnest wish to use
what influence I possess for its advancement."*

Louisa Mae Alcott

****

SCHNEIDER, MAJEL HORNING (1910-1993), of East Lansing; only
woman and non-medical member of the Board of Directors of the
Rehabilitation Medical Center at Lansing's Sparrow Hospital in
1957 and chair of the board in 1961; also chair of the board of the
Rehabilitation Industries in Lansing. A graduate of Michigan State
University with degrees in music education, Schneider was elected
secretary of the national council of Sigma Kappa Sorority, for which
she organized and served as first chair of the Lila M. Koch Memorial
Scholarship Fund. Her concern for the needs of the disabled
began in 1949 when her son was born with cerebral palsy. She
became a charter member of the Lansing chapter of the United
Cerebral Palsy Association of Michigan, for which she helped to
develop many local and state programs and services for the
disabled. She was also active with the Ingham County Easter Seal
Society. Working with Congress, she organized and directed a
nationwide lobby for more than three years to win support for the
Talking Book Act of 1966, which was an amendment to the Talking
Book Acts of 1931 and 1962 that provided books and magazines on
tape to the blind. The 1966 amendment extended the service to the
near blind, physically handicapped and the elderly. For her long
service to the physically and visually impaired, she received many

honors, including a Certificate of Appreciation from the United Cerebral Palsy Association of Lansing and B'Nai B'rith's Greater Lansing Human Relations Award. Ref.: 57 (Mar. 1, 1993, 2B)

SCHULTZ, LONNIE, see **TILLEY, BARBARA**

SCHUMAN, PAULA, of Detroit; first director of a clinic to treat women with AIDS, begun in 1991 at Hutzel Hospital in the Detroit Medical Center. In 1992 Schuman began directing a five-year federally funded study on women infected with the AIDS virus, to determine whether women die from AIDS faster than men and whether AIDS is linked to cervical cancer. Born in Detroit, Schuman received her medical degree from George Washington University in Washington, D.C.. Returning to Detroit, she worked in the city's health department where she led the fight for a physician's union, formed in 1988. Schuman left her position to study infectious diseases at Wayne State University's Medical School, joined its staff and became an AIDS specialist. Ref.: 117 (Winter 1993, 18-19)

SCHWANNECKE, FRANCES S., of Saginaw; first woman to be ordained as a deacon in the Episcopal Diocese of Michigan, in 1973; one of the first women to be ordained in Saginaw as an Episcopal priest, in 1978; first woman to be a dean in the Episcopal Diocese of Michigan, with her appointment as dean of the Saginaw Valley Convocation of the Episcopal Church in 1980 and her reelection in 1981. An accountant and owner of a rental business before starting her studies at the Whitaker School of Theology in Detroit, she has served as assistant rector of St. John's Episcopal Church in Saginaw. In her position as dean, she works with many parishes. Ref.: 105 (Oct. 25, 1992, C1)

SCRUGGS-TOOKES, ALLISON, of the Detroit area; first woman to coach a male sport at Wayne State University, as the Tartars' head men's tennis coach from 1980 to 1991. As the men's coach, she was named Great Lakes Intercollegiate Athletic Conference Coach-of-the-Year four times and won GLIAC titles in 1980 and 1981. Scruggs-Tookes was also the women's head coach from 1979 to 1988. As women's coach, she was named the GLIAC's top coach twice and earned titles in 1979, 1981 and 1982. She also served as intramural director and assistant athletics director. Scruggs-Tookes was inducted into the Wayne State University Athletic Hall of Fame in 1993. Ref.: 117 (Spring 1993, 20-21)

SEABROOKS, NETTIE H., of Detroit; first woman to be deputy mayor of Detroit, in 1994. She takes over the mayor's role during his temporary absence and serves as the city's link to the state and federal governments. Seabrooks holds a degree in chemistry from Marygrove College and a master's degree in library science from the University of Michigan. She was formerly director of government relations for General Motors Corporation. Ref.: 25 (Dec.12, 1993, 1A, 15A; Jan. 17, 1994, 1, 4)

SELDEN, ANNA BELL(E) SEARS (1863-1932), of Stambaugh and Iron River; founder and later president of the Iron River and Stambaugh chapter of the WCTU in 1892; founder of the Stambaugh Women's Club in 1910. Selden also co-founded the Presbyterian Church at Stambaugh. Ref.: 34 (273)

SELMON, BERTHA EUGENIA LOVELAND (1877-1949), of Battle Creek; co-founder in 1932 of the Maternal Health Center (a birth control clinic) in Battle Creek, serving as its clinician from 1932 to 1943; first president of the Michigan Branch of the American Medical Women's Association, 1934 to 1936; first historian of American women physicians, as history editor of the <u>Medical Women's Journal</u>. Born in Ohio, she graduated from Battle Creek College in 1898 and from the Medical Missionary College in 1902. Her post graduate studies were at Tulane University in New Orleans, New York Lying-In Hospital in New York City, University of Michigan, and Washington University School of Medicine at St. Louis. After her 1903 marriage to Dr. Arthur Selmon, the couple served as missionaries in China, where she was chief obstetrician at the Shanghai Sanitarium from 1917 to 1924. Following their return to Battle Creek, she established her practice in gynecology and obstetrics, and served on the staffs of the Nichols Memorial and Leila Post Montgomery Hospitals. She also practiced industrial medicine for the Kellogg Company Health Service from 1925 to 1932. Selmon made a monumental contribution to women's history by collecting pictures and life histories of America's women physicians. Her histories of Michigan's women physicians are at the Bentley Historical Library; her other histories of America's women physicians are at the Blackwell Foundation in Philadelphia. Selmon was also a member of the Shanghai Medical Society, China Medical Missionary Association, American Medical Association, Calhoun County and Michigan State Medical Societies, Battle Creek BPW and YWCA, and Seventh-day Adventist Church. Ref.: 204

SHAGONABY, SUSAN (1905-1978), of Harbor Springs; first curator (from 1956 until 1976) of the Andrew J. Blackbird Museum, a museum of Indian history in Harbor Springs. An Odawa Indian and a descendant of Chief Pogsigon, Shagonaby organized and directed Indian pageants for Harbor Springs and Cross Village from 1947 to 1960, teaching younger Odawas the dances, songs, and language of their ancestors. She also taught art classes, including her specialty of quill box making, and adult education Indian history courses. She was known for her annual Ghost Suppers, given in memory of deceased members of the Indian community and attended by as many as 150 of her fellow Indians, white guests and friends. She also served as a consultant to the Headlands Indian Health Careers Program at Mackinac City, where she taught traditional Indian herbal medicine. Shagonaby retired as curator of the Blackbird Museum in 1976, after developing it into one of the country's best collections of Indian cultural artifacts. Her successor was **Veronica Medicine**. Operated since 1990 by the Little Traverse Bay Bands of

Odawa Indians, the Museum is the first Indian-operated Indian Museum in Michigan and one of only ten in the U.S. Ref.: 164

SHARPE, EVA ALMA (1878-1940), of Howell; first woman to serve as a Livingston County School Commissioner, appointed in 1920, elected in 1922 and in every succeeding election until her death in 1940. She was a teacher in the Howell public schools. Ref.: 133

SHOOK, FRANCES (1901-1991), of Grosse Pointe; member of the first graduating class of dental hygienists at the University of Michigan in 1921 and co-founder in 1923 of both the Michigan Dental Hygienists Association and the American Dental Hygienists Association. Shook served three times as president of the MDHA and became president of the ADHA in 1935. During World War II she served in the Dental Hygiene clinics for the Army Air Force at San Antonio and Eagle Pass, Texas, and for the U.S. Atomic Energy Program at Oakridge, Tennessee. She was made the first life member of the MDHA in 1948 and of the Detroit District Dental Hygienists Society in 1949. In 1955 she began the MDHA Bulletin, a quarterly publication that she edited until 1962. Shook also served as liaison between the MDHA and the Michigan Dental Association. She was appointed in 1962 as one of the first dental hygienists to serve with the Michigan Board of Dental Examiners. For her many contributions to the profession of dental hygiene, she received the Outstanding Alumnae Award of the University of Michigan Dental Hygienists Alumnae Association and the Alfred C. Fones Award from the ADHA in 1984. An accomplished horseback rider, she also won several riding competitions. Ref.: 14 (Dec./Jan. 1992, 7-9)

****

"The Michigan Equal Suffrage Association stands for equal rights for men and women, socially, civilly, and politically and exists for the purpose of forming public opinion along these lines, continuing the work begun by its parent society in 1848."

Clara B. Arthur of Detroit

****

SIELOFF, ALICE F., of Brighton; founder, publisher and editor-in-chief of Detroit Metropolitan Woman, Lansing Metropolitan Woman, and Grand Rapids Metropolitan Woman magazines. A graduate of Northwood University, Sieloff has held public relations and marketing positions with The Detroit News and Crain Communications. She published Michigan Woman in 1989 and Detroit MarketPlace in 1990 before launching Detroit Metropolitan Woman in 1991, followed by the Lansing and Grand Rapids editions of the magazine. She is affiliated with the National Association of Women Business Owners, the Adcraft Club of Detroit, the National Press Club, and the Women's Economic Club of Detroit. Ref.: 205

SINGLETARY, SHERYL, of Lansing; first African American woman to join the Lansing Fire Department, in 1992. She was formerly an international flight attendant for 13 years. Ref.: 57 (Apr. 4, 1995, 1B)

SJUNNESON, SIGGAN (dates not known), of Detroit; first Michigan resident to be honored with the Gold Royal Vasa Medal of Sweden, awarded her by Sweden's King Gustaf VI Adolf in 1959, in recognition of her contributions to cultural achievements and her promotion of good will between the peoples of Sweden and the United States. A native of Stockholm, Sjunneson came to this country in the 1920s. She worked with the Swedish American Line in Chicago and the Swedish Pavilion at the 1933 Chicago World's Fair, before going to New York to manage a firm that imported Swedish art objects. In 1939 she and her husband founded "The Stockholm," a Detroit restaurant that introduced the first "Smorgasbord" to Michigan. The Stockholm Restaurant was host to many distinguished guests from throughout the United States and other countries, including heads of state, royalty, famous writers, artists, scientists, stars of the stage and screen, and numerous other celebrities. Scandinavian and other organizations held their meetings in its private dining rooms that were decorated with fine paintings and furnishings from Sweden. Sjunneson was known as "Detroit's International Hostess," a title she held until The Stockholm was sold in 1962. Ref.: 28 (Feb. 17, 1959); 29 (167)

SLOAN, MARTHA, of Houghton; first woman to be professor of electrical engineering at Michigan Technological University, 1969; first MTU faculty member to be named a Fellow of the Institute of Electrical and Electronics Engineers, 1991; first woman to be president of the IEEE, which has more than 320,000 members in 150 countries. After attending a summer session in engineering at Stanford University as a high school student, Sloan was recruited by Stanford for its engineering program and was the only woman in the 1961 graduating class of engineers. She received the 1994 Distinguished Engineering Educator Award at the Society of Women Engineers convention, held at Pittsburgh in June of 1994.
Ref.: 57 (Jun. 5, 1994, 3D)

SLOMAN, LOTTIE T. (1857-1941), of Detroit; first president of the Sisterhood of Temple Beth El, first president of the Michigan State Federation of Temple Sisterhoods, founder and director of the Priscilla Inn and the Girls Protective League. Ref.: 25 (May 16, 1941); 52 (107)

SMITH, FRANCES WHEELER (1850-1922), of Hastings; co-founder of the Hastings Woman's Club in 1893 (and its second president), the first lecture course in Hastings, and the anti-tuberculosis society. Born in Barry County, Smith taught in country schools before marrying M. Clement Smith, a circuit judge for Barry and Eaton counties. Beginning in 1900, she held various offices in the Michigan State Federation of Women's Clubs, serving as state president from 1906-1908. Ref.: 49 (203)

SMITH, LYDIA (dates not known), of Keweenaw County; first woman to be lighthouse keeper of the Manitou Island Light, off of Keweenaw Peninsula in Lake Superior, from 1855 to 1856. Ref.: 18 (163)

SMITH, MARIE DOANE (c. 1897-1993), of Grosse Ile; co-founder of the nature conservancy that became the Grosse Ile Bird Sanctuary. A Master Gardener, Smith organized and judged many flower shows. She also served as president of the Michigan Federated Garden Clubs. She was a graduate of Alma College and taught at Midland High School before her marriage in 1919. Ref.: 22 (Jun. 3, 1993, B4)

SNYDER, RUTH, of Munising; first woman to be mayor of the City of Munising, elected in 1985. Ref.: 2

SPEARS, EVELYN C., of East Lansing; founder in 1993 of Lansing's Institute for the Healing of Racism of Mid-Michigan, a volunteer organization that provides seminars where people can explore their own attitudes and beliefs about race and how understanding of differences can change communities. She has helped to establish similar institutes in Kalamazoo, Benton Harbor, Saginaw, Detroit, and Toledo. Spears, who holds a Ph.D. in agricultural economics and degrees in aerospace engineering, is also a motivational speaker, owner of a business, Change Option Associates, and the producer and director of a twice-weekly television program, "Focus on Women." She received the Communicator of the Year Award from the Yawn Patrol Toastmasters Club in July, 1994. Ref.: 57 (Jul. 13, 1994, 2D; Jul. 18, 1994, 8B)

STEARNS, SARAH BURGER, of Ann Arbor; first woman to apply for admission to the University of Michigan, in 1858. Turned down twice by U-M regents, Burger attended Ypsilanti State Normal School (now Eastern Michigan University). In 1863 she married Ozora Stearns, a young lawyer then serving as a colonel in the 39th U.S. Colored Infantry of the Union Army. While her husband was away at war, Sarah raised money for food, clothing, and hospital supplies for the Union Army, by lecturing throughout Michigan and other nearby states. After the war, the couple settled in Minnesota, where Ozora was elected to the U.S. Senate and later became a district judge. Sarah continued to lecture widely in favor of higher education and suffrage for women, served as president of the Minnesota Woman Suffrage Association, and vice president of the National Woman Suffrage Association. Her failed attempts to be admitted to the University of Michigan are said to have greatly contributed to her dedication to women's rights. Ref.: 68 (23-24)

STEBBINS, CATHARINE A. FISH (1823-1904), of Detroit; secretary for the first Woman's Rights Convention held in 1848 at Seneca Falls, New York, and one of the signers of the "Declaration of Sentiments," which demanded that women have "immediate admission to all the rights and privileges which belong to them as citizens of the United States." Among the eleven resolutions adopted by the Convention, the most daring was the ninth which read: "Resolved, that it is the duty of the women of this country to secure to themselves the sacred right to the elective franchise." Stebbins was also secretary for the second session of the Woman's Rights Convention held at Rochester, New York. Born into a Quaker family at Farmington, New York, she taught school in Rochester after receiving her teaching certificate in 1841. Following her marriage to Giles Stebbins in 1846, she and her husband became Garrison abolitionists and she served as secretary of the Rochester Anti-Slavery Society. Stebbins and her husband, by then members of the Unitarian Church, moved to Detroit in 1867, where she joined the Detroit Woman's Club. In 1871 she attempted to register to vote, following Detroiter **Nannette B. Gardner**'s successful registration and vote based on Gardner's status as a widow and taxpayer. (See **Gardner, Nannette B**. in Michigan Women: Firsts and Founders, Vol. I.) Although Stebbins argued for her own voting rights as a human being, she was prohibited from registering and voting. After her husband's death in 1900, she moved back to Rochester. Ref.: 154

****

"There is and can be but one safe principle of government -- equal rights to all. Discrimination against any class on account of color, nativity, sex, property, culture, can but embitter and disaffect that class, and thereby endanger the safety of the whole people."

Susan B. Anthony

****

STEFFENS, THERESA, see **SANDERS, MRS. JOSEPH**

STEVENSON, JAN, of Farmington; co-founder in 1989 of Affirmations Lesbian/Gay Community Center in Ferndale, serving as president of the board, 1989 to 1991, and first executive director from 1991 to 1995. In six years the center grew from a volunteer-run helpline to a community center with eight full-time staff persons, 1700 members and four main services, including a toll-free statewide helpline, a network of 27 weekly support groups, a community outreach and education program, and peer group sessions and mentoring for youth. Holding degrees in music from the University of Cincinnati in 1977 and Yale University in 1979 and a master's degree in finance from Drexel University in 1985, Stevenson was a bassist with the New Haven Symphony Orchestra and New England Chamber Orchestra before serving as assistant vice president of Provident National Bank in Philadelphia and second vice president of Manufacturers National Bank of Detroit. Ref.: 22 (Jun. 29, 1995, 4B); 207

STEWART, ROWENA, of Detroit; first professional executive director of the Motown Museum in Detroit, 1992. Previously Stewart was director of the Afro-American Historical and Cultural Museum in Philadelphia. She was appointed to her new post by Motown Museum founder and chairperson **Esther Gordy Edwards**.

(See Edwards, Esther Gordy in Michigan Women: Firsts and Founders, Vol. I.) Ref.: 22 (Oct. 28, 1992, B1; Jul. 11, 1993, G1)

STOCKMAN, LOTTIE (dates not known), of Charlevoix; first school teacher in Charlevoix, in 1861. For a salary of one dollar per week, Stockman taught twenty to thirty pupils, from three to twenty years of age, in the first schoolhouse, a sixteen-foot square log building. By 1867 more space was urgently needed and the women of the community organized to raise funds for a new school building which opened in 1868. Ref.: 9

STOVER, BETSY, see CORY, JERRE

STRAHL, MARION (dates not known), of Sault Ste. Marie; first woman news photoengraver in the country, at the Escanaba Daily Press in the 1930s. After graduating with a degree in art from the University of Wisconsin in 1935, Strahl began at the newspaper doing layouts, writing and advertising sales. When the newspaper installed a photoengraving department, she learned to use both a camera and the new photo-engraver and soon took over as press photographer and photoengraver. Over the years she produced thousands of pictures and engravings for her paper, as well as for major newspapers such as the Chicago Tribune and the Milwaukee Journal. Ref.: 100 (Feb. 1940, 26, 86-87)

STRICKLAND, MARTHA (b. 1853) of Detroit; first woman lawyer to argue cases in the Michigan Supreme Court, in the 1880s. Born at DeWitt, she grew up in St. Johns, received her law degree from the University of Michigan and was admitted to the bar in 1883. Although married to Leo Miller in 1875, she retained her own name. After serving three years as assistant prosecuting attorney for Clinton County, she moved in 1887 to Detroit, where she opened her own law office. Among the many cases Strickland successfuly argued before the Michigan Supreme Court was "Wm. S. Wilson vs. Genesee Circuit Judge", in which she upheld the right of women to hold the office of deputy county clerk. This case brought her wide recognition. Strickland was also well known as a powerful speaker on behalf of equal suffrage and the advancement of women. Ref.: 50 (132)

STRONG, MARTHA COCHRANE (1843-1926), of Jackson; first woman to practice medicine in Jackson, from 1875 to 1925. She was born in Ireland, the ninth of 11 children. In 1847 her father died and her mother brought her family to America, settling in Michigan near Wacousta and later moving to Onondaga. Strong began teaching school at the age of 16 and was married in 1870. Inspired by the examples of her older sister and younger brother, both graduates of medical schools, she entered the first class to admit women to the study of medicine at the University of Michigan and opened a practice in Jackson after graduating in 1875. She was active in the county and state levels of the American Medical Association, serving as president of the county chapter, and was also a member of the AAUW, the BPW, and the Women's Relief Corps. An enthusiastic supporter of the Woman Suffrage Movement, she brought to Jackson such speakers as English suffragists Emmeline and Sylvia Pankhurst. Ref.: 204

SUTTERLY, AULGA, see **GREENWOOD, MABEL S.**

SUTTON, SHARON, of Dexter; first African American woman in the United States to be named a full professor of architecture, at the University of Michigan's architectural school. Sutton, a musician who has also played the French horn professionally, studied and taught architecture at both Pratt Institute and Columbia University. In the early 1980s she joined the faculty at the U-M, where she promotes the concept of a more egalitarian "moral architecture" that incorporates environmentalism, feminism, a child-centered agenda and the civil rights movement. Ref.: 22 (Oct. 17, 1994, 5F)

SWANSON, G. MARIE, of Whitmore Lake; first woman to head a major cancer research center, as the first director of the Cancer Center at Michigan State University (CCMSU), founded in 1988. A nationally-recognized epidemiologist and expert on breast cancer, Swanson was appointed to her post in 1990. She has also served as president of the American Cancer Society-Michigan Division and the American College of Epidemiology, co-chair of the Michigan Cancer Consortium, chair of the Breast Cancer Task Force of the State Department of Public Health, and on both the Michigan Agent Orange Commission and the nation's first Special Commission on Breast Cancer. As part of its total program, the CCMSU includes the Comprehensive Breast Health Clinic, which provides a full range of breast health services, conducts breast cancer research and the education of health professionals. Ref.: 57 (Dec. 29, 1993, 1, 3C); 90 (Winter 1994, 22-25)

SWEENEY, FLORENCE (1898-1987), of Grosse Ile; first woman to be president of the Detroit Federation of Teachers, in 1931. Ref.: 27 (Mar. 31, 1993, 4)

TALLEY, BARBARA, of Southfield; first African American elected to public office in Southfield, with her election to the Southfield City Council in 1983. Talley, who holds a degree in business administration from Wayne State University and a master's degree in public administration from Central Michigan University, is a budget analyst for Oakland County. A Detroit native, she is a member of the Metropolitan LWV, helping to implement fair housing laws, and the Women's Conference of Concerns, for which she founded the Southfield Chapter. She received a human rights award from the Southfield Chamber of Commerce in 1983. Ref.: 22 (Dec. 1, 1983, 1A, 10B; Jan. 6, 1993, 8A); 71 (Nov. 19, 1983)

TAPP, ANN SCHWEIZER (c. 1902-1991), of Ann Arbor; first policewoman in Ann Arbor, appointed in 1940. Tapp was known for her skill in pistol shooting, winning many competitions and earning proficiency ratings in every weapon used by the police department. Her colleagues dubbed her "Annie Oakley" after the famous Western crack shooter. Later in her career, Tapp served as executive secretary to three police chiefs. Ref.: 4 (Feb. 12, 1992)

TAUBERT, GERTRUDE M. (1887-1972), of Iron River; first visiting nurse for Iron River area mining companies, c. 1912. Taubert came from her native Germany to the Iron River area at the age of sixteen. After graduating from the Illinois Training School of Nursing in Chicago in 1912, she returned to Iron River where she served the community as a visiting nurse for the Monroe Mining Company, making her rounds in a horse and buggy. In later years, she worked as a nurse at Mercy Hospital and Stambaugh General Hospital, before retiring in 1953. She was a member of the Iron County Nurses Club and the OES. Ref.: 34 (236); 127

****

*"Give woman her rights and she will lift the world
into a nobler and purer atmosphere."*

Susan B. Anthony
Speaking at the National American Woman Suffrage Association
Convention, Grand Rapids, 1899

****

TAYLOR, KRISTIN CLARK, formerly of Detroit; first African American woman to be the White House Director of Media Relations, appointed by President George Bush in 1988. A graduate of Michigan State University, Taylor joined the editorial board of USA Today in 1982, after an internship at the Detroit Free Press. She joined Bush's staff as assistant press secretary in 1987 and assumed her White House position after Bush was elected president. In 1990 she became director of communications for BellSouth in Washington, D.C. Taylor relates her experiences at the White House in her book, The First To Speak. Ref.: 22 (Jun. 30, 1993, F1)

TERRY, MARY L. (dates not known), of Escanaba; first lighthouse keeper of the Sand Point Light at Escanaba, from 1868 until 1886, when she died in a fire that destroyed the lighthouse. Terry's husband John was appointed first keeper of the new lighthouse but died of consumption before it was completed. In spite of objections from local officials, she was appointed to replace him and maintained the light for nearly 18 years. Because she was known to be very careful and efficient, many believed that she had been the victim of murder and arson, but this was never proved. Ref.: 18 (83-84, 164)

THOMAS, JACQUELINE, formerly of Detroit; first African American and one of few women to serve as Washington Bureau Chief of a major metropolitan daily newspaper, for the Detroit News, 1994. Prior to her appointment, Thomas worked at Kentucky's Courier-Journal and Louisville Times, the Chicago Sun-Times, was associate editor and editorial writer at the Detroit Free Press for six years, and joined the Detroit News as news editor in 1992. She became deputy Washington Bureau Chief in 1993. A graduate of Briarcliff College with a master's degree in International Affairs from Columbia University, she was awarded a Nieman fellowship at Harvard University during 1983-84. Thomas is a member of the National Association of Black Journalists and the American Society of Newspaper Editors. Ref.: 25 (Jul. 7, 1994, 1A, 10A)

THOMAS, PAMELA BROWN (b. 1817), of Schoolcraft; first public schoolteacher in Schoolcraft, after coming from Vermont in 1833. She and her husband, Nathan Thomas, helped hundreds of escaping slaves at their home, a major stop on the Underground Railroad from 1844 to 1860. Years later, Thomas recalled, "It is now between thirty and forty years since the last of that long train of fugitives stopped at our house on the road to freedom, and I, an old lady of seventy-six years, feel glad and proud of my small share in the glorious emancipation consummated by our martyr president." Ref.: 74 (Mar./Apr. 1986)

THOME, JOANNE, of Comstock Park; first woman to be chair of the International Apple Institute, a trade organization of 600 representatives from all segments of the apple industry, including 9,000 apple growers, in 1994. Ref.: 57 (Apr. 2, 1994, 3B)

TILLEY, BARBARA, of Southfield; founder of the Detroit Area Chapter of the Association for Women in Science (AWIS-DAC), in 1984. The AWIS is a national organization, with headquarters in Washington, D.C. Tilley, Director of Biostatistics at Henry Ford Hospital, was joined by **Melanie Hwaleck** and **Victoria Neale** of Wayne State University in forming the chapter's first board. Other organizers included **Lonnie Schultz**, **Christine Hampton** and **Renee Laya Boving**. Ref.: 129

TILLMAN, GEORGEANNA, see **THE MARVELETTES**

TIMMER, JOHANNA (1901-1978), of Grand Rapids; first dean of women at Calvin College, in 1927; founder, first acting president, dean and teacher of the Reformed Bible Institute (later called the Reformed Bible College) at Grand Rapids in 1940. Born in Graafschap, Timmer graduated from Calvin College, the University of Michigan, and the University of Chicago Divinity School. After three years as acting president at the RBI, she served as principal of a school in California and founded a high school in Philadelphia, before retiring to Holland in 1963. Ref.: 136; 183

TINSLEY-WILLIAMS, ALBERTA, of Detroit; founder of Citizens Against Billboard Advertising of Alcohol and Tobacco in 1988 to protest proliferation of tobacco and alcohol ads in poor and black communities; founder of Mack Alive in 1991, a neighborhood revitalization project to improve the quality of life in the Mack Avenue area. A graduate of Eastern Michigan University with a degree in social work and criminal justice, Tinsley-Williams is a project specialist at Job Connection, a federally-funded agency that provides employment counseling and training programs for Wayne County communities. She was elected to the Wayne County Board of Commissioners in 1987. Her campaign against billboard advertising of alcohol and tobacco resulted in an agreement with billboard companies not to run such ads within 500 feet of schools and churches. Ref.: 22 (Oct. 2, 1993, 3A)

TOEPPNER, SADIE DRAGO (1873-1961), of Bay City; founder of the Bay City Civic League in 1911; co-founder of the Wenonah and Roosevelt Parks. Known as the "Gardening Dean of Bay County," Toeppner was a member of several Bay City garden clubs, the Wild Flower Society and the Northeastern Gladiolus Society, and was recognized statewide as an authority on gardening and flower arranging. During World War II she served as chair of women's work on the State Federation's Victory Gardens Committee. Later she taught continuing education classes and spoke to many groups about flower arranging and gardening. In 1949 she was elected Bay County's "Woman of the Year" and on April 21, 1954, she was honored by an officially proclaimed "Sadie Toeppner Day." Ref.: 121 (22)

TORRE, SUSANA, of Bloomfield Hills; first woman to be director of the Cranbrook Academy of Art in Bloomfield Hills in the academy's 67-year history, with her appointment in 1994. Previously, she was chair of the Department of Architecture and Environmental Design at Parsons School of Design in New York. An internationally known architect, architectural critic and curator, Torre organized the first exhibition of work by women architects in the 1970s. She graduated in 1967 from the University of Buenos Aires in Argentina, her native country. After coming to the United States, she also studied at Columbia University and co-founded a feminist art journal, Heresies. Her architectural work includes a famous firehouse in Columbus, Indiana, designed to accommodate both male and female firefighters. Ref.: 22 (Sept. 16, 1994, 1G); 137

TOWSLEY, MARGARET DOW (1906-1994), of Ann Arbor; first woman to serve on the Ann Arbor City Council, from 1953 to 1957; co-founder in 1950 and later president of the Women's City Club of Ann Arbor; co-founder of the Ann Arbor Civic Ballet in 1956; co-founder in 1959, with her husband Harry Towsley, of the Harry A. and Margaret D. Towsley Foundation, which contributed more than $1 million to the University of Michigan; donor of more than $1 million toward scholarships awarded in her name by U-M's Center for the Education of Women, as well as gifts to the School of Music, where a wing of the North Campus facility bears her name, and to Schembechler Hall, where a sports museum is named for her. Towsley was born in Midland to Grace and Herbert Dow, the founder of Dow Chemical Company. A graduate of U-M and Columbia University, she was awarded honorary doctorates from

Eastern Michigan University in 1969, from Cleary College in 1981, and from U-M in 1993. Towsley was also co-founder of the Mid-Michigan Chapter of Planned Parenthood in 1934, founder and lifetime director of the Ann Arbor Children's Play School in 1935, co-founder of the Ann Arbor Community Center, and a member of P.E.O. Sisterhood and of Zonta International. Ref.: 4 (May 3, 1994, A1); 22 (May 8, 1994, 2C); 78 (June 1993, 9)

TRINKLEIN, LYNDA LITOGOT, of Grand Ledge; first woman elected to the Grand Ledge City Council, in 1976, and first woman to be mayor of Grand Ledge, elected in 1991 and re-elected in 1993 and 1995. Trinklein is the great-granddaughter of **Caroline Litogot**, the first woman to be the lighthouse keeper of the Mama Juda light on Grosse Ile. (See **Litogot Antaya, Caroline.**) Ref.: 211

TRUCKEY, ELIZA (dates not known), of Marquette; first woman lighthouse keeper of the Marquette Light in Marquette Harbor, Lake Superior, from 1862 to 1865, after the death of her husband, the previous keeper. Ref.: 18 (163)

****
"The time will come when one shall look back upon the arguments against granting the suffrage to women with as much incredulity as we now read the arguments against their education."

Mary E. Wooley
President, Mt. Holyoke College
****

TUANQUIN, ADORACION B. (1940-1994), of Dearborn; co-founder of the Philippine-American Association of Michigan, the Philippine-American Community Council, the Philippine Nurses Association in Michigan, and the Far Eastern Festival on the Detroit waterfront; founder of the Most Outstanding Filipino Award in Michigan. Born in the Philippines, she moved to Detroit in the early 1960s and worked as a registered nurse in various hospitals, retiring in 1983 from the Veterans Administration Medical Center in Allen Park. She was active in the Filipino community, where she was known as "Adoring," and helped many Filipino nurses find jobs in Michigan. She also assisted medical missions and religious ministries to the Philippines, hosted religious seminars and retreats, and sponsored religious speakers from other countries. Her awards included the Humanitarian Service Award from the Detroit City Council and the International Institute Service Award. Ref.: 25 (May 19, 1994, 2C)

TUFTY, ESTHER VAN WAGONER (1896-1986), of Kingston; first woman elected to the National Press Club, in 1971. The NPC lifted its forty-year ban against women members two days after the Women's National Press Club voted to admit men. Later, Tufty became the only woman elected president of the American Women in Radio and Television, the American Newspaper Women's Club, and the Women's National Press Club (now the Washington Press Club). A graduate of the University of Wisconsin, Tufty founded the

Tufty News Service in 1935, acting as president, editor, and writer. The news service covered Washington for many Michigan newspapers until 1985. Tufty was inducted into Sigma Delta Chi's Hall of Fame for Journalists in 1976. Ref.: 103 (452)

TULLOCH, JEAN S. (dates not known), of Grand Marais; founder and first president of the Grand Marais Woman's Club, in 1932. Ref.: 213

UHL, ALICE FOLLETT (1843-1917), of Grand Rapids; co-founder of the St. Cecilia Society in 1883, the first women's music club in the United States to have its own recital hall. Co-founder **Ella Matthews Pierce** served as the society's first president. Born in Ypsilanti, Uhl moved to Grand Rapids with her husband in 1876. As president of the St. Cecilia Society, Uhl organized the construction in 1893 of the St. Cecilia Society's hall, which now serves as a Center for the Performing Arts. In April of 1899 the hall was the site of the National American Woman Suffrage Association Convention. Uhl was also the first president of the National Federation of Women's Music Clubs of America and a member of the DAR. Ref.: 136; 183

VANDERMOLEN, MIMI, of the Detroit area; first woman to be an automotive designer at Ford Motor Co., 1970. Born in the Netherlands, Vandermolen moved to Canada as a child and later studied industrial design at the Ontario College of Art. At Ford Motor Co. she has been in charge of the small car and concept studios and supervised the design team for the 1993 Ford Probe. Ref.: 57 (Sept. 13, 1992, 5B)

VAN HOESEN, GRACE AMES (c. 1870-1959), of Grand Rapids; co-founder of the Grand Rapids League of Women Voters, in 1921. Other women who co-founded the League were **Christine M. Keck** (c. 1871-1946), **Mary Louise Hinsdale** (1866-1946), **Justina Hall Merrick Hollister** (c. 1863-1949) and **Jeanette Shelly Warner** (1888-1974). As president of the Kent County Equal Suffrage Association in 1915, Van Hoesen organized Suffrage groups in Bowne Center and in Paris, Mecosta County. She served as president of the Grand Rapids Equal Franchise Club in 1917. In 1931 she was elected as a Kent County supervisor, an office she held until 1935. Ref.: 42 (Oct. 1994, 4-5)

VAN MILLER, JOSEPHINE McBRIDE, see **CAMPBELL, CARINA**

VIVENTI, CAROL, of Okemos; first woman and first member of an ethnic minority to be elected Secretary of the Michigan Senate, in 1995. She previously served as Deputy Chief of Staff, Counsel to the Cabinet, and Director of State Policy for the governor, and Co-Counsel and Administrator to the Joint Committee on Administrative Rules in the Michigan legislature. A graduate of Michigan State University and Cooley Law School, Viventi has also taught at Western Michigan University. Ref.: 82 (Summer 1995, 7)

VOSS, B. MARGARET, of Rockford; first woman administrator at Davenport College in Grand Rapids, as Dean of Women and Dean of Students, 1962-1987; first woman elected to chair the governing board of Fountain Street Church in 1975 and the first woman member ordained to deliver a sermon from its pulpit, in 1982; first woman to be a member of the Greater Grand Rapids Economic Club in 1972 and first woman to serve as its chair, 1985-1987; first woman admitted to the Grand Rapids chapter of the International Torch Club in 1983 and the club's first woman president in 1984. As executive director of the Methodist Community House, Voss worked with **Ruth Johnson**, president of the Board of Directors, to found, design and direct the building of the first day care center in Grand Rapids and western Michigan, opened in December 1956. Ref.: 216

WALKER, FLORA, of Detroit; first woman to be president of the American Federation of State, County and Municipal Employees (AFSCME) Council 25, appointed in October 1992 and elected in January 1993 to complete an unexpired term. She was elected to her first four-year term in October 1993. The AFSCME is the largest public employee union in Michigan, with 63,000 members in eleven regions. Born in Mississippi, Walker has lived in Detroit since she was four years old. After graduating from Detroit High School of Commerce, she worked for Michigan Bell and then for the City of Detroit, where she and a friend organized the first union for 1,200 city clerical workers. Hired as the first woman staff representative of former Council 77, Walker received union staff training at the University of Maryland, Wayne State University Labor Studies, the Para-Legal Institute, and the George Meany Center of Labor Studies. She promotes the rights of public employees to fair wages, benefits and safe working conditions and is concerned with women's special health care issues. Citing love as her guiding principle, Walker says, "I have always known I am here to help people who need help." In 1995 she was honored as a "Champion of Hope" by the National Kidney Foundation of Michigan for her "devotion to helping others enjoy better lives both on and off the job." She has been active in New Detroit, Wayne County COPE, the Minority Women's Network Detroit Chapter, the Michigan Pay Equity Network, the Southeast Michigan Labor Management Committee, and the United Way of Michigan. Ref.: 84 (Nov. 13-26, 1994, 2, 6, 17; Apr. 2-15, 1995, 10)

WALKER, JANET, of Grand Ledge; founder and director of Critter Alley Wildlife Care Center, a non-profit federal and state licensed wildlife rehabilitation facility near Grand Ledge, in 1989. With the help of many volunteers, Critter Alley rehabilitates several thousand sick, injured and orphaned wildlife animals each year and returns them to their natural habitat once they are able to live independently. Critter Alley is the first and only wildlife rehabilitation center in Michigan that accepts all kinds of wildlife. The Center also serves as an educational resource to promote better understanding, treatment and appreciation of Michigan's wildlife population. One of its projects is an annual fine art show, "Art for Wildlife's Sake." Ref.: 39 (Dec. 6, 1994, 4); 57 (Sept. 1, 1993, 1D; Feb. 15, 1994, 1D)

WALSHAW, SALLY, of East Lansing; first woman to win the Bustad Companion Animal Veterinarian Award, in 1994. The award, named after Leo K. Bustad, a well-known American veterinarian and retired dean of the College of Veterinary Medicine at Washington State University, is given annually to a veterinarian who excels in the field of animal-human bonding. Walshaw, a professor of veterinary medicine at Michigan State University, helped found the Pet Loss Support Hotline to help people deal with the death of their pets. A graduate of the University of Pennsylvania veterinary school, she came to MSU in 1978 and has served as a professor and training coordinator of the University Laboratory Animal Resources. Her interest in human-animal bonding began in the 1980s when she began taking animals to Lansing-area nursing homes and saw the rapport established between the residents and the animals. She has stressed the importance of that bond and the need for compassion for animals with her students. Ref.: 25 (May 1, 1994, C1); 91 (May 19, 1994, 4)

****

While Europe's eye is fixed on mighty things,
The fate of empires and the fall of kings;
While quacks of state must each produce his plan,
And even children lisp the Rights of Man;
Amid this mighty fuss just let me mention,
The rights of Women merit some attention.

Robert Burns, November, 1792

****

WANGER, MARILYN MORRIS, of Lansing; first woman to serve on the Lansing Community College Board of Trustees, in 1967; first woman appointed as commissioner on the Michigan Court of Appeals, in 1973. A graduate of Michigan State University in 1955 and the University of Michigan Law School in 1959, Wanger was with the Michigan Court of Appeals until her retirement in 1994. Ref.: 57 (Apr. 24, 1994, 2G)

WARD, MARGARET McCALL THOMAS, of Detroit; founder of the Fred Hart Williams Genealogical Society in 1979, while serving as field archivist of the Burton Historical Collection of the Detroit Public Library. Ward is now librarian/archivist of the Louise Wright Research Library of Detroit's Museum of African American History. From 1939-1945 she was a writer and office assistant for the <u>Detroit Tribune</u>, a weekly newspaper owned and operated by her parents to provide a means of communication for the black community. Ref.: 89 (168-170)

WARNER, JEANETTE SHELLY, see **VAN HOESEN, GRACE AMES**

WARREN HILL, SUSAN (dates not known), of Copper Harbor; first school teacher in Copper Harbor, c. 1850. Warren, who was employed by Mr. Brockway to teach his children, taught the Brockway children and other children in the Brockway kitchen until a schoolhouse was built in 1851, just outside of the Brockway yard. She stayed for just one winter and later married Sam H. Hill. Ref.: 87 (49)

WARSAW, IRENE, of Bay City; first woman to be an officer of Peoples National Bank & Trust Company (now part of First of America Bank), where she began as a secretary and retired in 1974 as vice president and trust officer, administering trusts and estates. A nationally-recognized poet whose poetry has appeared in leading magazines and newspapers, Warsaw has published two books of humorous poetry, won many awards in national poetry competitions, judged numerous poetry contests, and conducted workshops at writers' conferences. She is active in many professional poetry organizations, including the National League of American Pen Women and the Detroit Women Writers. Warsaw was awarded an honorary Doctor of Letters degree from Saginaw Valley State College in 1980. Ref.: 121 (32); 162

WASHINGTON, JACQUELIN (JACKIE) EDWARDS, of Detroit; co-founder and first chair of the Violence Against Women Committee of the Detroit chapter of NOW in 1970, where she fostered community awareness of spouse abuse and changes in police response to abuse victims; co-founder and first president in 1975 of New Options, a personnel agency for placing women and minorities in desirable, non-traditional positions in business and industry; co-founder of the national NOW Minority Caucus, bringing about more involvement and leadership of minority women in NOW; first African American woman to serve as Director of NOW's Legal Defense and Education Fund, overseeing LDEF's role in issues of sex equity, sexual harassment, and employment discrimination; first woman to be President/CEO of the Pontiac Area Urban League, from 1988 to 1992, administering programs for minorities and the poor; first African American woman to serve as Executive Director of Planned Parenthood of Southeastern Michigan, in 1992; co-founder and president of the Sojourner Foundation, providing direct funding for projects for women. After earning her Master's Degree in Social Work at Wayne State University, Washington was a social worker in Detroit Public Schools from 1965 to 1975, when she began New Options. Washington was Human Resources Director for Bendix Corporation, Detroit, from 1980 to 1985, and for Vixen Motor Company, Pontiac, from 1985 to 1987. She has served on the boards of the Michigan Abortion Rights Action League, the National Association of Negro Business and Professional Women's Clubs, Inc., and the Michigan Metro Girl Scout Council, and is president of the Top Ladies of Distinction, Cite d'etroit Chapter. She is also a member of WINGS (Women Involved in Giving Support), the Women's Economic Club of Detroit and Alpha Kappa

Alpha. Among her awards are the Women Lawyers Association's
Female Pioneer award in 1975, the Sojourner Truth Award from the
National Association of Negro Business and Professional Women in
1985, the Hunger Advocate of the Year award in 1990, Detroit
NOW's Loretta Moore Award in 1991, and the Wonder Woman
Community Services Award in 1992. Washington was inducted
into the Michigan Women's Hall of Fame in 1995. Ref.: 184

WATERS, FLORENCE HILLS (1866-1956), of Grand Rapids; co-
founder of the Grand Rapids Furniture Museum; donor of the first
public playground in Grand Rapids, the Mary Waters Field in the
Coldbrook District; first official member of the Women's City Club
of Grand Rapids in 1924. A native of Ohio, she studied at Vassar
College and moved to Grand Rapids after her marriage in 1892.
She served as president of the Women's City Club, on the boards of
the Grand Rapids Public Museum and Blodgett Hospital, and as
head of the Red Cross women's activities during World War I. In
1949 she initiated the "Waters Award for Achievement in Furniture
Design." Ref.: 40 (Oct. 1993, 50)

WATKINS THOMPSON, RUTH MARIA (b. 1819), of Brooklyn,
Michigan; first schoolteacher in Brooklyn (then called Swainsville),
in 1834 at the age of fifteen. Watkins came with her family to
Michigan from Keene, New Hampshire, where her father had been
president of the Collegiate Institute. She taught school in
Swainsville until 1839, when she married Theophilus W.
Thompson. Ref.: 3 (197-198)

WATSON, SUSAN, of Detroit; first woman and first African American
to win the Knight-Ridder News/Editorial Award of Excellence, for
her column in the Detroit Free Press, in 1993. A University of
Michigan graduate, Watson has been with the Detroit Free Press
since 1965, working as a reporter from 1965 to 1979, assistant city
editor from 1979 to 1980, and as the first African American city
editor from 1980 to 1983, when she began her column. She has
also been a speech writer for Sen. Philip Hart and an administrative
assistant at New Detroit, Inc. Ref.: 22 (Jul. 1, 1993, B1)

WAX, ROBIN, of Ann Arbor; founder of an electronic tutoring
program for at-risk students to learn history, at Ann Arbor's Pioneer
High School in1992. The program connects Wax's high school
history students with University of Michigan students who tutor the
Pioneer students via computers. Her students discuss and debate
historical issues with their U-M mentors and then send their essays
for their mentors' comments. Wax also uses a multicultural
curriculum in her classroom, participates in the cable television
project "Migration," in which paired African-American and Jewish
students collect oral histories from senior citizens, and has initiated
a women's studies course in the Ann Arbor school district. In 1994
she was named by the National Education Association's National
Foundation for the Improvement of Education as one of five Christa
McAuliffe Educators nationwide for her use of creative technology

and multiculturalism in the classroom. She is the co-editor of
Remember the Ladies!: A Handbook of Women in American History,
published in 1980. Ref.: 4 (Jan. 27, 1994, B1; Jan. 31, 1994, A8)

WEBSTER, COLLETTE (1966-1993), of Sunfield; first American to
die in the Bosnian war, in 1993. Webster had gone to Bosnia to
help in any way she could, after seeing scenes of suffering on
television. She befriended orphan children, distributed aid in a
refugee camp, and fixed up old railroad cars for temporary
classrooms. Webster died when a grenade was fired into a window
where she had been standing. She was posthumously honored
with the annual human rights award given by the Reebok
Corporation, which endowed the Lansing Chapter of Big Sisters in
her name, inasmuch as Webster had been a Big Sister. Ref.: 39
(Oct. 25, 1994, 9)
****

*"Our responsibility does not cease with the granting of suffrage,
for now it is up to us, who have worked so hard for the vote, to
see that women appreciate the significance of their
enfranchisement."*
Grace A. VanHoesen, President
Grand Rapids Equal Franchise Club
****

WEBSTER-MAIER, CARLENE L., of Okemos; first woman appointed
to the planning commission of Meridian Township in Ingham
County, in 1973; first woman to be an officer on the Capital Area
Transportation Authority, as vice chair in 1979; first woman to be
elected Supervisor of Meridian Township, serving from 1980 to
1988. Webster-Maier was elected as a Trustee to the Meridian
Township Board in 1974 and served as the board's representative
on the Capital Area Transportation Authority from 1975 to 1985.
She also served as chair of the Tri-County Regional Planning
Commission for Ingham, Eaton and Clinton Counties, in 1982.
Ref.: 218

WELLS, AGNES ERMINA (1876-1959), of Saginaw; first woman to
have a residence hall named for her at Indiana University, with the
naming of the first women's dormitory. A graduate of the University
of Michigan in 1903 and of Carleton College, Minnesota, in 1916,
Wells became a high school principal in Crystal Falls, Michigan, in
1904, acting dean of women at U-M in 1917, and dean of women at
Indiana University in 1919, a position she held until 1938. Before
retiring in 1944, she taught mathematics and astronomy at I-U,
where the first women's dormitory was named for her. Wells served
as vice president of the national AAUW and belonged to many
organizations, including the DAR, the National Society of the
Daughters of 1812, the BPW, the American Association of Deans of
Women, the National Education Association, and Phi Beta Kappa.
In 1948, she became head of the National Woman's Party, which
had picketed the White House and endured imprisonment, hunger

strikes and forced feeding during the struggle for woman suffrage. Under her leadership, the National Woman's Party continued the crusade by advocating passage of the Equal Rights Amendment. Ref.: 85 (114-116)

WHEATLEY, MARY A. (dates not known), of Eagle Harbor; first woman to be lighthouse keeper of the Eagle Harbor Light on Lake Superior, from 1898 to 1905. Ref.: 18 (163)

WHITE, ELLEN G. HARMON (1827-1915), of Battle Creek; co-founder in 1861 (with her husband James White and Joseph Bates) of the Michigan Conference of Seventh-day Adventists (the first organization of Seventh-day Adventist churches), as well as the General Conference of Seventh-day Adventists in 1863, both organized in Battle Creek. Born and reared in Maine, Ellen White became a follower of the Baptist preacher William Miller, who proclaimed the imminent Second Coming of Christ. She had her first spiritual vision in December of 1844, shortly after the Millerites' disappointment over Christ not returning when they expected him. The 2,000 visions she experienced during her lifetime influenced the formulation of her religious beliefs and provided instruction in many areas of life in addition to religious matters, such as education, home and family life, and mental and physical health. She urged abstinence from meat, coffee, tea, drugs and alcohol, and advocated a diet of fruits, grains, nuts and vegetables. In 1855 Ellen White and her husband moved to Battle Creek, where the Seventh-day Adventist church was later organized. As a result of a vision, she also called for and helped to bring about the establishment of the Western Health Reform Institute (later renamed the Battle Creek Sanitarium) in 1866. Her visions were instrumental in the founding of Battle Creek College (now Andrews University) in 1874, with other schools to follow. Guided by her counsel, Seventh-day Adventists today operate the largest Protestant educational system in the world. Her many books, pamphlets and articles continue to be influential in the worldwide expansion of the church. She is the most-translated American author of either gender and the most-translated woman author of all time, with works available in about 150 languages. She is buried in Battle Creek. Ref.: 151

WHITE, MARY A. (1813-1901), of Grand Haven; first schoolteacher in western Michigan, at Grand Haven in 1835. Born in Ashfield, Massachusetts, White began teaching at the age of 16 at private schools in Ashfield and Amherst. She came to Michigan at the request of her sister, **Amanda White Ferry**, to teach the Ferry children. Amanda and her husband, Rev. William M. Ferry, had left their mission post at Mackinac Island to found a new mission at Grand Haven. After arriving in Grand Haven, White opened her school in the Ferry home, then moved to a nearby log hut. In 1836 a building was erected to serve as schoolhouse, church and courthouse, and in 1850 a township school was built. White taught at Grand Haven for sixteen years, then in another community for twelve years before returning to Grand Haven. She was known affectionately throughout the Grand Haven area as "Aunt Mary." Ref.: 210

WHITE, VIRGINIA L. CONVERSE, of Okemos; first woman elected as Clerk of Meridian Township, Ingham County, serving from 1972 to the present; founder of the 48-mile Pedestrian-Bicycle Pathway Program of Meridian Township. A graduate of Baldwin-Wallace College in Berea, Ohio, White taught in Ohio schools before moving to Michigan in 1969. She has also chaired the Meridian Township sesquicentennial celebration and the "People Make a Difference" recognition program, has served on county and state Republican committees, and is the author of a widely-used election procedure manual. In 1995, White received a "Tribute to Women Award" from the Republican Women's Federation of Michigan. Ref.: 57 (Apr. 24, 1995, 2D); 218

WHITE, ZAE ROBINSON (1894-1992), of Union City; first woman elected president of the Michigan Townships Association, in 1969. Born in Union City, White graduated from Union City High School and was Union Township Clerk for twenty years. She and her first husband, Fred Robinson, owned and operated the Union City weekly newspaper. Ref.: 79 (Dec. 2, 1992, 18)

WHITFIELD McENTEE, KAY, see **HILLARY EARHART, NOREEN**

WHITMYER, NAOMI WILKINS, of Williamston; first woman to be elected to the Meridian Township Board in Okemos, serving from 1951 to 1957 as treasurer. Ref.: 218

WHITTEMORE, SUSAN (d. 1993), of Detroit; founder of International Awareness Days, a cooperative venture of the League of Women Voters and the Detroit Public Libraries, c. 1988. She served as president of the Detroit LWV, as United Nations Chair of the LWV of Michigan and as president of the AAUW in Detroit. A graduate of Mills College in California, Whittemore worked for 20 years in advertising as Employee Communications Director for the J.L. Hudson Co. She served as the Michigan director for CARE for 13 years and on the Michigan Partners of the Americas Board, where she coordinated Partners and CARE programs in Michigan's partner countries of Belize and the Dominican Republic. She was also Public Relations Chair for the Metropolitan Detroit UNICEF. She produced and hosted the radio program, "It's a Small World," sponsored by the Detroit International Institute. In recognition of her International Awareness Days programming, Whittemore was presented with the Ethnic Heritage Studies Center Award for Recognition in 1989 and the Spirit of Detroit Award. She was the daughter of **Mrs. W. Nelson Whittemore**, who was chair of the Michigan Branch of the National Woman's Party in 1915, and the niece of **Margaret Whittemore**, an activist in the Woman Suffrage and Equal Rights Movements. Ref.: 80 (Mar. 1993, 1)

WHITTEN, ELOISE CULMER, of Detroit; co-founder of Homes for Black Children in 1967, when she helped change adoption agency requirements to ease adoption of black children; founder of the Lula Belle Stewart Center in 1969, one of the first centers in the country to provide services for single, black, low-income women; founder of Diversified Youth Services in 1979, an agency offering many social services to young people. As chair of the Planned Parenthood League education committee, she organized the first Detroit area conference on the problems of unwed pregnancy and single parents in 1964. Whitten was named a Distinguished Warrior by the Detroit Urban League in 1995. Ref.: 22 (Mar. 14, 1995, 1B)

WIDGEON, BETTY R., of Superior Township, Washtenaw County; first African American and first woman to serve as the 14-A District Court Judge in Washtenaw County, appointed by Gov. John Engler in 1994 and subsequently elected to the post. Prior to her appointment, she was Assistant Prosecuting Attorney for Washtenaw County. She has also taught law classes at Eastern Michigan University and for Spring Arbor College at Jackson State Prison. Widgeon holds bachelor and master's degrees from Wake Forest University in North Carolina and received her law degree from the University of Michigan Law School in 1980. Ref.: 115 (Mar. 18, 1994, 1A)

****

"VOTES FOR WOMEN!"

Popular slogan used on Suffrage posters and banners

****

WILCOX, LAURA, of Detroit; first woman to be promoted to Fire Engine Operator in the Detroit Fire Department, 1995. Wilcox, who joined the department in 1983, has worked in more than a dozen Detroit firehouses and began driving a fire engine in 1988. Ref.: 25 (Feb. 19, 1995, 1C)

WILCOX, LUCINDA SEXTON (1820-1884), of Detroit; first woman to practice medicine in Detroit, from 1864 to 1868. (**Lucy M. Arnold**, previously identified in Michigan Women: Firsts and Founders, Vol. I as the first woman to be a physician in Detroit, was the second.) A native of New York, she graduated from the Western College of Homeopathic Medicine at Cleveland in 1854, then practiced in Ohio and Louisiana before moving to Detroit, where she administered "electro thermal baths" for ladies only. Ref.: 220

WILLIAMS, CHARLOTTE, of Flint; first African American woman elected to public office in Genesee County; first African American woman to serve as chair of the Board of Commissioners of Genesee County; first African American (second woman) to be president of the National Association of Counties. Williams served on the Genesee County Board of Commissioners from 1965 to 1980. She has also been a nurse and active in Church Women United in the Flint area. Ref.: 72 (Feb. 1995, 3-4)

WILLIAMS, LULA MARGARET ROBERTS (dates not known), of Kalamazoo; co-founder of the Dorcas Club and Let Us Be Friends Club in Kalamazoo. A native of St. Joseph County and a graduate of Indiana State Normal College, Williams taught in the public schools of Lafayette and Columbus, Indiana, and in Haines Industrial and Normal School at Augusta, Georgia, before her marriage in 1906 to Henry Williams of Kalamazoo. The Dorcas Club, organized at Williams' home, was founded to provide needy African American children with enough clothing so that they could attend school. The Let Us Be Friends Club, a part of the YWCA, was organized in 1914 "to promote the spirit of friendliness" among young African American women of Kalamazoo and "to develop the highest type of womanhood." Ref.: 75 (32, 141)

WILLIAMS, REGINA, of Detroit; first African American elected president of the Michigan Nurses Association, in 1987. Williams holds a bachelor's degree from Ohio State University, a master's degree in nursing from Wayne State University, and a doctorate from the University of Michigan. She served for three years as a first lieutenant and staff nurse in the U.S. Army Nurse Corps at William Beaumont Army Hospital in El Paso, Texas, and was an instructor for seven years at Grant Hospital School of Nursing in Columbus, Ohio. Williams was also an instructor at Mercy School of Nursing in Detroit, assistant director of health careers at Schoolcraft College, professor and assistant dean of nursing at Wayne State University, and became head of Eastern Michigan University's Department of Nursing Education in 1990. She was presented with a Spirit of Detroit Award by the Detroit City Council in 1994, in recognition of her "exceptional achievement, outstanding leadership and dedication to improving the quality of life." Ref.: 32 (Mar. 15, 1994, 3)

WILLS-MERRELL, LUANNE, formerly of Lansing; first African American woman to be a licensed B-737 pilot, in 1994. Wills-Merrell won a scholarship from the Organization of Black Airline Pilots for her training at a United Airlines Flight Training Center in Denver. A graduate of Lansing Community College, where she majored in aviation flight technology, she was a flight instructor at LCC before becoming an aviation safety inspector for the Federal Aviation Administration in Des Plaines, Illinois. Ref.: 57 (Aug. 2, 1994, 2B)

WINCKLER, KATHRINE (1898-1976), of Okemos; one of the two first women, with **Alma Goetsch** (1901-1968) of Okemos, to be art instructors at Michigan State College, in 1926 and 1928, respectively. Both natives of Wisconsin, Winckler graduated from the University of Wisconsin in 1921 and Goetsch from the Art Institute of Chicago in 1928. Six years after each had completed an M.A. degree at Columbia University Teachers College, they were promoted to assistant professor, in 1941 and 1943. Just before retiring in 1965 they were both promoted to full professor.

Winckler, a painter and ceramist, was a co-founder of the Michigan Creative Education Association. Goetsch, who excelled in silkscreen and textile art, was instrumental in founding the Michigan Art Education Association. In 1938 they commissioned Frank Lloyd Wright to design a moderate-cost "Usonian" house for them in Okemos, incorporating features that reflected their special needs and interests. They moved into the house in 1940 and stayed until 1965, when they retired and moved to a new home in Arkansas especially designed for them by noted architect E. Fay Jones. Ref.: 120 (Fall 1991/Winter 1992, 15-19)

WINDSOR, PEARL (1888-1991), of Iron River; first woman to be superintendent of schools at Iron River, from 1938 to 1954. A native of Iron River, Windsor graduated from the University of Michigan in 1911 and began teaching English at Iron River High School, where she became principal in 1918. She was awarded a Master of Arts degree from Columbia University in 1932 and an honorary Master of Arts degree from Michigan State Normal College (Eastern Michigan University) in 1936. Ref.: 34 (213)

WITHEY, MARION LOUISE (1829-1912), of Grand Rapids; founder of a history class in 1869 that became the Ladies' Literary Club, with the goal of promoting education; co-founder and president of the Union Benevolent Association Hospital. Withey was the niece of **Lucinda Hinsdale Stone** of Kalamazoo. (See Michigan Women: Firsts and Founders, Vol. I.) Together with the Board of Education and the YMCA, the club began the Public School Library in 1871. The organization's nationally-recognized clubhouse was built in 1897. Its Town Hall Series has hosted many well-known guest speakers, including Presidents Grover Cleveland and Theodore Roosevelt and Susan B. Anthony. Other club activities include a "Books and Lunch" program, an annual children's writing contest, and the LLC Classical Theatre. Ref.: 40 (Oct. 24, 1993, 23-49)

WITHROW, PAMELA K., of Ionia; first woman to be in charge of a Michigan men's prison, as superintendent of the Michigan Dunes Correctional Facility at Holland, in 1982. Previously, Withrow was assistant deputy warden at Southern Michigan Prison at Jackson. She had also been the supervisor of a male prison camp, Camp Brighton at Pinckney, in 1977. By 1994 she was warden of the Michigan Reformatory at Ionia. Ref.: 23 (Sept. 18, 1994, 13)

WOLFE, DELIGHT J. (dates not known), of Hastings; first woman physician in Barry County, beginning her practice in 1878 after attending the first meeting of the Barry County Medical Society in January 1877. Ref.: 97

WOLFE, LAUREN, of Okemos; first Michigan girl to be a winning wrestler on a high school boys' team for a full season, at Okemos High School in 1992. According to the Michigan High School Athletic Association, Wolfe was eligible for the boys' team as long as no girls' wrestling program was offered. Wolfe, who has wrestled against boys since the first grade, also won the gold medal in her weight class at the 1991 U.S. Women's World Championship trials in Toledo but was barred from the world championships because she was three years under the minimum age requirement of 16. In 1992 she represented the U.S. in an international women's wrestling tournament in France. During her high school years, Wolfe won four varsity letters, competing on the boys' wrestling team. She won the national women's tournament in April of 1995, the Women's World Wrestling Team trials in June and represented the United States at the world freestyle championships in September at Moscow. Ref.: 23 (Feb. 9, 1992, 8-11); 57 (Jun. 23, 1995, 1C)

WOOD, JANE LUNDELL (1924-1993), of Grosse Pointe Woods; founder and director of the Detroit Swedish Council. Active in Swedish American cultural affairs, Wood often entertained the Swedish royal family during their visits to Michigan. In 1975 she was presented with a medal of appreciation by King Carl XVI of Sweden. Born in Detroit, Wood graduated from Grosse Pointe High School and from Briarcliff College in Briarcliff, NY. She was a past president of the Jenny Lind Club of Detroit and the Ibex Club, a cultural art appreciation organization. Ref.: 22 (Jul. 18, 1993, 6C)

WORDEN LATHROP, SAMANTHA (dates not known), of Okemos; first school teacher in Okemos, in 1844. The first school was housed in a log building two miles east of the village, where the first settler had arrived in 1839. Worden had five pupils in her first class, including **Mary Turner** who was the first child born in the settlement. In 1846 she married B. E. Lathrop. Ref.: 102

YAKELEY, ELIDA (dates not known), of East Lansing; first Registrar of Michigan Agricultural College (now Michigan State University), in 1908; co-founder of the American Association of Collegiate Registrars, organized at Detroit in 1910. From 1903 to 1908 she had been secretary to the college president. As Registrar for thirty years, she was responsible for admissions and was an early advocate of keypunching equipment to facilitate record keeping. Yakeley Hall, a women's residence on the MSU campus, was named in her honor in 1948. Ref.: 102

YANCHECK, GAIL, of Romulus; first woman to win at the Meadow Brook Historic Races, involving vintage sports cars, held at the Waterford Hills Road Racing Course in August 1993. The only woman entered in Class 5 with eleven other cars, she drove a Cosworth-powered Daren sports racing machine in the first race she had ever run. Yancheck had received a Rookie License from the Sportscar Vintage Racing Association, after attending two driving schools earlier in the year. She is president of Approved Aircraft Accessories, a company that rebuilds turbo compressors, hydraulic pumps, and other engine accessories for aircraft rebuilders throughout the U.S. and other countries. Ref.: 24 (Oct. 1993, 34)

YAO, CYNTHIA CHIN, of Ann Arbor; founder of the Hands-On Museum in Ann Arbor, 1982. With a master's degree in Museum Practice from the University of Michigan, Yao persuaded city officials to rent the old 1883 firehouse for a token fee, enlisted the help of many volunteers, and raised funds to renovate the building to showcase hands-on science exhibits. Since the museum opened in 1982, more than a million children and adults have visited its innovative exhibits, special events, workshops and classes. Yao also worked to establish a traveling science program that visits community centers during the summer months, in order to reach underserved young people in the Ann Arbor and Ypsilanti areas. Ref.: 4 (Oct. 14, 1992, B1)

YOUNG, WANDA, see **THE MARVELETTES**

ZIELINSKI, MARY ANN, of Center Line; first woman voted into public office in Center Line, with her election to the Center Line City Council in 1975. She was the first woman elected as Mayor of Center Line in 1981, serving until 1993. Ref.: 24 (Oct. 1993, 53); 195

****

"To get the word 'male' in effect out of the Constitution cost the women of the country fifty-two years of pauseless campaign. . . .

"Hundreds of women gave the accumulated possibilities of an entire lifetime, thousands gave years of their lives, hundreds of thousands gave constant interest and such aid as they could. It was a continuous, seemingly endless, chain of activity. Young suffragists who helped forge the last links of that chain were not born when it began. Old suffragists who forged the first links were dead when it ended. . . .

"It is doubtful if any man, even among suffrage men, ever realized what the suffrage struggle came to mean to women before the end was allowed in America. How much of time and patience, how much work, energy and aspiration, how much faith, how much hope, how much despair went into it. It leaves its mark on one, such a struggle. . . .

"Not all women in all the States of the Union were in the struggle. There were some women in every State who knew nothing about it. But most women in all the States were at least on the periphery of its effort and interest when they were not in the heart of it. To them all its success became a monumental thing."

Carrie Chapman Catt and Nettie Rogers Shuler, 1923

****

A SELECTED CHRONOLOGY OF MICHIGAN WOMEN'S HISTORY

1702   **Marie-Therese Guyon Cadillac*** and **Anne Picote de Belestre de Tonti*** join their husbands at Fort Pontchartrain (Detroit), becoming the first two European women settlers in Michigan.

1804   The first permanent trading post in Michigan is founded near present-day Ada by **Madeline LaFramboise*** and her husband Joseph.

1820   **Susan Johnston** (Ozhawguscodaywaquay, "Green Meadow Woman") is the first Native American woman within the Michigan territory to facilitate a treaty between her people and the U.S. government, the Treaty of Cession between the Ojibwa people and the United States, providing land for the founding of Fort Brady at Sault Ste. Marie.

1832   **Laura Smith Haviland*** and **Elizabeth Margaret Chandler*** found the Logan Female Anti-Slavery Society in Lenawee County, the first women's anti-slavery society in the Michigan territory, leading to one of the first Michigan stations of the Underground Railroad to Canada.

1837   Michigan becomes a state.

1846   Ernestine L. Rose, a reformer from New York, speaks to the Michigan Legislature "on the right and need of women to the elective franchise" but has little influence.

1848   The first Women's Rights Convention is held at Seneca Falls, New York. **Catharine Fish Stebbins** (who moves to Detroit in 1867) serves as the Secretary.

1849   A Senate committee, led by Senator Rix Robinson of Ada, proposes a universal suffrage amendment but it is not acted upon because of the "unusualness" and "needlessness" of the franchise for women.

1851   **Sojourner Truth** of Battle Creek speaks before the Women's Rights Convention in Akron, Ohio.

1852   The first women's club in Michigan, the Ladies Library Association of Kalamazoo, is founded by **Lucinda Hinsdale Stone***.

       Livonia Benedict* is the first Michigan woman to earn a Bachelor of Arts degree, at Hillsdale College.

1855   Suffragists from Lenawee County present petitions for woman suffrage, signed by many state citizens, to the Michigan Legislature.

The first college for Michigan women, the Michigan Female College, is founded at Lansing by **Abigail Rogers***.

1857   The Michigan Legislature gives greater attention to woman suffrage petitions but takes no action.

1859   A House committee considers the vote for black males but not for women, causing resentment among women.

1861-1865   The Civil War

1861   The nation's first Ladies Aid Society, for the purpose of providing aid to Civil War Soldiers at hospitals, camps, and battlefields, is organized in Detroit.

Jennie Hayes of Lansing is the first Michigan woman to enlist as a Civil War nurse in the First Michigan Regiment of Volunteers.

Ellen G. White of Battle Creek co-founds the Michigan Conference of Seventh-day Adventists (the first organization of Seventh-day Adventist churches) at Battle Creek; in 1863 she co-founds the General Conference of Seventh-day Adventists, also at Battle Creek.

Sarah Emma Edmonds* of Flint, the first Michigan woman to be a Civil War soldier, serves with the Second Michigan Volunteer Infantry Regiment as "Pvt. Franklin Thompson".

1866   The state's first bill on woman suffrage is defeated by one vote.

1867   The Michigan Legislature grants women taxpayers the right to vote for school trustees but rejects total woman suffrage.

1868   120 women vote unchallenged in the Sturgis school elections.

1869   The Fifteenth Amendment is passed by Congress, granting the vote to males regardless of race, color, or previous condition of servitude.

Susan B. Anthony and Elizabeth Cady Stanton form the National Woman Suffrage Association.

Lucy Stone leads the formation of the American Woman Suffrage Association.

1870   The Michigan State Woman Suffrage Association is formed at Battle Creek. The woman suffrage amendment is passed by the Michigan Legislature but vetoed by the governor.

Madelon Louisa Stockwell* of Albion is the first woman admitted to the University of Michigan, the first university to admit women. The University of Michigan medical school also accepts its first women students. Stockwell graduates in 1872.

Mary E. Green of Charlotte is said to be the first woman physician in the country to be admitted to any medical association, with her election to the New York Medical Society in ca. 1870.

1871   **Nannette B. Gardner*** of Detroit and **Mary Wilson*** of Battle Creek vote in city and state elections.

Amanda Sanford* is the first woman to graduate from the University of Michigan medical school.

The Ladies Library Association of Kalamazoo builds the first clubhouse in the nation for a woman's organization. In 1879 **Hannah Trask Cornell** becomes its first librarian.

Sarah Killgore Wertman is the first woman to graduate from the University of Michigan Law School and the first woman to practice law in Michigan.

1872   **Frances Armstrong Rutherford*** of Grand Rapids, **Ruth Geary*** and **Sibelia Baker*** are the first women physicians to be admitted to the Michigan State Medical Society.

The first public school kindergarten in Michigan is founded by **Fannie M. Richards***, the first African American teacher in Detroit's integrated school system, at the Everett School in 1871.

1874   The State Legislature puts a woman suffrage amendment on the ballot, but it is defeated, 135,957 to 40,077; the Michigan State Woman Suffrage Association disbands.

1875   The statewide Women's Christian Temperance Union is formed at Grand Rapids.

1878   **Virginia Watts*** of Ann Arbor is the first African American woman to enroll at the University of Michigan; in 1885 she becomes the first African American woman to graduate from the University.

1880   **Anna Howard Shaw*** of Big Rapids is the first woman in the nation to be a fully ordained minister in the Methodist Protestant Church.

1881   School suffrage is extended to parents and guardians of children of school age.

Emma Hall* of Tecumseh is the first woman to be head of a state institution, as Superintendent of the Reform School for Girls at Adrian, the first girls' reformatory in the U.S. run by an all-woman staff and a board of directors consisting mainly of women.

1880s   F. Elizabeth Palmer* of Albion is the first woman in Michigan elected to a board of education, under the new law granting school suffrage to women.

1884   The Michigan Equal Suffrage Association is formed in Flint with Mary L. Doe* of Bay City as the first president.

Michigan's Senator Thomas W. Palmer makes the first speech in the U.S. Senate in support of woman's suffrage.

1889   The Michigan Supreme Court upholds the right of Eva Belles* of Flint to vote in school board elections, after she was refused that right in 1888 (Belles vs Burr).

The National Woman Suffrage Association and the American Woman Suffrage Association merge to become the National American Woman Suffrage Association.

1890   The Michigan Women's Press Association is founded at Traverse City, with Belle McArthur Perry of Charlotte as its first president.

1893   The Michigan State Legislature passes municipal suffrage but the Michigan Supreme Court declares it unconstitutional on the grounds that "the legislature has no right to create a new class of voters".

1895   A proposed constitutional amendment to grant women suffrage is defeated in the House.

The Michigan State Federation of Women's Clubs is founded, with Clara A. Avery* of Detroit as its first president.

1898   Ellen May Tower* of Byron is the first U.S. Army nurse to die on foreign soil, of typhoid fever in Puerto Rico during the Spanish-American War, and is the first woman to receive a military funeral in Michigan.

The Michigan Association of Colored Women's Clubs is founded by Mary E. McCoy* of Detroit and Lucinda S. Thurman* of Jackson, with Thurman as president and McCoy as vice president.

1899 The National American Woman Suffrage Association holds its annual convention in April at the St. Cecilia Society hall in Grand Rapids, the only time the convention is held in Michigan.

1900 **Alice Chaney*** of Detroit is the first woman to be licensed as a ship's captain on the Great Lakes.

1902 **Agnes Nestor** of Grand Rapids co-founds the International Glove Workers Union.

1904 **Anna Howard Shaw*** of Big Rapids is elected president of the National American Woman Suffrage Association.

The Michigan Nurses Association is founded, with **Lystra Gretter*** of Detroit as its first president.

1907-8 At the State Constitutional Convention woman's suffrage is defeated 57 to 38, but women who pay taxes can vote on local bonding and tax issues.

1908 The first women's curling club in the country, the Grand Rapids Women's Curling Club, is formed.

1911 **Harriet Quimby*** of Branch County is the first woman in the nation (second in the world) to receive a pilot's license.

Annie Smith Peck, at age 61, is the first person to reach the peak of Peru's 21,150 ft. Mt. Coropuna, where she drives in a pennant declaring "Votes for women".

1912 Governor Charles S. Osborn successfully urges the Michigan State Legislature to put the suffrage question before the all-male electorate in November. **Clara B. Arthur*** of Detroit leads the campaign and the proposal appears to win. However, the opposition steals the election under suspicious circumstances.

Beginning in 1912, the Michigan State Grange, led by **Jennie Buell** of Ann Arbor and **Ida Chittenden** of Lansing, is the only state Grange to campaign actively for woman suffrage.

The Detroit Business Woman's Club, the first professional woman's club in the nation, is founded, with **Emily Helen Butterfield***, the first woman in Michigan to be a registered architect, as its first president.

1913 The Michigan Association Opposed to Equal Suffrage is formed. The suffrage proposal is again put on the ballot and again defeated.

1915 The American Women's Medical Association is founded, with **Bertha Van Hoosen*** of Rochester as its first president.

1916 **Frances Elliott Davis*** of Detroit is the first African
American nurse officially accepted into the American Red
Cross.

1917 The United States joins the Allies in World War I.

1917 **Ella H. Aldinger** of Lansing, **Betsy Graves Reyneau** and
Kathleen McGraw Hendrie of Detroit, and **Mrs. G. B.
Jennison** of Bay City join Alice Paul of the National
Woman's Party to picket the White House in support of
woman suffrage. Reyneau is arrested and sentenced to 60
days of hard labor in prison.

Governor Albert E. Sleeper signs a bill on May 8, granting
Michigan women the right to vote in presidential elections.

1918 Michigan male voters approve a state constitutional
amendment granting suffrage to Michigan women.

The Michigan Federation of Business and Professional
Women's Clubs is founded, with **Lena Lake Forrest*** of
Detroit as its first president.

1919 Michigan women vote for statewide offices for the first time.

The National Suffrage Amendment, the Nineteenth
Amendment to the U. S. Constitution, is passed by
Congress on June 5. Michigan is the second state to ratify
the amendment on June 10.

The National American Woman Suffrage Association
disbands and is replaced by the League of Women Voters.
The Michigan League of Women Voters is led by **Florence
Belle Brotherton*** of Detroit.

The first all-woman jury in Michigan is seated in Detroit on
March 19, with **Mabel S. Greenwood** of Detroit as foreman.

Ella C. Eggleston of Hastings is the first woman to be
appointed as a probate judge in Michigan.

Phoebe Ely Patterson* of Plymouth is the first woman in
Michigan to be a Justice of the Peace.

Anna Howard Shaw* of Big Rapids is the first woman in the
nation to receive the Distinguished Service Medal, for her
work as Chair of the Women's Committee of the Council of
National Defense.

1920 The 19th Amendment to the Constitution, granting the vote
to women, becomes law on August 26. Women vote for the
first time in the presidential election on November 2.

1921   **Eva McCall Hamilton*** of Grand Rapids is the first woman to serve in the Michigan Legislature with her election to the Michigan Senate.

1923   The Equal Rights Amendment is introduced in the U. S. Congress.

1925   **Cora Reynolds Anderson*** of L'Anse is the first woman elected to the Michigan House of Representatives.

1928   The Elliottorian Business Women's Club, the first African American business women's club in Detroit and Michigan, is founded by **Elizabeth Nelson Elliott*** of Detroit.

1930   The Detroit Housewives League, the first such league in the nation, is formed to encourage African American women to use their economic power to improve their own community. Founder **Fannie B. Peck*** of Detroit later becomes the first president of the National Housewives League formed in 1933.

       Ella Bareis Prochnow of Ann Arbor is the first woman in Michigan to own and manage an automobile dealership.

1930s **Grace Eldering*** and **Pearl Kendrick*** of Grand Rapids develop the first successful vaccine for whooping cough. They later develop the single innoculation for diphtheria, whooping cough and tetanus.

       The County Extension Program, to train farm women as leaders of homemaker groups and 4-H clubs, is founded at Michigan Agricultural College (Michigan State University) by **Edna V. Smith***.

1937   The Women's Emergency Brigade and UAW Women's Auxiliary, led by **Genora Dollinger**, support the sit-down strike for union organizing at General Motors Corporation in Flint.

1941   **Lila M. Neuenfelt** of Dearborn is the first woman to be a circuit court judge in Michigan, serving on the Wayne County Circuit Court.

1942   The United States enters World War II.

       The Women's Auxiliary Ferrying Squadron (later called the Women's Airforce Service Pilots or WASPS) is founded by **Nancy Harkness Love*** of Houghton, the first woman air ferry pilot in the nation in 1940.

       The nation's first chapter of the Blue Star Mothers of America (mothers of military men and women) is founded at Flint with **Adda Harris** as president.

1943   The All American Girls Professional Baseball League,
       formed while players on men's baseball teams are in
       military service, includes the Grand Rapids Chicks, the
       Battle Creek Belles, and the Muskegon Lassies; the League
       is active until the mid-1950s.

       Charlotte Plummer Owen of Ann Arbor founds the U.S.
       Marine Corps Women's Reserve Band, the official band of
       the women in the Marine Corps during World War II. She
       is the only woman to guest-conduct the U. S. Marine Band,
       in 1945 and again in 1993.

1944   U.S. Army Nurse **Aleda E. Lutz*** of Freeland is the first U.S.
       military woman to die in a combat zone during World War II
       when her hospital plane goes down on her 196th rescue
       mission.

1946   **Dorothy Waite Pearl** of Eastport founds Girls' Nation and
       Girls' State, to help high school girls throughout the country
       learn how their state and federal governments function.

1948   **Waunetta McClellan Dominic** of Petoskey co-founds the
       Northern Michigan Ottawa Association, to secure treaty-
       based rights for the non-reservation Ottawa and Chippewa
       people of Michigan.

1950   **Ruth Thompson*** of Muskegon is the first Michigan woman
       elected to Congress, in the House of Representatives where
       she is the first woman member of the House Judiciary
       Committee.

       Charline Rainey White* of Detroit is the first African
       American woman elected to the Michigan House of
       Representatives.

1952   **Cora Mae Brown*** of Detroit is the first African American
       woman elected to the Michigan Senate.

1953   **Irene M. Auberlin** of Detroit founds World Medical Relief, an
       organization that has provided medical supplies throughout
       the world for more than 40 years.

1961   **Clara Raven*** of Detroit is the first woman physician to be a
       full colonel in the U. S. Army Medical Corps.

1965   **Elly Peterson*** of Charlotte is the first woman to be state
       chair of a major political party in Michigan, as chair of the
       Republican Party.

       Viola Liuzzo of Detroit is the first white woman to be
       murdered as a civil rights worker, while working for the
       movement in Alabama.

1967   **Ann Holtgren Pellegreno*** of Saline is the first aviator in the U.S. to recreate the world flight of Amelia Earhart, to commemorate the 30th anniversary of Earhart's disappearance in 1937.

 Noreen Hillary of Grand Rapids and **Kay Whitfield** of Flint are the first women to become Michigan State Police Troopers.

1968   The Michigan Women's Commission is established by the Michigan State Legislature.

1969   Michigan's first chapter of the National Organization for Women is convened by **Patricia Hill Burnett*** of Detroit.

1970   **Cornelia Kennedy*** of Detroit is the first woman to be a federal judge, with her appointment to the U.S. District Court of the Eastern District of Michigan.

1971   The Women's Crisis Center is founded in Ann Arbor, one of the first two rape crisis centers in the nation.

1972   **Mary Stallings Coleman*** of Battle Creek is the first woman elected to the Michigan Supreme Court.

1973   The Michigan Women's Studies Association, the first women's studies association in the nation, is founded at Michigan State University

 The Equal Rights Amendment is reintroduced in Congress by Rep. **Martha Griffiths*** of Michigan, fifty years after it was first introduced.

 The first Title IX complaint against a university, charging gross discrimination against women in athletics, is filed by **Marcia J. Federbush*** of Ann Arbor.

 Carolyn King* of Ypsilanti, at age 12, is the first girl in the country to play in Little League Baseball.

1974   The Coalition of Labor Union Women (CLUW) is founded, with **Olga Madar*** of Detroit as its first president.

 The Michigan Criminal Sexual Conduct Act, which labels rape as a violent crime while insuring the victim's privacy, is passed after being drafted by **Virginia Nordby*** of Ann Arbor.

 Belita Cowan of Ann Arbor founds the National Women's Health Network, the only national consumer organization devoted to women's health.

1975   ERAmerica, with **Elly Peterson*** of Charlotte and Liz
       Carpenter as the first national co-chairs, is founded in
       Washington, D.C., to win support for the Equal Rights
       Amendment.

       The National Organization for Women's Wife Abuse Task
       Force in Washtenaw County establishes Michigan's first
       network of private homes to shelter survivors of domestic
       violence.

1976   ERAmerica is founded in Michigan by **Helen W. Milliken*** of
       Traverse City.

1978   **Margaret Brewer*** of Durand is the first woman to be a
       General in the U.S. Marine Corps.

1979   **Mary Stallings Coleman*** of Battle Creek is the first woman
       to be Chief Justice of the Michigan Supreme Court.

1980   **Marjorie Swank Matthews*** of Onaway is the first woman
       elected as a Bishop in the United Methodist Church.

1982   **Martha W. Griffiths*** of Romeo is the first woman elected to
       the office of Lieutenant Governor of Michigan.

       Martha M. Mertz of Okemos founds the ATHENA Award
       Program to honor outstanding business and professional
       women for their achievements, community service and
       assistance to other women in gaining leadership skills; the
       program becomes national in 1985 and international in
       1994.

1983   The annual Celebration of Michigan Women, at which
       historic and contemporary women are inducted into the
       Michigan Women's Hall of Fame, is founded by the
       Michigan Women's Studies Association.

1984   **Judith Craig*** of Royal Oak is the first woman to serve in
       Michigan as a Bishop of the United Methodist Church.

1986   **Catherine Comet** is the first woman in the country to be the
       official conductor of a professional orchestra, as conductor
       of the Grand Rapids Symphony Orchestra.

1987   The Michigan Women's Historical Center and Hall of Fame,
       the first historical center in the nation to focus on the
       achievements of the women of a single state, is opened at
       Lansing by the Michigan Women's Studies Association, with
       Gladys May Beckwith* as its first director.

       Teola Hunter* of Detroit is the first woman elected as
       Speaker Pro Tem of the Michigan House of Representatives.

1988   **Yolanda Alvarado-Ortega** of East Lansing founds the Hispanic Women in the Network of Michigan.

1990   **Susan Hershberg Adelman** of Southfield is the first woman to be president of the Michigan State Medical Society in its 124-year history.

1991   **Melissa Rathbun-Nealy** of Newaygo is the first U.S. Army woman to be a prisoner of war in the Persian Gulf War.

1992   **Merrily Dean Baker*** of Okemos is the first woman to be the Athletic Director at a Big Ten University, at Michigan State University.

A record number of women is elected to the U.S. Congress and the Michigan State Legislature, making a total of 47 women in the U.S. House of Representatives, six women in the U.S. Senate, 25 women in the Michigan House of Representatives and three women in the Michigan Senate.

1993   **Alta DeRoo** of Paw Paw is one of the first two women chosen for combat training as a U.S. Navy pilot.

Julie Krone of Eau Claire is the first woman jockey to win a triple crown event in the Belmont Stakes and the first woman to win five races in one day at Saratoga.

Collette Webster of Sunfield is the first American to die in the Bosnian War.

1994   **Margaret Dhaene** of Lansing is in the first group of women in the U.S. Navy assigned to a combatant ship.

Candice S. Miller of Macomb County is the first woman elected as Michigan Secretary of State.

The first on-campus domestic violence shelter in the country is founded at Michigan State University by **Joanne McPherson** of East Lansing.

1995   The first publicly-funded domestic violence shelter in the country is founded in Ann Arbor, with **Susan McGee** as its executive director.

Suellen Finatri of Roscommon is the first woman to ride horseback from St. Ignace to Anchorage, Alaska, starting out on February 1 and reaching Anchorage by December.

The 75th Anniversary of the Nineteenth Amendment, ratified on August 26, 1920, is celebrated throughout the year and those involved in the long struggle to win the vote for women are honored for their courage and commitment to the cause of equal suffrage.

THE MICHIGAN WOMAN SUFFRAGE HONOR ROLL

The Michigan Woman Suffrage Honor Roll is a listing of more than 3,000 Michigan women and men who were active in the long struggle for women's right to vote. Many of the names were found in accounts of Suffrage activities appearing in newspapers, Suffrage publications, and other periodicals. Other names were provided by organizations and individuals in the counties represented. Additional counties and names will be added to the Michigan Woman Suffrage Honor Roll as they are found or provided. The names are listed in alphabetical order by county. Wherever known, the home cities of the women and men follow their names. Corrections and additions to the names, cities and counties are welcomed.

ALCONA COUNTY

W. L. Chappell, Harrisville • Mrs. E. M. Green, Harrisville • Mrs. A. MacClatchey, Harrisville • Mrs. J. McIntyre, Harrisville • Mrs. M. Plow, Harrisville • Mrs. George Rutson, Harrisville • Mrs. O. H. Smith, Harrisville • Mrs. D. E. Storms, Harrisville

ALGER COUNTY

Mrs. Walter Bell, Grand Marais • George E. Friedly, Winters

ALLEGAN COUNTY

Mabel Barber, Plainwell • Mrs. George Bardeen, Otsego • Mrs. J. E. Botsford, Plainwell • Lillian Buskirk, Wayland • Mrs. F. I. Chichester, Allegan • Nellie Chrisman, Wayland • Mina Duel, Wayland • Mrs. Philo Duel, Wayland • Jane Estabrook • Bernice Ewing, Wayland • Mrs. Foster Fuller, Plainwell • Mrs. Fred D. Haines, Plainwell • Marcia Hall, Otsego • Lizzie Hudson • Mrs. H. W. McIntosh, Allegan • Mrs. H. D. Moore, Allegan • Mrs. Nevins, Otsego • Mrs. E. S. Nichols • Anna Pipp, Otsego • Metta Ross, Wayland • Laura Schroder, Allegan • Mrs. Artus Sherwood, Allegan • Mrs. Jay Sherwood, Plainwell • Mrs. Harry Sirrine • Mrs. Perry Sirrine, Allegan • Mrs. Malcolm Smith • Mrs. Walker, Otsego • Mr. Walker, Otsego • Mrs. John Webster, Plainwell • Mrs. William Woodhams, Plainwell • William Woodhams, Plainwell • Irene Yeakey, Wayland • Mrs. Joseph B. Zwemer

ALPENA COUNTY

Harriet Comstock, Alpena • William A. Comstock, Alpena • Mrs. William A. Comstock, Alpena • Miss Des Jardines, Alpena • Mrs. W. B. Dobson, Alpena • Mrs. Herbert M. Howe, Alpena • Mrs. Fred Le Blanc, Alpena • Mrs. Lewis Kline, Alpena • Mrs. MacKnight, Alpena • Mrs. Robert Rayburn • Mrs. I. W. Stewart, Alpena • Mrs. Andrew Wentz, Alpena • Mrs. E. H. Whedon, Alpena • Ella White, Alpena

ANTRIM COUNTY

Mrs. J. E. Bacon • Mrs. W. J. Brower, Mancelona • Mrs. C. H. Kay, Alden • Mrs. H. M. Coldren • Mrs. Charles Coy, Alden • Mrs. Robert Craven • Anna Doyle, Mancelona • Miss Eldred, Alden • Mrs. George Frink, Bellaire • Mrs. H. Hoffman, Mancelona • Mrs. W. Lambert, Mancelona • Mrs. McCracken, Alden • Elmer Mills, Mancelona • George W. Perry, Elk Rapids • Mrs. Perry, Elk Rapids • Mrs. Charles Towne, Elk Rapids • Miss Valleau, Alden • Mrs. L. G. Van Liew • Fern Wood, Mancelona

ARENAC COUNTY

Mrs. Drummond, Turner • Mr. Drummond, Turner • Owen Glover, Omer • Mrs. Goldrun, Turner • Mr. Hayes, Standish • Miss MacDonald, Omer • Mrs. MacDonald, Omer • Mr. MacDonald, Omer • Mrs. Mead, Omer • Ida Pomeroy, Standish • Mrs. Pomeroy, Standish Mrs. O. B. Shaw, Arenac • Mr. O. B. Shaw, Arenac

BARRY COUNTY

Bertha Bush, Delton • J. F. Edmonds, Hastings • Rep. Henry C. Glasner, Nashsville • Maud Glasner, Nashville • Mrs. Gould • Charles Ketchem, Hastings • John Ketcham, Hastings • Mrs. John Ketcham, Hastings • Mrs. P. R. Pancoast, Hastings

BARAGA COUNTY

Cora Reynolds Anderson, L'Anse

BAY COUNTY

Mrs. I. N. Baker, Bay City • May Baker, Bay City • Mrs. M. A. Ballard, Bay City • Isabel Ballou • Charlotte Bousfield, Bay City • Mrs. F. W. Braman, Bay City • Florence Browne, Bay City • Miss Clift Campau, Bay City • Mrs. F. H. Cash, Bay City • Mrs. Ward Coomer • Mrs. Coyle, Bay City • Matilda E. Daglish • Mrs. James A. Davidson • Mary L. Doe, Bay City • Mrs. Reuben Eger, Bay City • Mrs. John Every, Bay City • Richard Fletcher, Bay City • Mrs. Richard Fletcher, Bay City • Sen. Augustus H. Gansser, Bay City • Mrs. Augustus H. Gansser, Bay City • Mrs. S. M. Green • Mrs. J. D. Grinnell • Mr. Gustin, Bay City • Isabelle Hill • Mrs. Judge Holmes • Lottie Wilson Jackson, Bay City • Kathleen Jennison, Bay City • Mrs. G. B. Jennison • Frank P. Kelton, Bay City • Mrs. Frank S. Kelton, Bay City • May Stocking Knaggs, Bay City • Mary S. Knaggs, Bay City • John Wesley Knaggs, Bay City • Mrs. J. E. Knapp, Bay City • Hon. J. D. Lewis • Miss Lindsay, Bay City • Ida Grout Rust MacPherson, Bay City • Mr. F. McCormick, Bay City • Helen McGregor, Bay City • Mrs. A. M. Miller • Mrs. L. W. Oviatt, Bay City • Mr. L. W. Oviatt, Bay City • Mrs. A. W. Plum, Bay City • Mrs. H. M. Ready, Bay City • Martha Snyder Root, Bay City • Margaret Temple Smith, Bay City • Mrs. Louis J. Weadock, Bay City • Millie Webster, Bay City • Mrs. Norris Wentworth, Bay City • Helen D. Wilcox, Bay City • Mrs. James Wilcox, Bay City

BENZIE COUNTY

Mrs. H. Begold, Beulah • Mrs. E. H. Barrows, Nessen City • Mr. Cotton • Mrs. Cotton • Mrs. L. V. Dains, Beulah • Walter Damos, Honor • Mrs. Einar Erickson, Frankfort • Mabel Ford, Frankfort • Mrs. Hill • Mrs. A. Johnson, Elberta • Mrs. Sidney Johnson, Elberta • Leota Kane, Benzonia • Mrs. J. H. (or H. J.) Kinne, Frankfort • Mrs. Knapp, Frankfort • Mrs. A. E. Knight, Beulah • Mrs. Lewis, Frankfort • Mrs. A. S. Lobb, Frankfort • Mrs. F. Monroe, Beulah • Mrs. L. J. Nelson, Frankfort • Rose Conway Parker, Frankfort • Mrs. William Petitt, Beulah • Mrs. W. M. Powers • Mrs. G. Rose, Beulah • Mr. J. W. Saunders, Beulah • Mrs. James K. Savage • Mrs. Frank G. Snyder • Mrs. Alfred Upton, Frankfort • Harriet Van Deman • Myra Van Doman, Benzonia • Mrs. William Voorheis • Mrs. W. G. Voorheis, Elberta

BERRIEN COUNTY

Mrs. W. M. Alger • Mrs. Alfred Anderson, St. Joseph • Mrs. W. T. Ball, Coloma • Mrs. Ross Ballard, Niles • Mrs. Ralph Ballard, Niles • Mrs. H. G. Bartlett, St. Joseph • Ebbie Best, Buchanan • Mrs. E. A. Blakeslee, St. Joseph • Charles H. Cavanaugh • Mrs. F. B. Christopher, Benton Harbor • Margaret Christopher • Dean Clark, Buchanan • Sarah Clute, St. Joseph • Mrs. W. E. Cook, Benton Harbor • Mrs. Charles Coombs, Benton Harbor • Mrs. W. L. Curtis • Katie Putnam Emery, Benton Harbor • Mrs. Philip Friday,

BERRIEN COUNTY (CONTINUED)

Coloma • Mary M. Gibson, Benton Harbor • Helen Gore, Benton Harbor • Mrs. V. M. Gore, St. Joseph • Victor M. Gore, St. Joseph • Congressman Edward L. Hamilton, Niles Mrs. Edward L. Hamilton, Niles • Mrs. John Hamilton, Benton Harbor • Mrs. Charles Hanry, Sodus • Mrs. H. C. Hill, Benton Harbor • Emma Hinkley, St. Joseph • Mrs. O. B. Hipps, St. Joseph • Mrs. A. W. Hudson, Niles • Mrs. C. D. Kent, Buchanan • Mrs. Henry Kephart, Berrien Springs • Mrs. Thomas Kuykendall, Benton Harbor • Mrs. J. H. Langley, St. Joseph • Mrs. R. J. Lass • Mrs. Wallace Martin, St. Joseph • Jane McCartney, Benton Harbor • Mrs. B. F. McConnell • Helen McDowell, St. Joseph • Gerald McDowell, St. Joseph • Mrs. Julius J. Miller, St. Joseph • Ida Orr, St. Joseph • Mrs. John T. Owens • Mrs W. O. Pratt, Benton Harbor • Frank Rhoades, South Bend • Mrs. Frank Rhoades, South Bend • Mrs. Frank Rough, South Bend • Mrs. Jacob Rough, Niles • Lucille Schaus, Benton Harbor • Sara Schaus, Benton Harbor • Mrs. D. S. Scoffern, Niles • Harriet Sorge, St. Joseph • Hon. Levi Sparks • Rosalie Springsteen, St. Joseph • Mrs. D. R. Starkweather, St. Joseph • Mrs. A. H. Stoneman, St. Joseph • Mrs. A. T. Vail, St. Joseph • Mrs. John Wallace • Charles K. Warren, Three Oaks • Anne (Anna) Watson Mrs. J. E. Webster, St. Joseph • Mrs. T. N. Wells, South Bend • Mrs. C. A. White, St. Joseph • Mrs. H. S. Whitney, Benton Harbor

BRANCH COUNTY

Harriet J. Boutelle • Lorena E. Brown, Bronson • Mabel Stewart Buell, Union City • Elizabeth Cleveland, Coldwater • Melissa Rudd Fisk, Bronson • Cora Fulton, Sherwood • Grant Hadley, Coldwater • Cornelia Hodgman, Coldwater • Loa Lindsey, Bronson • Hon. Jonas H. McGowan, Coldwater • Mrs. Palmer, Coldwater • Judge Palmer, Coldwater • Hattie Parsons, Union City • Mrs. A. E. Robinson, Coldwater • State Sen. Henry E. Straight, Coldwater • Mrs. Henry E. Straight, Coldwater • Ella Taggart, Bronson • Mrs. Burton Taggart, Bronson • Grace V. Taylor • Celia Woolley

CALHOUN COUNTY

Mrs. A. W. Austin, Albion • Mrs. Bangham, Albion • Dr. Bangham, Albion • Morgan Bates Ethel Bedient, Albion • Mrs. Homer C. Blair, Albion • Homer C. Blair, Albion • Mrs. S. O. Bush • Mrs. E. L. Calkins, Battle Creek • Mrs. Frank Carleton, Albion • Prof. Carlton, Albion • Mrs. O. S. Clark, Battle Creek • Mr. O. S. Clark, Battle Creek • Mrs. R. J. Comstock, Albion • Jessie Davis, Albion • Mrs. E. L. Ford • Mrs. Robert Glascoff, Albion • Ann E. Lapham Graves, Battle Creek • Judge Graves, Battle Creek • Mrs. Green, Albion Prof. Green, Albion • Rena Louisa Tompkins Hamilton • Maude Harroan, Albion • Mrs. A. C. Hebble, Battle Creek • Dr. Betsy Hicks, Battle Creek • C. H. Hoagland, Battle Creek • Dr. G. P. Jocelyn • Dr. John H. Kellogg, Battle Creek • Mrs. John H. Kellogg, Battle Creek Mrs. Leroy Lewis, Ceresco • Mrs. Thomas Lloyd, Albion • Clara MacDiarmid, Battle Creek Martha Matthews, Battle Creek • Mrs. F. D. Miller, Marshall • Rev. Thornton Anthony Mills • Mr. W. F. Neil • Mrs. Peet • Mrs. E. W. Pendill, Battle Creek • Carrie Phillips, Ceresco • Clara Ross, Battle Creek • Frances Titus, Battle Creek • Josephine Stone, Battle Creek • Sojourner Truth, Battle Creek • Ellen Wartman, Albion • Elizabeth Willard, Battle Creek • Mary Wilson, Battle Creek

CASS COUNTY

Hannah Ackerman, Dowagiac • Estelle Adamson, Cassopolis • Ida Atkinson, Cassopolis Mrs. Essig, Dowagiac • Mrs. Charles Glasgow, Dowagiac • Carrie Frost Herkimer, Dowagiac • William J. Jacques • Mrs. Arthur Jewell, Dowagiac • Mabel Lee Jones, Dowagiac • Hon. G. C. Jones, Dowagiac • Mrs. Floyd Lanibeck, Dowagiac • Jennie Lyle, Dowagiac • Eula Nagler, Dowagiac • State Sen. Edgar A. Planck, Union • Mrs. Edgar A. Planck, Union • Kate Redner • Mrs. Boyd Redner, Dowagiac • Mr. Rice • Mrs. Harsen D. Smith • Mrs. M. P. White, Dowagiac • Mrs. John Wooster, Dowagiac

CHARLEVOIX COUNTY

Marcia Burdick, Boyne City • Mrs. A. L. Coulter, Charlevoix • Cora B. Coulter, Charlevoix Cynthia Galin, Charlevoix • Mrs. C. Gates, Boyne City • Mrs. E. E. Hall, East Jordan • Cassie Hart, Charlevoix • Jessie Himes • Mrs. Sabin Hooper, Boyne City • Mrs. James Howey, East Jordan • Alice Ann Round Malpass, East Jordan • Edith Wilkinson, Charlevoix

CHEBOYGAN COUNTY

Mr. H. F. Baker, Weadock • Mr. W. S. Barr, Cheboygan • Mabel Dixon, Cheboygan • Emma Eck, Wolverine • Mrs. Walter Elliot, Cheboygan • Phoebe Kennedy, Cheboygan • Dr. E. J. O'Brien, Cheboygan • Mrs. John P. Och, Cheboygan • Rev. Francis Piaskowski, Cheboygan • Mrs. C. C. Post, Cheboygan • Mrs. A. W. Ramsay, Cheboygan • Mildred Reed, Wolverine • Mr. C. S. Reilley, Cheboygan • Ada C. Sangster, Cheboygan • Mrs. C. V. Sutherland, Cheboygan

CHIPPEWA COUNTY

Mrs. J. S. Donnelly, Sault Ste. Marie • Mrs. R. F. Endress • Mrs. Otto Fowle, Sault Ste. Marie • Mrs. J. J. Lyons • Mrs. James T. Moore, Sault Ste, Marie • Patrick O'Shea • Annie Rooney • Mrs. Charles Shepherd • Spotted Tail

CLARE COUNTY

Dr. Louis L. Kelley, Farwell • Mrs. Louis L. Kelley, Farwell • Mrs. H. L. Kirshbaum, Harrison • George Langworthy, Clare

CLINTON COUNTY

Mr. G. W. Allen • Ida Brink, DeWitt • Abbie E. Dills, DeWitt • Mrs. Grole • Sally Hendryx • Mrs. Lee • Nellie Luce • Irwin Luce • Galusha Pennell, St. Johns • Mrs. Spaulding, St. Johns • Hon. Randolph Strickland • Florence Whelan • Mrs. Hoyt Whelan • Mrs. A. H. Walker, St. Johns • Alma Wisner

CRAWFORD COUNTY

Mrs. George Alexander, Grayling • Mr. Connine, Grayling • Nancy Deckrow, Grayling • Mr. Gregory, Grayling • Minnie Gregory, Grayling • Mrs. H. Hanson, Grayling • Mr. H. Hanson, Grayling • Mrs. Marius Manson, Grayling • Mrs. Olaf Michelson, Grayling • State Sen. Lee J. Morford, Grayling • Mrs. Lee J. Morford, Grayling • Perry Ostrander, Grayling • Oscar Palmer, Grayling

DELTA COUNTY

George Jensen • Selma Lindell, Escanaba • Mrs. J. E. Strom

DICKINSON COUNTY

Mrs. Dan Mallory, Foster City • Mrs. R. S. Powell, Iron Mountain

EATON COUNTY

Mrs. Barnum, Charlotte • Hon. J. Chance • Alice M. Charles, Bellevue • Mrs. B. J. Culbertson, Charlotte • Mary L. Dann, Charlotte • Mrs. DeFoe • Mr. E. A. Foote • Mrs. E. A. Foote • Cynthia Green, Charlotte • Miss Grisson, Grand Ledge • Mrs. M. P. Hart, Charlotte • Dr. Hixon, Grand Ledge • Dr. Martha Hixon, Grand Ledge • Mr. Nathan P. Hull, Dimondale • Rev. Alfred W. Hutchins, Charlotte • Minnie Keyes, Olivet • Dr. Miller, Olivet • Mrs. J. Musgrave • Meda Hess Patchell, Charlotte • Belle McArthur Perry, Charlotte • Dr. Stanka, Grand Ledge • Edith Steffener Stanka, Grand Ledge • Marian Marsh Todd, Eaton Rapids • A. K. Warren • Mary F. Youngblood, Charlotte

EMMET COUNTY

M. Kate Bachus, Harbor Springs • Emma L. Barnes, Petoskey • Mrs. C. Call • Mrs. Leon Chichester, Petoskey • Mrs. C. E. Churchill, Petoskey • Mrs. Alton Cook, Petoskey • Minnie M. Cross, Petoskey • Mrs. E. E. Cross • Mrs. William L. Curtis, Petoskey • Mrs. Cushman • Mrs. Englebeck • Mr. C. F. Erwin, Harbor Springs • Mrs. C. F. Erwin, Harbor Springs • Zella Goldstein, Petoskey • Jessie C. Grosenbaugh, Petoskey • Mrs. C. Hanky, Petoskey • Mr. H. Hinckley, Petoskey • Mrs. P. J. Howard, Petoskey • Mrs. J. McCune, Petoskey • Mrs. James Oldham • Mrs. Charles Pratt, Petoskey • Mrs. M. F. Quaintance • Alice Rosenthal, Petoskey • Mrs. H. Sweeney, Petoskey • Mrs. Joseph Warnock, Harbor Spring • Mrs. G. Welling, Petoskey

GENESEE COUNTY

Gov. Josiah B. Begole, Flint • Eva R. Belles, Flint • Mrs. W. G. Billings, Davison • Mrs. E. D. Black, Flint • Dr. Daniel Clark, Flint • Caroline C. Davis, Fenton • Dr. William E. DeKleine, Flint • George Durand, Flint • Rev. R. C. Hufstader, Flint • Mrs. A. Jenney •

GENESEE COUNTY (CONTINUED)

E. T. Middleton, Flint • Jane Payne, Flint • Mrs. O. Stewart • Mrs. M. S. Tucker, Flint • Mr. J. B. Walker, Flint • Emily West, Flint • Dr. J. C. Wilson, Flint

GLADWIN COUNTY

Mrs. G. S. Bliss, Gladwin • Mrs. M. Leibrand, Gladwin • Gertrude Reymore, Beaverton

GOGEBIC COUNTY

Janet Goudie, Ironwood • O. W. Johnston, Ironwood • Mrs. P. Vander Hagen, Ironwood • Delphia Westerman, Ironwood • Mrs. E. B. Williams, Ironwood

GRAND TRAVERSE COUNTY

Mrs. H. D. Alley • Mrs. J. D. Alley, Traverse City • Mrs. C. D. Alway • Grace Bartholomew, Traverse City • Clara Bates, Traverse City • Mrs. C. M. Buell • Mrs. Frank Carver • Dr. Sara Chase, Traverse City • Matt Connine • Mrs. C. G. Covell, Traverse City • Mrs. W. P. Croster • Ruth Davis, Grawn • Mrs. C. L. Dayton • Mr. C. L. Dayton • Mr. Parm Gilbert, Traverse City • Mrs. William Grant, Traverse City • Anah Grelick, Traverse City • Mrs. C. L. Greilick, Traverse City • T. T. Henderson • Jennie Maria Burnett Hendricks, Traverse City • Francis Heney • Mrs. John Heuss • Mrs. John Hoxsie, Acme Township • Mrs. E. L. Hughes, Traverse City • Mrs. Carey Hull, Traverse City • Mrs. James Johnson • Mrs. Edgar Kent • Mrs. William Love, Traverse City • Mrs. J. B. Martin, Traverse City • Mrs. John V. McIntosh • Mrs. Joseph McIntosh • Mrs. F. T. McNamara, Traverse City • Hildegarde Grawn Milliken, Traverse City • Mrs. J. T. Milliken • Hon. W. H. C. Mitchell • Mrs. J. D. Munson • Hon. J. G. Ramsdell • Mrs. J. G. Ramsdell • Mrs. Loren Roberts, Traverse City • Mrs. J. J. Sanburn • Mrs. M. S. Sanders, Traverse City • Mrs. John R. Santo • Mrs. Frank Shannon • Mrs. Frank H. Smith, Traverse City • Mrs. Shiloh Smith, Traverse City • Mrs. Levi Soule, Traverse City • Elvin L. Sprague • John Straub, Traverse City • Mrs. William Striker, Lakeview • Mrs. Walter Thirlby • Mr. L. L. Tyler, Traverse City • Mrs. L. L. Tyler, Traverse City • Mrs. D. E. Wyncoop

GRATIOT COUNTY

Mrs. Andrews, St. Louis • Mrs. W. A. Balke, Alma • Mrs. A. E. Branch, St. Louis • Frances Burns, St. Louis • Mrs. J. N. Day • Mrs. F. E. Ellsworth, Alma • Hon. Ralph Ely • Rev. S. B. Ford • Jennie M. Hanley, St. Louis • Mrs. Francis King • Grace Messenger, Alma • Sadie Messenger, Alma • E. H. Mudge, St. Louis • Mrs. Wilbur Nelson, Ithaca • Dr. A. H. Olmstead, St. Louis • Mrs. A. H. Olmstead, St. Louis • Mr. F. G. Palmer, North Star • Mrs. Timby, Alma • Rev. E. H. Vail

HILLSDALE COUNTY

Kate Baker • Adah Benedict, Litchfield • Edna Blair, Hillsdale • Mrs. E. V. Blakeman, Osseo • Eva Bliss • Mrs. Asher Blount, Osseo • C. M. Bohen, Pittsford • Louisa Brainard Flossie Bump • Pearl Porter Chamberlain, Osseo • Mrs. Cheney • Mrs. Charles Clark, Cambria • Mrs. Frank Cook • Mary Corbett • Eva Crane, Camden • Mrs. George Darrow • Mrs. George Deal, Jonesville • Charles M. DeWitt, Osseo • Mrs. M. C. Dey • Mrs. Fowler • Mrs. S. J. Gier, Hillsdale • Mr. S. J. Gier, Hillsdale • Archie Gilbert, Litchfield • Mrs. L. A. Goodrich, Hillsdale • Mr. L. A. Goodrich, Hillsdale • Nellie Goutfrey, Camden • Mrs. D. W. Grandon, Hillsdale • Mr. D. W. Grandon, Hillsdale • Asher Hadley • Bertha Hall • Mrs. John Haskell, North Adams • Mrs. Victor Hawkins, Jonesville • Mrs. Charles Hayes • Charles Hayes • Ralph W. Hayes, Hillsdale • Adelle Hazlett, Hillsdale • Mrs. Hunker • Mrs. W. F. Jerome, Hillsdale • Rev. W. F. Jerome, Hillsdale • Mrs. Edward Kennebrook, Litchfield • Mrs. William Kilby, Jonesville • Mrs. Larrabee • Prof. Larrabee • Prof. C. A. Mack • Mrs. Joseph Mauck • Joseph Mauck • Mrs. Harry McClave, Hillsdale • Harry McClave, Hillsdale • Professor Frances Stewart Mosher, Hillsdale • Mrs. James O'Neill • Julian Palmer, Camden • Mrs. M. A. Pendill, Hillsdale • Mrs. W. H. Porter, North Adams • Mary Pratt • Mrs. D. B. Reed • Prof. D. B. Reed • Mrs. Reffner • Myra Remmele • Mrs. F. A. Roethlisberger • Mr. F. A. Roethlisberger • Betsy Russell, Reading • Mrs. E. Samm • Walter H. Sawyer, Hillsdale • Mrs. Walter H. Sawyer, Hillsdale • Mrs. Ralph Smith, Mosherville • Mrs. Frank Stewart, Hillsdale • Frank Stewart, Hillsdale • Edith Strong, Jerome • Mrs. Swift • Mrs. Lewis Taylor, Osseo • Mrs. Tinker • Mrs. D. W. Ward, Hillsdale Mr. D. W. Ward, Hillsdale • Berthe Wetmore, Jonesville • Mrs. Burr Wilbur

HOUGHTON COUNTY

Mrs. E. J. Abrams, Dollar Bay • Ruth Gibson Butler, Houghton • E. Belle Delft, Calumet
Lydia E. Haire, Hancock • Frances Hubbard, Houghton • L. L. Hubbard, Houghton • Mrs.
L. L. Hubbard, Houghton • Congressman Frank W. James, Houghton • Mrs. Frank W.
James, Houghton • Lucille James, Calumet • Marie James, Calumet • Cora Doolittle
Jeffers, Painesdale • Frederick A. Jeffers, Painesdale • Edith H. Marvin, Lake Linden •
Judge O'Brien, Calumet • Mildred I. Ramsdahl, Calumet • Margaret Scallon, Hancock •
Ann Trimingham, Calumet • Emma L. Uren, Houghton • Katherine Wieber

HURON COUNTY

Grace Greenwood Browne, Harbor Beach • Mrs. J. J. Campbell, Pigeon • Mrs. John Clark,
Pigeon • Mrs. P. L. Fritz, Pigeon • Mrs. B. Hamill, Pigeon • Mrs. Peter Priemer, Ruth • Mrs.
F. A. Ryckman, Elkton • Mrs. P. N. Sawyer, Bad Axe • Gov. Albert E. Sleeper • Mr.
Trumbull, Elkton • Mrs. L. L. Wright, Bad Axe • Mrs. A. W. Yale, Pigeon

INGHAM COUNTY

Mrs. T. C. Abbott • Ella H. Aldinger, Lansing • Rev. F. C. Aldinger, Lansing • Mrs. B. H.
Anderson, Lansing • Mrs. H. B. Armes • Henry B. Baker • Hon. J. H. Bartholomew,
Lansing • Constance Bennett • Mrs. S. D. Bingham • S. H. Brigham, Lansing • Ethelyn
Britten, Lansing • Mrs. Charles Broas • A. R. Burr • Mrs. Luther Burton, Lansing • Mrs.
J. J. Bush • Mrs. L. L. Calkins, Lansing • Augusta Jane Chapin, Mason • Mrs. C. A.
Chaplin, Williamston • Ida Chittenden, Lansing • Hattie Clark, Lansing • Mrs. C. A. Cobb,
Lansing • Fannie Foster Cowles, Lansing • Mr. A. E. Cowles • Mrs. L. B. Curtis, Lansing •
Mrs. R. C. Dart • Miss Edmunds • Mrs. S. E. Emory, Meridian • Marie B. Ferrey, Lansing •
State Sen. Charles W. Foster, Lansing • Mrs. Charles W. Foster, Lansing • Mazie
Getchell, Lansing • Mrs. E. A. Gilkey, Lansing • Dr. Grace Hendrick, Lansing • Carrie W.
Holmes • Mrs. J. W. Holmes • Grant Hudson, Lansing • Mrs. Grant Hudson, Lansing •
Ruth Inglehart, Lansing • Mrs. O. A. Jenison • Minnie E. Johnson • Mrs. Frae Johnson,
Lansing • Congressman Patrick H. Kelley, Lansing • Mrs. Patrick H. Kelley, Lansing •
Mrs. Latterman • Mr. W. L. Larned • Mrs. J. I. Mead • May Ross Moore, Lansing •
Samanthy Newbrough, Lansing • R. E. Olds, Lansing • Mrs. R. E. Olds, Lansing • Mrs. R.
H. Person, Lansing • Judge Rollin Person, Lansing • Rep. Seymour H. Person, Lansing •
Mrs. Seymour H. Person, Lansing • Mrs. G. W. Phelps • Dr. O. J. Price, Lansing • Bertha
Ray, Lansing • Mrs. J. W. Robinson • Mrs. T. R. Robinson, Lansing • Richard Scott,
Lansing • Mrs. Richard Scott, Lansing • Lillian Shipman • Luella Smith, Lansing • Marie
C. Spencer, Lansing • Rev. J. Straub, Lansing • Harriet A. Tenney, Lansing • Ila B.
Thomas • Belle Towne, Lansing • Mathilde Victor, Lansing • Mrs. C. S. Watters, Lansing
Mrs. E. L. Westcott, Lansing • Dean Georgia White, Lansing • Mrs. Kenneth Whitman,
Lansing • Fred L. Woodworth, Lansing • Mrs. Fred L. Woodworth, Lansing • Dr. S. W.
Wright

IONIA COUNTY

Sara Baldwin, Portland • Mrs. Chaddock • Anna Curtis, Ionia • Mrs. Frank Daniels,
Saranac • Sylvia Eaton, Belding • Joy Harrison, Belding • Major Lomas, Ionia • Mrs. N. C.
Neilson, Belding • Mrs. Morley E. Osborne, Belding • Morley E. Osborne, Belding •
Elizabeth Shaw, Belding • Mr. J. B. Smith • Mrs. Fred A. Washburn, Belding • Mrs. A.
Williams

IOSCO COUNTY

Laura V. Braddock, Tawas City • Mrs. C. A. Currey, Tawas City • Mrs. E. L. King, East
Tawas • Rose McDonald McKay, East Tawas • Mrs. Charles Pinkerton, Tawas City • Ezoa
Thomas, East Tawas

IRON COUNTY

Mrs. R. B. Webb, Crystal Falls

ISABELLA COUNTY

Mrs. George Chatterton, Mt. Pleasant • State Sen. John Adams Damon, Mt. Pleasant •
Mrs. John A. Damon, Mt. Pleasant • Mrs. B. A. Hills, Mt. Pleasant • Mr. B. A. Hills, Mt.
Pleasant • Mrs. Douglas Nelson • Mrs. R. M. Rathburn

JACKSON COUNTY

Mrs. W. H. Barry, Jackson • Katherine Bennett, Jackson • Margaret Bennett, Jackson • Mrs. John Bennett, Jackson • Mrs. Walter Bennett • Nevada Blagdon, Jackson • Mrs. Burt Blair, Rives Junction • Kate Bloomfield, Jackson • Florence Breck Bulson, Jackson Minnie Deline, Pulaski • Catherine Dunham, Jackson • Mrs. E. C. Edsell, Jackson • Mrs. E. M. Edsell, Jackson • Miss Zelie P. Emerson, Jackson • Mrs. Zelie P. Emerson, Jackson Catherine Falihee, Jackson • Mrs. Rayner Field • Larua Ford, Jackson • Mrs. E. L. Fuller, Jackson • Mrs. J. S. Geiger, Springport • Beatrice Haskins, Jackson • Mary Green Hayes, Jackson • Dr. Rhoda Grace Hendrick, Jackson • Mrs. Harry D. Heywood • Mr. J. W. Hutchins, Hanover • Harry L. Jors • Mary Lathrop • Tidus Livermore • Mrs. A. M. McGee, Jackson • Mrs. E. L. Moore • Mary Dunham Murray, Jackson • Mrs. C. G. Parnall, Jackson • Elva Frink Pelham, Jackson • Elvalene Pelham, Jackson • Mrs. John L. Senior, Jackson • Ella Wing Sharp, Jackson • Dr. Martha C. Strong, Jackson • Rev. J. B. Thompson, Rives Junction • Hon. W. H. Withington

KALAMAZOO COUNTY

C. Louise Anderson • Mrs. J. B. Balch, Kalamazoo • Mrs. E. A. Balyeat, Kalamazoo • Elizabeth Beckman, Kalamazoo • Mrs. D. C. Blakeman, Kalamazoo • Mrs. Carl Blankenburg • Mrs. C. C. Blood • Helen S. Brander, Kalamazoo • Mary Ahnafeldt Brander, Kalamazoo • Mrs. William L. Brownell • Mrs. Julius C. Burrows, Kalamazoo • Mrs. J. J. Campbell, Richland • Mrs. F. L. Chappell, Kalamazoo • Nellie Sawyer Clark, Kalamazoo • Winnifred S. Clark • Mrs. G. Cobb, Schoolcraft • Emeline Cope • Dr. Augustine Warren Crane, Kalamazoo • Caroline Bartlett Crane, Kalamazoo • Col. F. W. Curtenius • Mrs. E. N. Dingley, Kalamazoo • Ellen A. Doolan, Kalamazoo • Blanche Draper, Kalamazoo • C. H. Farrell, Kalamazoo • Anna L. Fellows, Schoolcraft • Arta Fisher, Scotts • Mr. Freeman, Kalamazoo • Dee Garrison • Maud Glenn, Portage • Carrie L. Harrison, Schoolcraft • Mrs. William P. Hobart, Comstock • Mrs. F. M. Hodge, Kalamazoo • John L. Hollander, Kalamazoo • May M. Hough, Comstock • Jennie E. Hurlburt, Richland • Mr. H. E. Johnson, Kalamazoo • W, O. Jones, Kalamazoo • Mrs. M. N. Kennedy • Caroline Kleinstuck, Kalamazoo • Irene Kleinstuck, Kalamazoo • Dr. Ella A. Knapp, Galesburg • Mrs. S. R. Light, Kalamazoo • Harriet A. Marsh, Kalamazoo • Alice L. McDuffee, Kalamazoo • Sue McKee, Kalamazoo • Miss McLaughlin, Kalamazoo • Mrs. Ward J. Miller, Comstock • Florence G. Balch Mills, Kalamazoo • Merritt Moore • Mrs. J. H. Norris, Comstock • Mrs. C. W. Oakley • Mrs. Oldfield • Mrs. F. R. Olmstead • Jessie Ostrander • Mrs. B. F. Parker, Kalamazoo • Rev. H. C. Peck • Miss Pierce, Kalamazoo • Mrs. Neal Romance, Portage • Mrs. F. N. Root • Rosalie Rudow, Kalamazoo • Marvin J. Schaberg, Kalamazoo • Mrs. William Shakespeare Jr. • Hermann Simmerer, Kalamazoo • Vida Smith, Portage • Bess Southwell, Portage • Mrs. F. I. Southwell, Portage • Della Sprague, Kalamazoo • Juliet Starkweather • Mrs. C. H. Stearns • W. H. Stewart, Kalamazoo • Mrs. W. A. Stone, Kalamazoo • Dr. Harriet McCalmont Stone • Lucinda Hinsdale Stone, Kalamazoo • James H. Stone, Kalamazoo • Dr. (Rev.) J. B. Stone, Kalamazoo • Fannie D. Stuart, Schoolcraft • Mrs. E. R. Swift, Comstock • Dr. N. Thomas • W. E. Upjohn, Kalamazoo • Samuel H. Van Horn • Celia J. Weed, Schoolcraft • Maude White, Kalamazoo • Cora Fuller Williams • Mrs. L. S. Woodhams

KENT COUNTY

Gertrude Abels, Sand Lake • Mrs. J. W. Adams, Grand Rapids • Sarah K. Adsit, Grand Rapids • Mrs. E. Anderson, Sparta • Mrs. William H. Anderson, Grand Rapids • Maude Austin, Kent City • Rachel Bailey, Grand Rapids • Lucy Ball, Grand Rapids • Sherry Ballard, Sparta • M. H. Barber, Grand Rapids • Rev. H. B. Bard, Grand Rapids • J. B. Barlow, Grand Rapids • Minnie Brazee Barlow, Grand Rapids • Mrs. E. W. Barnes, Rockford • Marie Wilson Beasley, Grand Rapids • Mrs. Beasom, Grandville • Anna S. Benjamin, Grand Rapids • Mrs. F. E. Berge, Grand Rapids • Charles Berkey, Grand Rapids • Rev. Edwin Bishop, Grand Rapids • Anna Sutherland Bissell, Grand Rapids • M. R. Bissell, Grand Rapids • Mrs. Aldi L. T. Blake, Grand Rapids • Dorothy Blake, Grand Rapids • William F. Blake, Grand Rapids • Mrs. M. C. Bliss • Hon. Delos A. Blodgett, Grand Rapids • Daisy Peck Blodgett, Grand Rapids • M. L. Bocher, Grand Rapids • Mrs. Lucius Boltwood, Grand Rapids • Mrs. R. Boyland, Lowell • Mrs. R. L. Boynton, Grand Rapids • Della Bradstrum, Sparta • Mrs. C. W. Brayman, Cedar Springs • Cornelia Fitch Briggs, Grand Rapids • Mrs. J. O. Briggs, Sand Lake • Mrs. J. D. Brooks, Grandville • Goldie Brown, Cedar Springs • Mrs. A. E. Carpenter, Grand Rapids • Emma Rathbone

KENT COUNTY (CONTINUED)

Carpenter, Grand Rapids • Anna Caulfield, Grand Rapids • Mrs. A. B. Cheney, Sparta • Mrs. John Cheney, Grand Rapids • E. P. Churchill • Mrs. M. J. Clark, Grand Rapids • Mrs. R. S. Coleman, Sparta • Maud Northrop Collins, Casnovia • Mae F. Conlon, Grand Rapids Mrs. Benn M. Corwin, Grand Rapids • Belle Cotton, Rockford • Judge Harry L. Cresswell, Grand Rapids • A. A. Crippen, Grand Rapids • F. M. Davis, Grand Rapids • Sarah J. Davis, Grand Rapids • Hattie De Jonge, Grand Rapids • Mrs. A. E. DeWar, Cedar Springs • Mrs. C. R. Dockery, Rockford • H. Margaret Downs, Grand Rapids • Mrs. Charles Doyle, Lowell J. M. Dudley, Grand Rapids • William H. Eastman, Grand Rapids • C. L. Fitch, Grand Rapids • Mrs. M. L. Fitch, Grand Rapids • Mary Fitzgerald, Grand Rapids • Mrs. C. C. Follmer, Grand Rapids • Mrs. Charles Foote, Grand Rapids • Miss Ford, Grand Rapids • Fred French, Grandville • Bertha French, Grandville • D. W. Giddings, Grand Rapids • Mrs. D. W. Giddings, Grand Rapids • Mr. I. B. Gilbert, Grand Rapids • Julia Goldsmith, Grand Rapids • Mrs. Theron H. Goodspeed, Grand Rapids • Josephine Ahnefeldt Goss, Grand Rapids • Lucy Gould, Grand Rapids • William A. Greeson, Grand Rapids • Mrs. M. C. Greene, Lowell • Alice B. Grimes, Grand Rapids • Mrs. H. P. Grover, Grand Rapids • Genevieve W. Hain, Grand Rapids • Sherwood Hall, Grand Rapids • Evelyn Hamilton, Grand Rapids • James Hamilton, Grand Rapids • Myrtle Hamilton, Grandville • Ida O. Hanson, Lincoln Lake • Hon. B. A. Harean • Laura Harris, Cedar Springs • Mrs. Allan Hartman, Grandville • Mrs. M. Hass, Sparta • Mary G. Hay, Grand Rapids • Mrs. Loren Henry, Grand Rapids • Mrs. A. S. Hicks, Grand Rapids • Ella Hill, Grand Rapids • Mrs. A. W. Hine, Grand Rapids • Elida Hodges, Lowell • Mrs. Martin H. Holcomb, Grand Rapids • E. G. D. Holden • Josiah R. Holden, Grand Rapids • Justina Merrick Hollister, Grand Rapids • Angie L. Hooker, Lowell • Mrs. L. B. Hopkins, Grand Rapids • Mrs. Myron Hopkins, Grand Rapids • Mrs. Joseph Horner, Grand Rapids • Mrs. H. B. Houghton • Miss Howell, Grand Rapids • Loraine Immen, Grand Rapids • Dr. L. Burton Jacques, Grand Rapids • Jessie Jenison, Grandville • Marion L. Jennings, Grand Rapids • Dell Jewell, Grand Rapids • A. T. Johnson, Grand Rapids • Dr. Collins H. Johnson • Edward Johnson, Grand Rapids • Lois M. Jones, Grand Rapids • N. P. Judd, Grand Rapids • Martha A. Keating, Grand Rapids • Christine Keck, Grand Rapids • Mrs. Bruce Keister, Sparta • Grace Kelley-Freehouse, Grand Rapids • C. B. Kelsey, Grand Rapids • Mary Atwater Kelsey, Grand Rapids • Emily B. Ketcham, Grand Rapids • Mrs. Ketchum, Grand Rapids • Smith D. Ketcham, Grand Rapids • Clara Knee, Lowell • Mrs. T. K. Lamb, Rockford • Frank Leavenworth, Grand Rapids • Mrs. Ben H. Lee, Grand Rapids • Nona Loop, Sparta • Alice Luton, Grand Rapids • Mrs. E. E. Mamoreaux • Sen. Carl E. Mapes, Grand Rapids • Julia Pike Mapes, Grand Rapids • Mrs. Ruben Maurits, Grand Rapids • Mary A. McConnelly, Grand Rapids • Kate G. McDonald, Sand Lake • Hon. W. F. McKnight, Grand Rapids • Mrs. William F. McKnight, Grand Rapids • Mr. F. H. McNaughton, Ada • Mrs. H. S. Miller, Kent City • Hon. James Miller • Charles H. Mills, Grand Rapids • Nora Mitchell, Sparta • Mrs. Bruce Moore, Grand Rapids • Emma Morley, Cedar Springs • Mrs. Roland Morley, Grand Rapids • Ione L. Morley, Grand Rapids • Mr. W. K. Morley, Grand Rapids • E. A. Mosley, Grand Rapids • Roy K. Moulton, Grand Rapids Edith Powers Moulton, Grand Rapids • Minnie Munshaw, Bowne Township • Mrs. J. Newton Nind, Grand Rapids • Mrs. Edwin Owen, Grand Rapids • Mrs. Jules Panigot • Mrs. H. Parker, Grand Rapids • Mrs. Charles S. Parks, Kent City • Charles S. Parks, Kent City Adella Pearsall, Cedar Springs • Mrs. Carroll Perkins, Grand Rapids• Cyrus E. Perkins, Grand Rapids • Bertha Phillips, Grandville • Frances Patterson Powers, Grand Rapids • Katherine Prager, Grand Rapids • Mrs. L. A. Prager, Kent City • William F. Quigley, Grand Rapids • Mary Remington, Grand Rapids • Mrs. John H. Rempis, Grand Rapids • Cora M. Riggs, Grand Rapids • Sen. Rix Robinson, Ada • Mrs. Fred N. Rowe, Grand Rapids • Mrs. W. E. Rowe, Grand Rapids S. Clark Rowlson, Grand Rapids • Clara Comstock Russell, Grand Rapids • Huntley Russell, Grand Rapids • Mrs. Russell, Cedar Springs • Dr. Frances Armstrong Rutherford, Grand Rapids • Mrs. George Savage, Grand Rapids • Mrs. Secord, Grandville • Mrs. R. E. Shanahan, Grand Rapids • Mrs. F. E. Shattuck, Sand Lake • Frank E. Shaw • Mrs. W. B. Sinclair, Sand Lake • Alice Smith, Grandville • Mrs. Fred Smith, Bowne Township • Henry Smith, Grand Rapids • Mrs. James A. Smith, Grand Rapids • Nana Osterhout Smith • William Alden Smith • Mrs. J. Spangenburg, Sparta • Mrs. Henry Spring, Grand Rapids • Mrs. Fred Stark, Rockford • Frank Stone, Grand Rapids • Bertha T. Stowell, Grand Rapids • F. W. Strahan, Grand Rapids • Mrs. F. K. Swain, Caledonia • Hon. Edwin F. Sweet, Grand Rapids • Sophia Fuller Sweet, Grand Rapids • Mrs. F. Taylor, Sparta • Cora S. Trowbridge, Grand Rapids • Mrs. I. M. Turner,

KENT COUNTY (CONTINUED)

Grand Rapids • Mrs. H. A. Van Antwerp, Rockford • Agnes Van Buren, Grand Rapids • Arthur Vanderburg, Grand Rapids • Lena Van Harten, Grandville • Grace Van Hoesen, Grand Rapids • Yaida Udel, Grand Rapids • Mary Vine, Grand Rapids • F. A. Voight, Grand Rapids • Ruby P. Walbrink, Cedar Springs • Myron N. Walker, Grand Rapids • Mrs. David A. Warner, Grand Rapids • Mrs. C. F. Waters, Grand Rapids • Mrs. Frank Weatherly, Grand Rapids Emma Wheeler, Grand Rapids • Lynette White, Grand Rapids • Minnie White, Grand Rapids • Helen A. Williams, Grand Rapids • Mrs. Ernest H. Williams, Grandville; • Jessie Williams, Lowell • Margaret Williams, Grand Rapids • Miss Wilson, Grand Rapids • Mrs. F. H. Wilson, Grand Rapids • Mrs. S. H. Wilson, Grand Rapids Mrs. E. D. Winchester, Grand Rapids • Rev. A. W. Wishart, Grand Rapids • Hon. S. L. Withey Minnie Wollett, Grand Rapids • Mrs. F. B. Woodward, Grand Rapids • Mrs. E. C. Woodworth, Cedar Springs • Louise Wooster, Grand Rapids • Mrs. Claude O. Wykes, Grand Rapids • Gert Young, Grand Rapids

KEWEENAW COUNTY

Maggie Walz (Margareeta Niranen), of Calumet

LAPEER COUNTY

Mr. W. E. Brown • Hon. Ira Butterfield • Congressman Louis C. Crampton, Lapeer • Mrs. Louis C. Crampton, Lapeer • Ada Davenport • Sarah White Davis • Mrs. Charles E. Gibbons • Mr. Lamb • Ettie V. Schanck • Charles Scully, Almont • Mrs. Charles Scully, Almont • Mrs. Stephen Slater • Mrs. J. H. Taylor, Lapeer • Florence Vincent, Lapeer • Lucy White Williams, Lapeer • Mr. J. B. Wilson

LEELANAU COUNTY

Olive Brooks • Mrs. O. A. Chappelle, Leland • Mrs. E. McKercher • Mrs. Levi Pheatt • Levi Pheatt • Elizabeth Ray, Leland • Mrs. D. H. Scott, Northport

LENAWEE COUNTY

Helen Anderson • Mrs. Howard Anderson, Adrian • Alice Angell, Adrian • Mrs. A. L. Bliss, Adrian • Mr. C. H. Bramble, Tecumseh • Mrs. C. H. Bramble, Tecumseh • Mrs. N. B. Bramble, Tecumseh • Miss N. E. Brewster, Hudson • Clara Brittain • Mrs. R. H. Brooks, Hudson • Mrs. Charles E. Brown, Hudson • Mrs. W. S. Brown, Hudson • John Carr, Adrian • Emma J. Cheney, Jasper • Carilyne Curtis, Adrian • Alice E. Daniels, Onsted • Mary E. Deery, Tecumseh • Winnifred W. Dodge, Adrian • Mrs. C. C. Fisher • Mrs. Frank Fisher, Franklin Township • Nancy Fleming • Mrs. B. J. Foster, Hudson • Mrs. Fox • Edward Frensdorf, Hudson • Florence Frensdorf, Hudson • Mrs. N. Geddes • Mrs. L. O. Hall, Blissfield • Harriet Halsted, Hudson • Jennie C. Law Hardy, Tecumseh • Dr. W. B. Hartzog • Mrs. Fred Harvey, Adrian • Mrs. W. B. Hartzog • Laura C. Haviland, Adrian • James Helme, Adrian • Rose E. Helme, Adrian • Mrs. Edd Hendryx, Franklin Township • Fred H. Hughes, Adrian • Caroline Humphrey, Adrian • Mrs. A. E. Illenden • Mrs. M. T. James, Hudson • Mrs. Thomas James • Mrs. William Jibb, Adrian • Matie E. Kirby, Hudson • Mary Knapp, Hudson • Lucinda Knapp • Mrs. W. H. Knight, Adrian • Mrs. C. H. Lamb, Blissfield • Edith Lamkin, Tecumseh • Mrs. H. M. Lowe, Hudson • Mrs. Irving Luce, Franklin Township • Mary Mapes, Tipton • Hattie Mead, Morenci • Mrs. Frank Meadford, Jasper • Hon. Charles E. Mickley • Mrs. O. N. Miles, Hudson • Nellie Mingay • Julius Moeller, Adrian • Florence Montague, Adrian • Ada Mumford, Adrian • Mrs. C. O. Myers, Adrian • Electra Myers • Orilla Foote Niles, Adrian • Mrs. D. E. Owen, Hudson • Betsy P. Parker • Clara Pease, Hudson • Ruth Mosher Place, Blissfield • Mrs. S. W. Raymond, Adrian • Mrs. J. M. Robertson, Blissfield • Mrs. F. A. Rowley • Mrs. John Schull, Tecumseh • Mrs. Philip Seewald, Hudson • Will Spaulding, Franklin Township • Mrs. C. B. Showell, Hudson • Nellie Stansberry, Cement City • Mrs. L. D. Tallman, Hudson • Alma Tate, Clinton • Mrs. Alva Waring • Mrs. W. Westerman, Adrian • Mrs. Hoyt Whelan, Tipton • Hoyt Whelan, Tipton • Hon W. S. Wilcox • Ada Wright, Jasper • Gertrude Zibble, Deerfield

LIVINGSTON COUNTY

Mrs. Charles Adams • Mrs. R. H. Baird • Mrs. Henry Beurmann • Mrs. Miller Beurmann • Carrie Bordman • Mrs. Joseph S. Brown • Mollie Burt • Mrs. Fred Chase • Mrs. W. E. Cleave • Clara Ellsworth • Mrs. Will Farnsworth • Mrs. William Fraser • Mrs. Alfred

LIVINGSTON COUNTY (CONTINUED)

Garland • Mrs. Arthur Garland • Mrs. J. D. Gilbert • Mrs. C. A. Goodnow • Mrs. E. P.
Gregory • E. P. Gregory • Mrs. E. Hadsall, Cohoctah • Sarah Hotcheler • Mrs. Eugene
Howe • Mrs. George Howe • May Hoyt • Mrs. William Huntington, Howell • Mrs. G. O
Hutchings • Mrs. F. M. Lansing • Mrs. J. F. LaRue • Mrs. F. J. Lee • Mrs. Perry Lewis,
Cohoctah • Mrs. Littlejohn • Mrs. H. A. McPhaerson • Mrs. Clark Miner • Mrs. A. A.
Montague • Helen Norton • Mrs. Horace Norton, Jr. • Mrs. A. J. Parker • Mrs. J. C.
Parsons • Mrs. Adelbert Peavy • Mrs. Howard Reed • Mrs. R. R. Smith • Julia Teasdale •
Mrs. W. P. Van Rinkle • Mrs. H. C. Weimeister • Mrs. A. N. Wells • Mrs. George Windles •
Mrs. John Wrigglesworth, Cohoctah • Mrs. D. L. Young

LUCE COUNTY

Carrie Dutcher

MACOMB COUNTY

L. D. Anderson, Armada • Mrs. Ambrose Campbell • Mrs. W. H. Crawford • Mrs. J. H.
Dussenberry • Mrs. John Lungerhausen • Mark T. McKee, Mt. Clemens • Mrs. Mark T.
McKee, Mt. Clemens • John M. Potter • Esther A. Reed, Richmond

MANISTEE COUNTY

Mr. Allen, Copemish • Elmer J. Alway, Manistee • Mrs. S. W. Baker, Manistee • Mrs. S. M.
Barnes, Manistee • Alice Bolton, Manistee • Mrs. William J. Bolton, Manistee • Rolo
Britton, Manistee • Ida M. Brownrigg, Manistee • Dr. Kathryn M. Bryan, Manistee •
Chester Burnais • Anna Chandler, Manistee • Mrs. Henry Cosier, Bear Lake • Georgia
Curtis • Hon. B. M. Cutcheon • T. G. Elton, Manistee • Mr. Filer, Manistee • Joseph Fisk,
Manistee • Fannie Holden Fowler, Manistee • Hon. Samuel W. Fowler • Mrs. P. C.
Gensen, Manistee • Mr. F. M. Gleason, Copemish • Miss A. M. Golden, Manistee • Mr. A.
Green • Mrs. George Hart • Mrs. O. C. Hawley, Manistee • Kitty E. Hull, Arcadia • G.
Iverson • Will H. Jarman, Copemish • Mrs. P. C. Jensen • Louise E. Jones, Manistee •
Mrs. Keddie, Bear Lake • Sarah A. Kies, Manistee • Dr. A. J. Kirkland, Manistee • Dr. Lee
A. Lewis, Manistee • Mrs. J. E. Lipe, Manistee • Mrs. William Lloyd, Manistee • John
Miller, Brethren • Mrs. Harry Musselwaite, Manistee • Harry Musselwaite, Manistee •
Rose Conway Parker, Manistee • Miss Lou Peache • Mr. T. J. Ramsdell • Eva Reed,
Copemish • Rev. Rood, Copemish • Alice Russell, Manistee • Floyd Schaab • May Wright
Sewall • Susan Seymour, Manistee • Lula Shults • Dr. L. Verna Simons, Manistee •
Thomas Smurthwaite, Manistee • Mrs. L. T. Stansell, Manistee • Dr. S. Szudrawski •
Alice Chapman Turner • Katherine Van Buskirk, Manistee • Nellie Walker, Manistee •
Mrs. J. E. Wilkinson, Manistee

MARQUETTE COUNTY

Sidney Adams • Mrs. Edgar Bell, Marquette • Matilda Schneider Blemhuber, Marquette •
Charlotte G. Kaufman Breitung, Marquette • Lida Bronson, Ishpeming • Hiram A. Bur •
Mrs. T. B. Catlin, Marquette • Mrs. W. S. Cook, Marquette • Mrs. Allen Cowden,
Marquette • Mrs. Henry Cunningham, Marquette • Mrs. M. Daniels, Marquette • Mrs. A.
W. Deadman, Marquette • Mrs. W. J. Ellison, Marquette • Mrs. Edward Farnham,
Marquette • Miss Sydney Harring, Marquette • Mrs. S. A. Houck, Marquette • Mrs. L. W.
Howe, Marquette • Mrs. Charles J. Johnson, Marquette • Mrs. James H. B. Kaye,
Marquette • Mrs. Daniel Keough, Marquette • Mrs. John Kreiger, Skandia • Hon. John
D. Mangum, Marquette • Mrs. J. D. Mangum, Marquette • Catherine Ellen Maxwell,
Marquette • Mabel McIntosh, Marquette • Ellen Monteith, Marquette • Mrs. H. R. Patrick,
Marquette • Susan J. Crawford Pearce, Marquette • Abby Beecher Longyear Roberts,
Marquette • Sen. Alton T. Roberts, Marquett • Mrs. M. J. Sherwood, Marquette • Ruth
Stafford, Marquette • Mrs. J. A. St. John, Marquette • Lillian A. Saari Vashaw, Marquette
Helen Vierling, Marquette • Olga O. Von Zellen, Marquette • Sigrid A. Von Zellen,
Marquette

MASON COUNTY

Emma Fisher, Ludington • Mr. Foster • Mrs. Elias Hall, Ludington • Mrs. F. W. Hawley •
Mrs. A. P. John • Graeme O'Geran • J. S. Stearns, Ludington • Mr. L. M. Stearns,

MASON COUNTY (CONTINUED)

Ludington • Kate G. Stufflebeam, Ludington • Mrs. G. O. Switzer, Ludington • Mrs. William A. Toby, Free Soil • Mrs. M. V. Young, Scottville • Mrs. O. C. Zook, Ludington

MECOSTA COUNTY

Mrs. C. C. Barnes, Big Rapids • Mrs. C. W. Doe, Big Rapids • Hon. Woodbridge N. Ferris, Big Rapids • Mrs. Albert Guild, Paris • Mrs. C. L. Kiefer, Morley • Mrs. G. A. Masselink, Big Rapids • Emma McCrath, Paris • Lucy Foote Morehouse, Big Rapids • Rachel Newcom • Stella B. Roben, Big Rapids • Dr. Anna Howard Shaw, Big Rapids • Mrs. B. S. Travis, Big Rapids

MENOMINEE COUNTY

Mrs. Ralph Seward, Stephenson • Ralph Seward, Stephenson • Mrs. J. A. Shernick, Wallace • Mrs. H. A. Vennema, Menominee

MIDLAND COUNTY

Minnie Ball, Midland • Congressman Gilbert A. Currie, Midland • Mrs. Gilbert A. Currie, Midland • Sarah E. Van DeVort Emery, Midland • Oscar Inman, Averill • Celia A. Jackson, Edenville • Dr. E. Jennings • Mrs. C. A. McDonald, Midland • Edith Price, Midland • Mrs. Summer

MISSAUKEE COUNTY

Mrs. E. M. Allen • Nellie Armstrong, Lake City • Mr. S. W. Davis • Mrs. J. W. Decker, Lake City

MONROE COUNTY

Mrs. E. E. Brown, Dundee • Mr. J. E. Burroughs, Dundee • Mrs. Wesley Dodd, Monroe • Helen Doehme, Monroe • Judge Franche, Monroe • Mrs. W. J. Hubble, Monroe • Mr. J. E. Husted, Dundee • Nora Lauer, Monroe • Jennie Sawyer, Monroe • Hon. J. J. Summer • Hon. Talcott E. Wing

MONTCALM COUNTY

Alice Allsopp, Carson City • Mrs. John Bale, Lakeview • Jennie Foley, Stanton • Mrs. Kelsey, Lakeview • Mrs. S. F. Kennedy, Lakeview • Mrs. C. C. Larke, Greenville • Mrs. F. O. Linquist, Greenville • Bess Northrop, Lakeview • Ella Bower Parkhurst, Greenville • E. J. Rawley, Greenville • Mrs. Louis Roenigk, Greenville • Mrs. Hiram Smith, Greenville • Mrs. Peter Van Deinse, Greenville • Mrs. Cory Vining, Lakeview

MONTMORENCY COUNTY

Rose Farrier, Hillman • Tibbie Farrier, Hillman • Mr. Ostrander, Hillman • Mrs. Whipple, Hillman

MUSKEGON COUNTY

Mrs. Barney • Grace Moon Beardsley, Muskegon • Mrs. C. C. Billinghurst, Muskegon • Miss Frazel Boucher, Muskegon • Mrs. M. A. Boynton • Mrs. Richard H. Browne, Muskegon • Mrs. William A. Campbell, Muskegon • Mrs. William J. Campbell, Muskegon • Mrs. William Carpenter, Muskegon • Mrs. O. H. Clark, Muskegon • Mary Covell, Muskegon • James M. Donnelly, Muskegon • Mrs. Thomas W. Donnelly, Muskegon • Thomas W. Donnelly, Muskegon • Dr. Eames (Mrs.), Muskegon • Lillian Freeman, Twin Lake • Mrs. Charles A. French, Muskegon • Emma Gee, Montague • Emma D. Giles, Muskegon • Mrs. A. R. Gold, North Muskegon • Mr. A. R. Gold, North Muskegon • May Gordon • Mrs. S. W. Gritzner, Montague • Lt. Gov. H. H. Holt • Anna O. Holthe, Muskegon • Mrs. Housemann • Mrs. H. J. Hoyt, Muskegon • Mrs. O. B. Ingersoll • Cora Jackson, Muskegon • Mrs. Howard C. Lawkins, Muskegon • Mrs. George W. March, Muskegon Heights • Mrs. Markley, Holton • Mrs. M. J. McConnell, Muskegon • Leah McCormick, Fruitport • Congressman James C. McLaughlin, Muskegon • Mrs. James C. McLaughlin, Muskegon • Mrs. Paul Moon, Muskegon • Mrs. Fred G. Neumeister • Blanche Orthwaite, Muskegon • Ransom I. Sanford, Muskegon • Franz Schoenberg, Muskegon • Mrs. Francis Smith, Muskegon • S. Shirley Smith, Muskegon • Gertrude Sullivan, Muskegon • Mrs. J. E. Sullivan, Muskegon • Mrs. Anson Temple, Muskegon • Margaret Turner, Muskegon • Mrs. Henry J. Van Zalingen, Muskegon •

MUSKEGON COUNTY (CONTINUED)

Mrs. A. A. Whipple, Muskegon • Mercedes Wiswell, Muskegon • Mrs. Will S. Wood, Muskegon • Rep. Carl Young, Muskegon • Mrs. Carl Young, Muskegon

NEWAYGO COUNTY

Hon. E. L Gray • Rep. Wayne R. Rice, White Cloud • Mrs. Wayne R. Rice, White Cloud • Mrs. William Robertson, Fremont • Lucy Utley

OAKLAND COUNTY

Mr. C. Adams, Rochester • Miss S. E. Adams, Rochester • Mrs. Alexander • Mrs. Frederick Arthur • Mrs. C. F. Arthur • Mrs. C. T. Arthur, Pontiac • Lillian Drake Avery, Farmington • Blanche Avery, Pontiac • Cora C. Bailey, Pontiac • Mrs. Fred Bailey, Pontiac Bertha E. Bails, Pontiac • Mabel E. Baldwin, Royal Oak • Mr. C. H. Bartlett, Pontiac • Mrs. Leo Beaudette, Pontiac • Mrs. John Betzer, Pontiac • Mrs. E. A. Brace, Pontiac • Mrs. R. J. Brace, Pontiac • Elizabeth P. Bradfield, Pontiac • Mrs. F. Brooks, Rochester • Mrs. Guy Brown, Pontiac • Mrs. Henry Carsner • Mrs. H. S. Chapman, Pontiac • Mrs. Harry Coleman, Pontiac • Mrs. N. B. Colvin, Pontiac • State Sen. Frank L. Covert, Pontiac • Mrs. Frank L. Covert, Pontiac • Ella Dawson, Pontiac • Mrs. W. L. Day, Pontiac • Elizabeth Dewey, Pontiac • Mr. G. W. Dickinson, Pontiac • Mrs. G. W. Dickinson, Pontiac • Rev. George L. Durr, Lake Orion • Elizabeth Edwards, Pleasant Ridge • Laura Efforts, Pontiac • Mrs. S. A. Farnum, Pontiac • Mrs. R. Y. Ferguson, Pontiac • Viva Flaherty, Royal Oak • Mrs. D. B. Fox • Mrs. T. B. Fox, Rochester • Mrs. Wallace Frost, Birmingham • Mrs. H. George, Pontiac • Mrs. H. J. Gerls, Pontiac • Fidelia Wooley Gillette, Rochester • Mrs. D. A. Green, Pontiac • Mrs. H. C. Guillot, Pontiac • The Misses Harrington, Pontiac • Pauline Harris, Pontiac • Mrs. C. H. Hartung, Pontiac • Catherine Henderson, Pontiac • Mrs. George T. Hendrie, Birmingham • Mrs. Richard Hewitt, Birmingham • Richard Hewitt, Birmingham • Mrs. J. B. Hoffer, Pontiac • Mrs. Conrad Hoffman, Pontiac • Mr. J. Holman Jr.• Georgia Hoyt, Pontiac • Mrs. M. D. Hubbard, Pontiac • Mrs. F. S. Ingoldsby, Pontiac • Mrs. Jamison, Birmingham • Lt. Gov. Patrick H. Kelley • Helen Marr Kessell • Mrs. S. A. Kessell, Pontiac • Mrs. William Kessels, Pontiac • C. F. Kimball • Mrs. F. J. Laidlow, Oxford • Kate Leggett • Sarah LeRoy, Pontiac • Myrta Lockwood, Holly • Mrs. C. N. Lounsberry, Walled Lake • Mrs. Austin Lynch, Pontiac • Mrs. Lyons, Pontiac • Cora B. Metz, Oxford • Mrs. Charles Matthews • Mrs. G. W. Miller, Birmingham • Mrs. Mitchell, Birmingham • Mr. Mitchell, Birmingham • Ann Murphy, Pontiac • Mr. M. Newberry, Rochester • Mrs. J. Norton, Rochester • Mr. J. Norton, Rochester • Minette Osmen, Pontiac • Grant N. Oxford, Lake Orion • The Misses Page, Pontiac • Mrs. P. J. Pool, Pontiac • C. L. Randall, Oxford • Anna B. Rees, Clarkston • Mrs. Judd J. Robbins, Pontiac Louisa M. Shepherd, Pontiac • Mrs. J. L. Sibley, Pontiac • Addie Sly, Birmingham • Ella Smith, Pontiac • Nellie M. Snook, Rochester • Mrs. Charles Staff, Pleasant Ridge • Mrs. C. T. Starker, Pontiac • Mrs. Wm. O. Stevens, Bloomfield Hills • Mrs. J. C. Stockwell, Pontiac • Mrs. P. H. Struthers, Pontiac • Chloe Crofoot Sullivan • Gov. Fred M. Warner, Farmington • Mrs. Fred M. Warner, Farmington • Mrs. E. E. Wheeler, Holly • Ida Wiley, Pontiac • Mrs. Harry Winston, Birmingham • Mrs. Frank Willets • Mrs. J. Wilson, Rochester • Mrs. Frank E. Wodell, Pontiac • Margaret Youngs, Pontiac

OCEANA COUNTY

Etta E. Crofoot, Hart • Rosa Goodrich, Cobmossa • John Halsted • Ella L. Leland, Hart • Mrs. B. B. Maxson • Edith Gotts Munger, Hart • Nina DeLong Sands, Pentwater • Bertha Skeels

OGEMAW COUNTY

Mrs. W. P. Hayes, West Branch • Mrs. James Scott, West Branch

ONTONAGON COUNTY

Mr. F. Green, Ontonagon

OSCEOLA COUNTY

Lizzie Anderson, Tustin • Mrs. F. C. Beeman, Reed City • B. F. Gooch • Mrs. William Homer, Reed City • Mrs. C. L. Lane, Reed City • Mrs. P. E. Robertson, Tustin • Mrs. Charles Smith, Evart • Mrs. Strong, Reed City • Dr. Wells, Evart

OSCODA COUNTY

Mrs. Perry Deyarmond, Biggs • D. L. Holly, Comins

OTSEGO COUNTY

Mrs. L. A. Aldrich, Gaylord • Clara Alexander, Gaylord • Weltha Alexander, Gaylord • Elberta Allen, Gaylord • Mrs. James Allen, Gaylord • Jennie Allis, Gaylord • Mrs. D. Anderson, Gaylord • Sadie Anderson, Gaylord • Mrs. Archie Armstrong, Gaylord • Addie M. Bailey, Gaylord • Mrs. R. D. Bailey, Gaylord • Mr. R. D. Bailey, Gaylord • Mrs. Perry Bala, Gaylord • Clara Banner, Gaylord • Mrs. Frank Barber, Gaylord • Minnewell D. Barlow, Gaylord • Agnes Barnes, Gaylord • Kate Barnes, Gaylord • Belle Barnum, Gaylord • Agnes Barr, Gaylord • Minnie E. Barr, Gaylord • Mrs. William Barrett, Gaylord • Emma Beatty, Gaylord • Lovey Beck, Gaylord • Lila C. Bellinger, Gaylord • Louise M. Bengal, Gaylord • Dorothea Benthien, Gaylord • Tillie Bergey, Gaylord • Mrs. John E. Berry, Gaylord • Olive Bertsch • Emma Bettis, Gaylord • Mrs. Louis Bigelow, Gaylord • Edna Bilow, Gaylord • Pearl Bilow, Gaylord • Alice Bingham, Gaylord • Lena Blanchard, Gaylord • Clarribel S. Blodgett, Gaylord • Irene Blong, Gaylord • Helen Borowiak, Gaylord Lottie Borowiak, Gaylord • Maryanna Borowiak, Gaylord • Rose Borowiak, Gaylord • Mrs. Valentine Borowiak, Gaylord • Jennie Bridge, Gaylord • Helen C. Bright, Gaylord • Mrs. Harold Briley, Gaylord • Mae Brintnell, Gaylord • Mrs. Anthony Broger, Gaylord • Mrs. Clark Brown, Gaylord • Gladys Brown, Gaylord • Lena S. Brown, Gaylord • Mary Brown, Gaylord • Mrs. John W. Brown, Gaylord • Irene Bruder, Gaylord • Mrs. Sanford W. Buck, Gaylord • Mrs. Edward Buckler, Gaylord • Mrs. Frank Buckler, Gaylord • Marianna Burchal, Gaylord • Mrs. Burlingame, Gaylord • Edna Burlison, Gaylord • Mabel Burr, Gaylord • Franciska Butka, Gaylord • Mrs. John Bwavak, Gaylord • Mrs. William E. Byrd, Gaylord • Mrs. Virgil A. Byrd, Gaylord • Marian Caffy, Gaylord • Rebecca Caister, Gaylord Catherine Campbell, Gaylord • Christina Campbell, Gaylord • Phemia Campbell, Gaylord Bessie Carl, Gaylord • Mrs. Otis H. Carpenter, Gaylord • Mrs. William Carpenter, Gaylord • Dell Carr, Gaylord • Rose Carroll, Gaylord • Lina Case, Gaylord • Ruby C. Case, Gaylord • Hattie Cataline, Gaylord • Mrs. Henry Celaspiel, Gaylord • Nina R. Chaloux, Gaylord • Ella Chantell, Gaylord • Louise Chase, Gaylord • Maggie Cherwinski, Gaylord • Edithe Choate, Gaylord • Hulda Christenson, Gaylord • Olulda Christenson, Gaylord • Jennie Clapper, Gaylord • Mrs. H. Clapper, Gaylord • Mrs. Lyle Clapper, Gaylord • Alice V. Clark, Gaylord • Rena Clink, Gaylord • Eifa Close, Gaylord • Alta Cogswell, Gaylord • Mrs. Bert Cole, Gaylord • Maud Coleman, Gaylord • Helen A. Collier, Gaylord • Hattie Comstock, Gaylord • Nora O. Congdon, Gaylord • Clyda Cook, Gaylord • Ella Cook, Gaylord • Mrs. George A. Cook, Gaylord • Luella M. Cook, Gaylord • Hattie M. Cook, Gaylord • Celia R. Cooley, Gaylord • Maude Cooley, Gaylord • Jennie Coppins, Gaylord • Mrs. Francis Corbin, Gaylord • Margaret Costello, Gaylord • Nina Coultes, Gaylord • Lizzie Cremeans, Gaylord • Melissa Cremeans, Gaylord • Mrs. Tom Cullacut, Gaylord • Flora E. Culliton, Gaylord • Mrs. James Cumming, Gaylord • Mrs. Charles Cushman, Gaylord • Mrs. Boleslaus Czarkowski, Gaylord • Elizabeth M. Daily, Gaylord • Mrs. Robert Dailey, Gaylord • Alice Darby, Gaylord • Mrs. Sam Davis, Gaylord • Mary Deichelbohr, Gaylord • Myrtle De La Matep, Gaylord • Anna Demerest, Gaylord • Mrs. I. S. Demerest, Gaylord • Maude Deming, Gaylord • Mrs. H. G. Deming, Gaylord • Mrs. Charles Derby, Gaylord • Mary E. Dickason, Gaylord • Carrie Dipzinski, Gaylord • Mrs. Alvin G. Dolen, Gaylord • Iva M. Doten, Gaylord • Esther Double, Gaylord • Jennie Dreffs, Gaylord • Blanche M. Duff, Gaylord • Minnie Dyer, Gaylord • Mary Ejray, Vanderbilt • Bertha Eldridge, Gaylord • Anna Ellsworth, Gaylord • Mrs. George W. Ellwanger, Gaylord • Pearl Engel, Gaylord • Mrs. Guy Ervin, Gaylord • Jennie Erwin, Gaylord • Mrs. Amil Evans, Gaylord • Christina Evans, Gaylord • Minnie Evans, Gaylord • Viola Evans, Gaylord • Mary Fabish, Gaylord • Eva Falk, Gaylord • Mrs. Andrew Falk, Gaylord • Susie Fat, Gaylord • Mary Ferris, Gaylord • Ruth M. Ferris, Gaylord • Mary E. Fields, Gaylord • Mrs. Edw. Fitzpatrick, Gaylord • Loretta Fitzpatrick, Gaylord • Mae Fitzpatrick, Gaylord • Elizabeth Fler, Gaylord • Mrs. John Florenski, Gaylord • H. Onalee Ford, Gaylord • Neenah M. Ford, Gaylord • Ora Ford, Gaylord • Dr. Ruey Ford, Gaylord • Ella E. Fox, Gaylord • Mary Fox, Gaylord • Mrs. Charles Fox, Atlanta • Laura Frazer, Gaylord • Carolina Frederickson, Gaylord • Esther Frederickson, Gaylord • Sophia Freeman, Gaylord • Mrs. Chris Freiberg, Gaylord • Hannah E. French, Gaylord • Henrietta French, Gaylord • Mrs. Seth M. French, Gaylord • Elizabeth Fulmer, Gaylord • Nellie M. Fulmer, Gaylord • Mrs. Earl Gales, Gaylord • Maude Gardner, Gaylord • Mrs. Amos Gary, Gaylord Bessie Galloway, Gaylord • Lizzie Garovonska, Gaylord • Ethel Gary, Gaylord •

OTSEGO COUNTY (CONTINUED)

Cora M. Gault, Gaylord • Mrs. Frank Gero, Gaylord • Mrs. Otha Getts, Gaylord • Maggie Gibbs, Gaylord • Mrs. George Gibson, Gaylord • Mrs. James Giffin, Gaylord • Mrs. Carl Gillette, Gaylord • Mrs. Charles Glasser, Gaylord • Leda Glasser, Gaylord • Loretta Glasser, Gaylord • Eulah M. Gocha, Gaylord • Anna Goden, Gaylord • Carrie L. Goff, Johannesburg • Daisy Goodrich, Gaylord • Elsie Goslow, Gaylord • Mary Green, Gaylord Nina A. Griffith, Gaylord • Minnie Griswold, Gaylord • Ida Groesbeck, Gaylord • Rolyn Groesbeck, Gaylord • Mary E. Grosley, Gaylord • Mrs. Harold Grow, Gaylord • Jazela Gruszynski, Gaylord • Hazel Gust, Gaylord • Mrs. Thomas Gutteridge, Gaylord • Mrs. Sam Hagadorn, Gaylord • Mrs. Joe Hale, Gaylord • Rebecca Hall, Gaylord Winnifred Hall, Gaylord • Ella F. Hand, Gaylord • Frances Gunn, Gaylord • Minnie Hackert, Gaylord • Grace Haley, Gaylord • Lizzie Haller, Gaylord • Mary Hamilton, Gaylord • Marion Hanson, Gaylord • Lillian Harrington, Gaylord • Meirabell A. Harrington, Gaylord • Hannah Harris, Gaylord • Lillie Harris, Gaylord • Mrs. E. J. Harris, Gaylord • Mrs. L. A. Harris, Gaylord • Irean M. Hartzell, Gaylord • Anna Haskill, Gaylord • Mrs. David Haskell, Gaylord • Elizabeth Haskill, Gaylord • Mary Haskill, Gaylord • Lena Haskill, Gaylord • Sarah Haskill, Gaylord • Inez Heath, Gaylord • Lizzie Hecox, Gaylord • Mildred Herrick, Gaylord • Mrs. Earl Bass Hetherton, Gaylord • Anna Hicks, Gaylord • Lilla Hilton, Gaylord • Eleanor Hodges, Gaylord • Charlotte Honeywell, Gaylord • Cora House, Gaylord • Mary House, Gaylord • Bertha Howe • Mary Hoyt, Gaylord • Nellie Hoyt, Gaylord • Rev. W. Huck, Gaylord • Mrs. J. M. Hudson, Gaylord • Amelia Huey, Gaylord • Phoebe Huges, Gaylord • Flora E. Humphrey, Gaylord • Hattie Humphrey, Gaylord • Anna Hurd, Gaylord • Myrtle H. Hurd, Gaylord • Lou Ethel Hutchins, Gaylord Marguerite Lundeen Hutchins, Gaylord • Mary Hutchins, Gaylord • Alice Ikens, Gaylord Jennie Inman, Gaylord • Mary Ish, Gaylord • Agnes Jackson, Gaylord • Elizabeth Jackson, Gaylord • Lea Jackson, Gaylord • Mrs. Wendal Jackson, Gaylord • Etta Jacoby, Gaylord • Martha Jarisel, Gaylord • Marie Jarnuszkiew, Gaylord • Mrs. Frank Jarvenski, Gaylord • Mrs. Frank Jasinski, Gaylord • Gertie Jenkins, Gaylord • Mrs. William Jensen, Gaylord • Lizzie Johnson, Gaylord • Bertha Johnston, Gaylord • Flora Jones, Gaylord • Nancy R. Jones, Gaylord • Jessie Karslake, Gaylord • Mrs. Frank Katowski, Gaylord • Mary Kelley, Gaylord • Georgia Kelso, Gaylord • Inez Ketzheck, Gaylord • Ora Keyworth, Gaylord • Ruby Kimberly, Gaylord • Lula King, Gaylord • Selma E. King, Gaylord • Elta Kitchen, Gaylord • Mary Kline, Gaylord • Pearl C. Knapp, Gaylord • Mary Kobylezak, Gaylord • Stanislawa Kobylezak, Gaylord • Konstantine Kondralowicz, Gaylord • Loinda Koril, Gaylord • Bessie Kramer, Gaylord • Hazel V. Kramer, Gaylord • Lillian Kramer, Gaylord • Rae E. Kramer, Gaylord • Agnes Kugs, Gaylord • Mrs. Jacob Kujawa, Gaylord • Josephine Kwapis, Gaylord • Mrs. Stanley Kwapis, Gaylord • Mrs. Valentine Kwapis, Gaylord • Mrs. Frank Kyckileski, Gaylord • Mrs. Thomas Kyle, Gaylord • Mary Lambert, Gaylord • Mary Lang, Gaylord • Mrs. Peter Latuzsek, Gaylord • Martha Laubley, Gaylord • Kate Lawsk, Gaylord • Mildred Leachman, Gaylord • Mamie Lemons, Gaylord • Mrs. F. C. Leonard, Gaylord • Fern Leonard, Gaylord • Emma Libcke, Gaylord • Mabel Liggetti, Gaylord • Edith Linendoll, Gaylord • Lael Linendoll, Gaylord • Mrs. S. W. Lister, Gaylord • Cora Long, Gaylord • Pauline Long, Gaylord • Alice Lount, Gaylord • Mrs. A. Lorentz, Gaylord • Mrs. Frank Lorentz, Gaylord • Esther I. Losey, Gaylord • Hattie H. Losey, Gaylord • Mrs. Charles Lursaw, Gaylord • Mrs. M. C. Lux, Gaylord • Mrs. Edward Lynch, Gaylord • Nellie Lynch, Gaylord • Katherine Mackowiak, Gaylord • Blanche MacMillan, Gaylord • Catherine MacMillan, Gaylord • Mrs. Carl Madsen, Gaylord • Gilpha D. Mafford, Gaylord • Mary Mallsks, Gaylord • Ida E. Manier, Gaylord • Barbara Mankowski, Gaylord • Mrs. John Marcenkowski, Gaylord • Emma Marshall, Gaylord • Alice Mae Martin, Gaylord Cora Martin, Gaylord • Edith Martin, Gaylord • Lizzie Martindale, Gaylord • Ellen McDonald, Gaylord • Mrs. Alex McGeachey, Gaylord • Mrs. Donald McKenzie, Gaylord • Mrs. Georghe McKenzie, Gaylord • Mabel McKibbon, Gaylord • Elizabeth McKinnon, Gaylord • Mrs. Jeff McKinnon, Gaylord • Lydia McKinnon, Gaylord • Mrs. Verne Meade, Gaylord • Clare Meadsker, Gaylord • Alice R. Menzies, Gaylord • Daisy M. Menzies, Gaylord • Martha Merkiel, Gaylord • Mrs. Charles Merry, Gaylord • Lena Merry, Gaylord • Lillian Merry, Gaylord • Dora Meryers, Gaylord • Autie S. Miles, Gaylord • Mrs. J. Milford • Cora Miller, Gaylord • Mrs. J. C. Mills, Gaylord • Jennie F. Miner, Gaylord • Marie Miner, Gaylord • Eunice Mitchell, Gaylord • Ione Mitchell, Gaylord • Julia Mitchell, Gaylord • Mary Mitchell, Gaylord • Grace Moffitt, Gaylord • Mrs. James Montgomery, Gaylord • Florence I. Mooney, Gaylord • Cora D. Moore, Gaylord • Mrs. E. A. Moore, Gaylord • Grace I. Morford, Gaylord • Mae Morford, Gaylord • Mary Morgan, Gaylord •

OTSEGO COUNTY (CONTINUED)

Catherine Morrison, Gaylord • Martha Mothersell, Gaylord • Minnie Murray, Gaylord • Mrs. Wacel Narocki, Gaylord • Mrs. A. Neithereut, Gaylord • Esther Nelson, Gaylord • Stella Nessel, Gaylord • Maley Nestle, Gaylord • Louise Nevills, Gaylord • Anna Newsome, Gaylord • Mary Nicholl, Gaylord • Anna Nichols, Gaylord • Mrs. John Nichols, Gaylord • Mrs. Nield, Gaylord • Antonia Nietoerwicz, Gaylord • Mrs. Mike Nivaska, Gaylord Mrs. Frank Noa, Gaylord • Mary Nofsinger, Gaylord • Sylvia Norton, Gaylord • Brunislawa Nowaczy, Gaylord • Nettie E. Nowlin, Gaylord • Bessie O'Connor, Gaylord • Mrs. Fred Ogden, Gaylord • Gladys Ogden, Gaylord • Maud Ogden, Gaylord • Rhoda E. Olund, Gaylord • Nellie M. Osborn, Gaylord • Bessie Partie, Gaylord • Florence Peak, Big Rock • Maude Peck, Gaylord • Mattie Peck, Gaylord • Mrs. Otis Peck, Gaylord • Mrs. William Peck, Gaylord • Maggie Pelham, Gaylord • Mrs. H. Pelton, Gaylord • Emma Perry, Gaylord Mrs. George Pethers, Gaylord • Victoria Petroski, Gaylord • Jennie Phelps, Gaylord • Rose Piehl, Gaylord • Eliza Pike, Gaylord • Zadie Pines, Gaylord • Mrs. Anthony Pjut, Gaylord • Lizzie J. Power, Gaylord • Jennie Pratt, Gaylord • Florence Pressland, Gaylord • Maude Provost, Gaylord • Minnie Publow, Gaylord • Kate Purall, Gaylord • Rosa Purple, Gaylord • Mrs. Andrew Pyke, Gaylord • Lucy Qua, Gaylord • Mrs. Reuben Qua, Gaylord • Lillian Queal, Gaylord • Celia A. Quick, Gaylord • Mae Quick, Gaylord • Mrs. Adrian Quick, Gaylord • Mrs. Wilhelm Quick, Gaylord • Stella Ralston, Gaylord • Minnie Rankin, Gaylord • Laura E. Rather, Gaylord • Minnie Rhodes, Gaylord • Florence Rich, Gaylord • Lillian Rich, Gaylord • Ella M. Robbins, Gaylord • Mrs. William J. Rooke, Gaylord • Imogene Rowlander, Gaylord • Elsie Runnels, Gaylord • Emma C. Rupp, Gaylord • Elsie Rutan, Gaylord • Maggie Sanders, Gaylord • Alora Schlichter, Gaylord • Mrs. Myron Schoolcraft, Gaylord • Mrs. Allen Schreur, Gaylord • Mrs. Dirk Schreur, Gaylord • Sarah Schreur, Gaylord • Lucy Schuyler, Gaylord • Mrs. John Schuyler, Gaylord • Carrie Scott, Gaylord • Mrs. Wm. H. Scott, Gaylord • Belle Seiwell, Gaylord • Erma Seiwell, Gaylord • Alda Selleck, Gaylord • Clara B. Sellers, Gaylord • Lillie E. Sexton, Gaylord • Mabel Shannon, Gaylord • Mrs. J. H. Shell, Gaylord • May Shell, Gaylord • Julia Shepard, Gaylord • Vieva P. Shipp, Gaylord • Anna Shorey, Gaylord • Mrs. Francis Shravisski, Gaylord • Alice Simmons, Gaylord • Ella Simpson, Gaylord • Gertrude Sisson, Gaylord • Phoebe Skelton, Gaylord • Helena Skwiertz, Gaylord • Lavina Slade, Gaylord • Fannie Sly, Elmira • Vera Sly, Gaylord • Lilia Small, Gaylord • Mabel Smart, Gaylord • Elizabeth Smith, Gaylord • Emma Smith, Gaylord • Lottie Smith, Gaylord • Mary M. Smith, Gaylord • Sarah A. Smith, Gaylord • Helena Smolasz, Gaylord • Anna Soderburg, Gaylord • Cilina Soderburg, Gaylord • Nellie Soderburg, Gaylord • Mrs. Nels Soderburg, Gaylord • Mildred H. Soules, Gaylord • Mrs. C. W. Stafford, Gaylord • Sarah M. Starks, Gaylord • Annis M. Stevenson, Gaylord • Mabel Stevenson, Gaylord • Mrs. Arthur Stevenson, Gaylord • Jennie Stewart, Gaylord • Mary Stewart, Gaylord • Isa A. Stout, Gaylord • Mrs. Martin Strwynski, Gaylord • Mary Summerix, Gaylord • Mrs. John Summerland, Gaylord • Mrs. Frank Switalski, Gaylord • Josephine Szczipaniak, Gaylord • Jozela Szicinska, Gaylord • Mrs. F. Szocinski, Gaylord • Cecilia Szunanski, Gaylord • Grace Taylor, Gaylord • Marguerite Taylor, Gaylord • Marie Tcherberg, Gaylord • Mrs. George A. Teeter, Gaylord • Mary Teeter, Gaylord • Lizzie Thayer, Gaylord • Cora Thomas, Gaylord • Dolly Thomas, Gaylord • Ora A. Thumm, Gaylord • Elizabeth Tiller, Gaylord • Mrs. Francis Tiller, Gaylord • Vina Tinsman, Gaylord • Francis Tobias, Gaylord • Fannie A. Townsend, Gaylord • Marie Treichel, Gaylord • Elizabeth Troup, Gaylord • Mrs. Arthur Turner, Gaylord • Mrs. James Turner, Gaylord • Blanche Van Buren, Gaylord • Luella Van Doran, Gaylord • Hattie Van Duzen, Gaylord • Elsie A. Van Dyne, Gaylord • Helen Van Horn, Gaylord • Marguerite Van Horn, Gaylord • Eva Van Luven, Gaylord • Mrs. F. J. VonKraenel, Gaylord • Mary Wagner, Gaylord • Mary Walcak, Gaylord • Vera Walker, Gaylord • Ena L. Weaver, Gaylord • Mrs. Alex Weaver, Gaylord • Mrs. H. A. Webster, Gaylord • Cora E. Welch, Gaylord • Pearl B. Welch, Gaylord • Myrtle A. Wertman, Gaylord Louisa Werts, Gaylord • Ada S. Wertz, Gaylord • Mrs. O. W. Wertz, Gaylord • Abbie Western, Gaylord • Bertha Wheeler, Gaylord • Adelaide M. Wickett, Gaylord • Bessie E. Wickett, Gaylord • Edna Wickett, Gaylord • Lucille Wickett, Gaylord • Mrs. W. J. Wickett, Gaylord • Hattie E. Wicks, Gaylord • Mrs. C. E. Wilcox, Gaylord • Anna Wildfunn, Gaylord Pearl Wilks, Gaylord • Rose Willis, Gaylord • Nellie Wilson, Gaylord • Sarah Wilson, Gaylord • Mrs. Andrew Winiecka, Gaylord • Esther M. Winters, Gaylord • Leonie M. Winters, Gaylord • Nina E. Wise, Gaylord • Mabel Witherall, Gaylord • Mrs. Casmer Wojciekowski, Gaylord • Mrs. Jerry Wolcott, Gaylord • Emma Woodford, Gaylord • Mabel Woodrox, Gaylord • Bereniece Woodruff, Gaylord • Bertha Woods, Gaylord •

OTSEGO COUNTY (CONTINUED)

Ella Woodward, Gaylord • Sally Wotjkewiak, Gaylord • Ada A. Wright, Gaylord • Beulah Osborn Wright, Gaylord • Cora Wright, Gaylord • Bell Wyman, Gaylord • Ida Yuill, Gaylord • Mrs. John Yuill, Gaylord • Mrs. Thomas Yuill, Gaylord • Maryanna Zyski, Gaylord

OTTAWA COUNTY

Mrs. D. W. Andrews, Grand Haven • Margaret J. Bilz, Spring Lake • Mrs. C. C. Coburn, Grand Haven • Dwight Cutler • Emma Decator, Hudsonville • Gerrit J. Diekema, Holland • Mr. A. DeKenif, Zeeland • Mrs. R. N. Demerell, Holland • J. C. DenHerden, Zeeland • Hon. Thomas W. Ferry, Grand Haven • Hon. William C. M. Ferry, Grand Haven Elsie Gowdy, Holland • John Holkje, Zeeland • Grace Inman, Holland • Mr. A. LaHuis, Zeeland • Mrs. A. H. Landwehr, Holland • Mrs. Charles H. McBridge, Holland • Mrs. Nystrom, Holland • Margaret O'Brien, Grand Haven • Katherine Post, Holland • Mrs. J. C. Post, Holland • Mr. G. W. Rogers, Holland • W. C. Sheldon • Mrs. B. P. Sherwood, Grand Haven • Mrs. Charles R. Shupe, Grand Haven • Mrs. Ned B. Spencer, Nunica • Ned B. Spencer, Nunica • George H. Stickney, Grand Haven • Mr. F. Titus, Zeeland • Anna Whelan, Holland • Mrs. Van I. Witt, Grand Haven

PRESQUE ISLE COUNTY

Mrs. Merritt Chandler, Onaway

ROSCOMMON COUNTY

Cora M. Coon, Roscommon • Mr. Davis, Roscommon • Fred L. DeLamarter, Herbert • Mr. Hall, Roscommon

SAGINAW COUNTY

Mrs. O. Baker, Saginaw • Mrs. E. J. Baxter, Saginaw • Anna Beach, Bridgeport • Mrs. C. H. Becker, Saginaw • Mrs. George Benedict, Saginaw • Mrs. Charles Benjamin, Saginaw Mrs. Francis Bliss, Saginaw • Arthur Boone, Brant • Elsie Boone, Brant • Blanche Booth, Saginaw • John Boutin, Merrill • Mrs. Otto Bowser, Birch Run • Mrs. J. F. Boynton • Rev. N. S. Bradley, Saginaw • Mrs. C. E. Buell, Saginaw • Mr. W. P. Burdick • C. W. Cheeney, Chesaning • Mrs. Christian, Chesaning • Lizzie Crane, Brant • Mrs. Fred B. Crego, Saginaw • E. A. Crosby, Merrill • Mrs. W. B. Cubbage, Freeland • Mrs. Fred W. Culver • Hon. C. V. DeLand • Mr. J. F. Driggs, Saginaw • G. C. Eastwood, Saginaw • F. L. Eaton, Saginaw • David E. Ellis, Bridgeport • G. E. Ellis, Bridgeport • Kate V. English, Saginaw • Mrs. Eynon, Saginaw • Congressman Joseph W. Fordney, Saginaw • Mrs. Joseph W. Fordney, Saginaw • Mrs. Glover Gage, Saginaw • Mrs. Gamble • Louise Germain • Rev. Gibson, Chesaning • Mrs. E. W. Glynn, Saginaw • James Gordon, Merrill Mrs. James C. Graves, Saginaw • Mrs. C. H. Green • Mrs. Norris Grover, Merrill • Ella Hanks, Saginaw • Meta Peters Hedrick, Saginaw • Clara Hodgman, Bridgeport • Robert T. Holland, Saginaw • Etta Hunsberger, Saginaw • George Hunsberger, Bridgeport • Blanche Ingalls, Chesaning • Mrs. Irelalnd, Chesaning • Mrs. James H. Jerome, Saginaw Mrs. J. A. Keeler, Saginaw • Mrs. W. R. Kendrick, Saginaw • Mr. W. R. Kendrick, Saginaw • Mrs. C. A. Koehler, Saginaw • Ida Rust MacPherson, Bay City • Rev. J. M. McCarthy, Saginaw • Clara B. McClure • Mrs. C. W. McClure, Saginaw • Grace McClure, Saginaw • Mr. W. J. McCron • A. McDonald, Merrill • Mrs. James McNally, Saginaw • Evelyn Mershon • Irene Miner, Brant • Mrs. S. S. Mitts • Louise W. Moore • Mrs. S. C. J. Ostrom, Saginaw • Patrick O'Toole, Merrill • Mr. H. F. Paddock, Saginaw • Marcia Potter, Saginaw • Harriet Putnam, Saginaw • Mrs. Howard C. Richardson • Hon. Archibald Robertson, Saginaw • Mrs. Archibald Robertson, Saginaw • Mrs. William Robertson, Saginaw • Mrs. J. R. Sackett • Albert Seavyer, Bridgeport • Mrs. S. S. Smitts, Saginaw • Mrs. Harry R. Stark, Saginaw • Rev. Harry Stark, Saginaw • Mrs. F. F. Summers, Saginaw • Dr. D. H. Sutherland, Merrill • Ruth Symons • Mrs. A. H. Totten, Birch Run • Mrs. S. B. Tubbs, Saginaw • Hattie Turner, Saginaw • Mrs. W. Parke Warner • Mr. E. C. Warriner, Saginaw; Agnes Ermina Wells, Saginaw • Mrs. Whiting • Mrs. W. L. Whitney • Mrs. Earl F. Wilson • Edna Wright • Mrs. W. S. Wright, Saginaw • Mrs. F. Y. Wyncoop • Hon. H. M. Youmans, Bridgeport

SANILAC COUNTY

Mrs. O. H. Babcock, Sandusky • Mrs. George Brown, Carsonville • Mrs. E. E. Burget, Marlette • Colon Coldon, Croswell • Mrs. William Cook, Croswell • P. O. Decker, Carsonville • Mrs. J. W. Dexter, Croswell • Mr. J. W. Dexter, Croswell • Mrs. Victor Ford, Port Sanilac • Victor Ford, Port Sanilac • Mrs. J. H. Hanley, Marlette • Margaret Irving, Croswell • Rev. C. L. Keene, Carsonville • John Kipp, Lexington • Mrs. H. A. Macklin, Marlette • Mrs. C. C. McGregor, Carsonville • Mrs. John McIntyre, Croswell • Edith Meddeaugh, Crosville • Mrs. James P. Mugan • Mrs. A. R. Niles, Carsonville • F. G. Pomeroy, Croswell • Fred Raymond, Port Sanilac • Mrs. George E. Scott, Brown City

SCHOOLCRAFT COUNTY

Rev. E. R. Clark • Mr. J. L. Clark • Mrs. Perry Fletcher, Hiawatha • Mrs. Fred Graham, Manistique • James Nesbitt • Mrs. William Reed, Gulliver • Mrs. John Riley, Manistique • Fannie D. Stuart

SHIAWASSEE COUNTY

Flora Galligan, Laingsburg • Hon. J. M. Goodell • Mrs. Frank Greenman, Owosso • Mr. J. H. Hartwell • Lettie Higby, Perry • Mrs. Jones, Owosso • Dr. King • Hon. James M. McBride, Burton • Ann McCarty, Laingsburg • Dr. (Mrs.) Parkill • Mr. S. W. Pulver • Blanche Scoville, Perry • Jessie Ullrey

ST. CLAIR COUNTY

Lincoln Avery, Port Huron • Mrs. Lincoln Avery, Port Huron • Mrs. J. W. Berry, Marine City • Mrs. C. L. Boynton • Frances Brown, Port Huron • Mrs. Canty, Port Huron • Mary Coat, Capac • Elizabeth Cote, Port Huron • Mrs. B. F. Crampton, St. Clair • Mrs. Charles Doyle, Marine City • Mrs. J. Fitzgerald, Port Huron • Laura Weting Griffith, Port Huron • Edith Harvey, Port Huron • Harriet Hatch, Marine City • Hon. B. W. Jenks • Lily Lanridge, Algonac • Mrs. William Manley, Marine City • Mrs. H. R. Moore, Algonac • Emma O'Dell, Port Huron • Mrs. T. H. Parkinson, Yale • Mrs. S. A. Peck, Port Huron • Hon. Albert Stevenson, Port Huron • Mrs. George L. Ward, St. Clair • Bina M. West, Port Huron

ST. JOSEPH COUNTY

Mrs. Addison • Mrs. B. E. Andrews • Mrs. Charles Bateman, Three Rivers • Mrs. H. H. Beeman • Mrs. Bell • Dr. M. Britton • Rev. J. D. Brosy, Three Rivers • Mrs. Burdsell, Three Rivers • Mrs. R. M. Cauffman, Three Rivers • Mrs. W. A. Cavin, Sturgis • Mrs. John Comin • Mrs. Curtis • Ella Custard, Mendon • Lena Doll • Laura Driesbach • Fannie Dukette, Mendon • Florence Ellett • Mrs. James Ellett, Three Rivers • Miss Fairchilds, Three Rivers • Frances Fletcher, Mendon • Caroline Gibson, Constantine • Mrs. E. B. Gray, Sturgis • Dr. Blanche M. Haines, Three Rivers • Mrs. L. B. Hechelman, Mendon • Mr. L. B. Hechelman, Mendon • Helen Helm, Constantine • Mrs. Huss • Mrs. Robert Keith • Mrs. Clara Koch, Three Rivers • Mrs. William Kyte, Sturgis • Mr. W. S. Moore • Mrs. Charles Pashby, Constantine • Mary Peck • Mrs. W. C. Perin, Three Rivers • Mrs. L. B. Perrin, Three Rivers • Mrs. Phibbs, Three Rivers • Mrs. A. E. Porter, Three Rivers • Mrs. W. J. Predmore • Lelia Rachor, White Pigeon • May Rix, Three Rivers • Rebecca Shelly, Three Rivers • Mrs. E. E. Salisbury, Parkville • Mr. E. E. Salisbury, Parkville • Mrs. A. W. Scidmore, Three Rivers • Mrs. Taylor Simanton, Three Rivers • Bishop Simpson, Sturgis • Mrs. Charles Spence, Sturgis • Mrs. J. C. Tracy, Constantine • Mr. J. C. Tracy, Constantine • Mrs. Wilbur F. Thomas, Constantine • Mr. R. J. Wade, Three Rivers • Mrs. R. J. Wade, Three Rivers • Mrs. Nellie Walton, Three Rivers • Mrs. George Yaple, Mendon Judge George Yaple, Mendon

TUSCOLA COUNTY

Meta Gage Clark, Vassar • Mrs. Terry Corliss, Mayville • Sen. Terry Corliss, Mayville • Mr. A. S. Dyckman • Mr. Gallery, Caro • J. P. Hoyt • Mrs. H. J. Miller • Mr. H. J. Miller • Maud McComb Stilson • Mr. C. D. VanVechten • Mrs. C. D. VanVechten

VAN BUREN COUNTY

Rachel A. Bailey, Paw Paw • Hon. S. H. Blackman, Paw Paw • Mrs. M. D. Buskirk, Paw Paw Elnora Chamberlain, Hartford • Mrs. Albert Chase, South Haven • Mrs. Cornish • Mrs. Curtiss • Pauline T. Heald, Hartford • Katherine Herriman, South Haven •

VAN BUREN COUNTY (CONTINUED)

Belle Johnson, Paw Paw • Mecca Marie Varner, Paw Paw • Rev. Olivia J. Carpenter-Woodman, Paw Paw

WASHTENAW COUNTY

Mr. H. J. Abbott, Ann Arbor • Mrs. George B. Angell, Ann Arbor • Congressman S. W. Beakes, Ann Arbor • Mrs. S. W. Beakes, Ann Arbor • Mrs. Willis Bellows, Ypsilanti • Dr. Emma E. Bower, Ann Arbor • Jennie Buell, Ann Arbor • George Burke, Ann Arbor • Marshall Byrne, Ypsilanti • Mrs. John Campbell, Ypsilanti Township • Anna Caulfield, Ann Arbor • Leona Chamberlain, Ypsilanti • Mrs. P. R. Cleary, Ypsilanti • Mr. P. R. Cleary, Ypsilanti • Mrs. Albert Coe • Olive Cook, Milan • D. Cramer • Alice Crocker, Ann Arbor • Rev. Florence Kollock Crooker, Ann Arbor • Mrs. M. J. Davis, Ypsilanti • Mrs. de Nancrede, Ann Arbor • Mrs. A. L. De Green, Ypsilanti • Mrs. J. W. DeRatt, Ypsilanti • Estelle Downing, Ypsilanti • Florence Eldridge, Ypsilanti • Jennie Eldridge, Ypsilanti • Leona T. Field, Ann Arbor • Mary E. Foster • Laura Fountain, Ypsilanti • Jennie Gauntlett, Milan • Louise George, Ann Arbor • Mrs. S. W. George, Ypsilanti • Mrs. Conrad J. George, Sr., Ann Arbor • Mrs. Glaser, Ann Arbor • Mrs. Green, Ypsilanti • Leonora Grey, Milan • Marcia Hall, Ypsilanti • Olivia B. Hall, Ann Arbor • William B. Hatch, Ypsilanti • Mrs. William B. Hatch, Ypsilanti • Miss Haviland, Ann Arbor • Frances Hettich, Ypsilanti • Frances L. Hickok, Ann Arbor • Dr. Mary Hinsdale, Ann Arbor • Phebe Howell, Ann Arbor • Miriam Hubbard, Ann Arbor • Mrs. Richard Hurdley, Ypsilanti Mrs. L. L. James, Ypsilanti • Mrs. Mark Jefferson, Ypsilanti • Mrs. L. B. Johnson, Milan • Myra B. Jordan, Ann Arbor • Bert Kenny, Webster Township • Julia King, Ypsilanti • Miss Kinzey, Ypsilanti • Mrs. Theran S. Langford, Ann Arbor • Miss A. Langley, Ann Arbor • Sybil Lawrence, Ann Arbor • Rev. H. Addis Leeson, Ypsilanti • Mildred Lipe, Ypsilanti • Alice May Martin, Ypsilanti • Charles McKenny, Ypsilanti • Kathleen Mendenhall, Ypsilanti • Emma Minor, Ypsilanti • State Rep. Henry Wirt Newkirk, Ann Arbor • Mrs. Henry W. Newkirk, Ann Arbor • Georgia Owen • Mrs. George W. Patterson, Ann Arbor • Webster M. Pearce, Ypsilanti • Mrs. Frederick B. Perkins, Ann Arbor • Jessie Phelps, Ypsilanti • Dr. Elsie Pratt, Ann Arbor • Mrs. D. L. Quirk Jr., Ypsilanti • Mr. H. C. Rankin, Ypsilanti • Rev. S. Reed, Ann Arbor • Mrs. Seth Reed • Mrs. R. B. Rouse, Ypsilanti • Mrs. H. A. Sanders, Ann Arbor • Mr. T. J. Sanford, Ann Arbor • Mrs. T. J. Sanford, Ann Arbor • Helen Smith, Ypsilanti • Mr. J. L. Smith, Salem Township • Congressman J. M. Smith, Ann Arbor • Mrs. J. M. Smith, Ann Arbor • Rev. Bastien Smits, Ypsilanti • O. P. Stearns, Ann Arbor • Sarah Burger Stearns, Ann Arbor • Thelma Stevenson, Ypsilanti • Mrs. John S. P. Tatlock, Ann Arbor • Edward Turner, Ann Arbor • Mrs. C. F. Unterkircher, Saline • Mrs. Varney • Dr. Victor C. Vaughan, Ann Arbor • Mrs. Victor C. Vaughan, Ann Arbor • Mrs. John Waite, Ann Arbor • Mrs. F. C. Waldron, Ann Arbor • Mr. Chang Ping Wang, Ann Arbor • Dr. A. S. Warthin, Ann Arbor • Mrs. A. S. Warthin, Ann Arbor • Marian Wilson, Ann Arbor • Mr. George Wing, Scio Township • Eleanora Young, Milan

WAYNE COUNTY

Lawrence Abbott • May Leggett Abel • Mrs. Frederick Abel • Margaret Ableson • Myron A. Adams • Mrs. G. M. Aiken, Detroit • Mrs. Ralph Ainsworth, Detroit • Mrs. G. Edgar Allen, Detroit • Mary A. Alt, Detroit • Edith V. Alvord • Clara Blanche Arthur, Detroit • Lillian Ascough, Detroit • Delphine Dodge Ashbaugh • Louise Warrren Atkinson, Detroit • Georgia W. Austin, Detroit • Clara A. Avery, Detroit • Eloise Backus • Anna Bagg • Mrs. John J. Bagley, Detroit • Governor Bagley, Detroit • Catherine Baisley, Detroit • Buda Baker • Mrs. Frederick Balch • Martha Baldwin • Mrs. Carrie S. Ballin, Detroit • Dr. Gertrude Banks • Mrs. Noble Banks • Mrs. George H. Barbour • Levi L. Barbour • Mrs. James Bartlett, Detroit • G. W. Bates • Octavia W. Bates, Detroit • Miss Baxter • Dr. C. S. Beadle • Dr. Helen Beadle, Detroit • Jennie E. M. Bean • Mrs. C. U. Bear, Detroit • Jennie Patton Beatie, Detroit • Mr. Berman, Detroit • Frank Bigler, Detroit • Mrs. Frank Bigler, Detroit • Emily M. Birmingham, Detroit • Mrs. John Bischoff, Detroit • Emma H. Black, Detroit • Mrs. William J. Black, Detroit • Father Henri Blanchot, Detroit • Warren Blauvelt • Leah Bleazby, Detroit • Mrs. Walter Blinn, Detroit • Mrs. William H. Blodgett, Detroit • Mrs. Louis D. Bolton • Jessie Bonstelle, Detroit • Minnie E. Booth, Detroit • Alice M. Boutell, Detroit • Mrs. Norman G. Bowbeer, Wyandotte • Dr. Emma Bower, Detroit • Mrs. A. G. Boynton, Detroit • Esther Boynton, Detroit • Isabel G. Brewer, Detroit • Lotta B. Broadbridge, Detroit • Z. R. Brockway • Barbara Brooks, Detroit •

Mrs. J. M. Brooks, Detroit • Marian E. Bross • Florence Belle Brotherton, Detroit • May Brownell • Mary Brumfield, Detroit • Aileen K. Buchanan, Detroit • Lou F. Buller, Detroit Winifred G. Burdick, Detroit • Mary E. Burnett, Detroit • Frances E. Burns, Detroit • Mrs. Charles Burnside • Maude Burrows • Dr. Richard Burton • Mrs. C. E. Butterfield • Minnie Cage, Detroit • Mrs. Adolphe Caille • Mrs. E. B. Calkins, Detroit • Bertha Callahan, Detroit • Elizabeth A. Callahan, Detroit • Miss Campbell • Colin Campbell, Detroit • Mrs. Frank Carleton, Detroit • Mrs. G. G. Caron, Detroit • Hattie Carstens, Detroit • May B. Carvin • Clara N. Caswell, Detroit • Dr. Charles Chadsey, Detroit • Mrs. Charles Chadsey, Detroit • Mrs. R. C. Chase • Mrs. Ralph E. Chedister, Detroit • Miss Lesley Church, Detroit • Mabel M. Clark, Detroit • Mary Strickland Clark, Detroit • Mrs. E. H. Coatsworth, Detroit • Euphemia Cochrane, Detroit • Mary Stuart Coffin, Detroit • Dr. Stanton Coit • Mrs. Ralph E. Collins, Detroit • May Condgeau, Detroit • George M. Condon, Detroit • Mrs. Hugh Connolly, Detroit • Anna L. Cooley, Detroit • Mrs. Robert Cooper, River Rouge • James Couzens • Leila Corn, Detroit • Anna Corbett, Detroit • Josephine Costigan, Detroit • Laura Cramer, Detroit • Mary Cryderman • Mrs. Arthur Cushman • August Cyroski, Detroit • Florence Davies • Mrs. Emerson Davis, Detroit • Lillian E. Davis, Detroit • Marion B. Davis • May Demer, Detroit • Louise B. Denton, Detroit • Mrs. Russell Dexter • Elizabeth Sackett Dixon, Detroit • Mary T. Dohany, Detroit • Rev. J. G. Doherty, Detroit • Lena Harris Doty • Lucy Lockwood Stout Dowd, Northville • Mr. E. H. Doyle, Detroit • Alberta Droelle, Detroit • Dr. Francis Duffield • Helen Muir Duffield, Detroit • Mrs. A. O. Dunk, Detroit • Edith Dunk • William T. Dust, Detroit • Clara E. Dyar, Detroit • Mrs. John B. Dyar • Dorothy Earle, Detroit • Mrs. Frank Eastman, Detroit • Frances Ellair, Detroit • Georgia Emery • Mrs. John Everson, Detroit Agnes Stevens Farrell, Detroit • Lillian Feldman, Detroit • William Muir Finck, Detroit • Julia Finster, Detroit • Mrs. O. E. Fischer • Charles Flowers, Detroit • Margaret Foley • Mary B. Folsom, Detroit • Rev. Joseph Folta • Mrs. John B. Ford • Lena B. Forest • Emma Augusta Fox, Detroit • Rabbi Franklin • Mrs. Frazee, Detroit • Ada Freeman • Alta Fulchur • Hazel Furman, Detroit • Alex A. Gage, Detroit • Mrs. Alex A. Gage, Detroit • Nannette B. Ellingwood Gardner, Detroit • Bess Garner, Detroit • Mrs. E. Gerard, Detroit • Catherine R. Gilchrist, Detroit • Elizabeth Goan, Detroit • Mrs. William H. Gordon, Detroit • Nettie Gorton, Detroit • Maybelle Gorthey, Detroit • Helen M. Green, Detroit • Thomas C. Greenwood, Detroit • Mabel S. Greenwood, Detroit • Lucia Voorhees Grimes, Detroit • Emily Grimes, Detroit • George L. Grimes, Detroit • Mary Hamilton Grosvenor, Detroit • Mrs. H. J. Maxwell Grylles, Detroit • Henry A. Haigh • Mrs. Andrew Hair, Detroit • Kate Hargreaves • Katherine Harrow, Detroit • Olive Hart • Mrs. Henry J. Hartz, Detroit • Mrs. J. F. Hartz, Detroit • Caroline Harvey • Mrs. James R. Hayes • Mae Hayes, Detroit • Mrs. Leon Haywood • Mr. D. J. Healy • Mrs. Henderson, Detroit • Mrs. Thomas Henderson, Detroit • George T. Hendrie • Kathleen Hendrie, Detroit • Mabel G. Herald, Detroit • Catherine Herlehy, Detroit • Clara C. Hickey, Detroit • Frederica Higbee, Detroit • Elizabeth S. Hitchcock • Lyda Hitchcock • Mrs. Floyd Hitchcock • Mrs. Charles H. Hodges, Detroit • Charles H. Hodges, Detroit • Mrs. Luther Hoffman • Mrs. William S. Holman, Detroit • Frederick Holt, Detroit • Lillian Silk Holt, Detroit • Julia Horton • Mr. J. B. Howarth, Detroit • Hon. W. N. Hudson • Rev. Percival Huget, Detroit • Augusta Hughston • Olive E. Hulburt, Detroit • Isabella Hull, Detroit • Edith Hume, Detroit • Harry E. Hunt, Detroit • Mrs. W. I. Hunt • Alexandria Hurst • Isabel Hurst • Helen Hyland, Detroit • Jennie A. Jackson, Detroit • Col. Oscar Janes • Mrs. Edward J. Jeffries, Detroit • Grace Jeffries • Minnie Stott Jeffries, Detroit • Mrs. Andrew Jelly • Helen Philleo Jenkins, Detroit • Mrs. George Johnston, Detroit • Mrs. S. L. Jones, Detroit • Dr. S. L. Jones, Detroit • Mrs. Fred Jotham, Detroit • Josephine Nevins Keal, Detroit • Mary Keil, Detroit • Rose Keller, Detroit • U. S. Rep. Patrick H. Kelley • Katherine Kennedy, Detroit • Ann F. Kinney, Detroit • Mrs. Otto Kirchner, Detroit • Otto Kirchner, Detroit • Bertha A. Koon, Detroit • Angela Kosanski, Detroit • Arthur Koscinski, Detroit • Mrs. F. S. Kratzet, Detroit • Mrs. Henry A. Krolik, Detroit • Irene F. Lamm, Detroit • Mrs. H. A. Langell, Detroit • Sara J.ane La Tour, Detroit • Mrs. Franklin Latham, Detroit • J. Fred Lawton, Detroit • Mr. E. O. Lee • Mrs. Ernest Lee, Detroit • Elizabeth Seaman Leggett • Lucy A. Leggett, Detroit • Frank B. Leland, Detroit • Mrs. Frank B. Leland, Detroit • Rev. Joseph Lempke, Detroit • Mrs. E. S. Leonard, Detroit • Melba M. Levin, Detroit • Ella Levine • Gladys Lloyd • Mrs. Horace Lobenstine • Mrs. Howard Longyear • Minnie C. Loud, Detroit • Helen MacDonald, Detroit • Lelah MaCauley, Detroit • Mrs. John E. MacDonough • Jean MacLennan, Detroit •

Margaret Mannebach • Rev. Samuel Marquis, Detroit • Theresa D. Marsano, Detroit •
Mrs. W. L. Marsh, Detroit • Alice Martin • Stevens T. Mason • Mrs. Stevens T. Mason •
Mrs. Frank Mathauer, Detroit • Lillian Matthews, Detroit • Emilie L. Max, Detroit • Rev.
W. D. Maxon, Detroit • Rev. Lee McCollister, Detroit • Frances McFarland, Detroit • Lizzie
Parker McCollister, Detroit • Mrs. Alex McDonald • Mrs. R. G. McDonnell • Harriet Story
McFarlane • Mrs. C. C. McGlogan, Detroit • Mrs. Monroe McGrath • Harriet Robinson
McGraw, Detroit • Annie McIntyre, Detroit • Mrs. P. S. McMahon, Detroit • Augusta
Meiser • Mrs. Charles Metcalf, Detroit • Jessie Miller, Detroit • Matilda Mitchell, Detroit •
Mrs. • W. E. Moss, Grosse Pointe • Selah W. Mullen, Detroit • Aleta Munger, Detroit •
Phoebe C. Munnecke, Detroit • Alfred Murphy, Detroit • Alicia Nangle, Detroit • Rilla A.
Nelson, Detroit • Mrs. Frank L. Newman, Detroit • Nesta Newman, Detroit • Vesta
Newman, Detroit • Mrs. Wesley Nutten • Robert Y. Ogg • Mrs. Robert Y. Ogg, Detroit •
Mrs. James O'Halloran, Detroit • Carrie Church Oostdyk, Detroit • Dr. Louise Orleman
Kathleen Ortisi, Detroit • Laura F. Osborne, Detroit • Liza Osterholm, Detroit •
Gertrude E. Oswald, Detroit • Agnes Palmer, Detroit • U. S. Sen. Thomas W. Palmer,
Detroit • Mr. W. T. Parker • Julia Parker, Detroit • Robert Parket, Detroit • Hatti
Urbanowica Pasternacki, Detroit • Nellie Stanley Payne, Detroit • Eleanor Hazard
Peacock, Detroit • Gertrude Pelletier, Detroit • Ida May Peppers, Detroit • Gov. Hazen S.
Pingree, Detroit • Mrs. Gustavus Pope, Detroit • Mrs. Willard Pope • Mrs. Sterling E.
Porter, Detroit • Phyllis Povah, Detroit • Louella E. Pruett, Detroit • Mrs. Quinn, Detroit
Mrs. P. F. Reuss, Detroit • Betsy Graves Reyneau, Detroit • Grace Palmer Rice • Detroit
Mrs. J. C. Rice-Wray • June Richards, Detroit • Peggy Riley • Jane Bancroft Robinson,
Detroit • Ethel Rowe • Helen Rozanska, Detroit • Rosa Rozanska • Della Runkel, Detroit
Elise Russian, Detroit • Mrs. W. R. Rutson • Kate Ryric, Detroit • Alice M. Salmoni,
Detroit • Mrs. Morris Sample, Detroit • Sarah Bradshaw Sampson, Detroit • Mrs. Joseph
Sanders, Detroit • Emelia Schaub, Detroit • Florence Schemel, Detroit • James
Schermerhorn, Detroit • Augusta Schober, Detroit • Mrs. E. H. Sellers, Detroit • Susan
Macklem Sellers, Detroit • Geraldine Sheehan, Detroit • Mrs. Alfred Sheppard, Detroit •
Mrs. Henry G. Sherrard, Detroit • Rev. Eugene Shippen, Detroit • Mrs. Eugene R.
Shippen, Detroit • Valerie Shissler, Detroit • Dorothy Simmons, Detroit • Mrs. Don
Simpson, Detroit • Mrs. H. L. Simpson, Detroit • Sarah Skinner, Detroit • Harriet
Smalley • Mrs. James Smith, Detroit • John W. Smith, Detroit • George B. Smith,
Detroit • Lillian Snedicor, Detroit • Florence J. Spaulding, Detroit • Hinton E.
Spaulding, Detroit • Dr. Anna Starring, Detroit • Mrs. A. Stearns • Mrs. Frederick
Stearns, Detroit • Mrs. Isaac Stearns, Detroit • Catharine A. Fish Stebbins, Detroit •
Giles B. Stebbins, Detroit • Eloise Steele, Detroit • Mrs. Henry Steffens, Detroit •
Theresa Steffens • Dr. Mary Thompson Stevens, Detroit • Dr. Rollin H. Stevens • Mrs.
Stanley G. Stevens • Grace Stiles, Detroit • Mrs. J. A. Stilson, Detroit • Mrs. E. W.
Stoddard• Mrs. Rae Stralse • Martha Strickland, Detroit • Mrs. Sullivan • Aulga Sutterly,
Detroit • Allan A. Templeton, Detroit • Mrs. Allan A. Templeton, Detroit • Dr. Marie
Timpona, Detroit • Mrs. Harold H. Tireman, Detroit • Margaret Tireman, Detroit • Julia
E. Todt, Detroit • Mrs. E. A. Torrey, Detroit • Harriet Trix, Detroit • John Trix, Detroit •
Mrs. M. G. Tryon • Mrs. J. C. Tufford, Detroit • Esther Urbanowica, Detroit • Dr. Lucy
Utter, Detroit • Mrs. Calvin Pitts Vary, Detroit • Joseph Vedda, Detroit • Augusta Voight
Johanna Von Wagner • Paul Voorhees • Ethel Ridgely Vorce, Detroit • Mattie B.
Walburn, Detroit • George Harmon Waldo, Detroit • Mrs. James E. Walsh, Detroit •
Mary Waring, Detroit • Isabella H. Warnke, Detroit • Major Charles B. Warren, Detroit •
Mrs. F. W. Waterworth, Detroit • Mrs. John Watling • Eva A. Werbe, Detroit • Mrs. J. D.
Werner, Detroit • Mrs. West, Detroit • Mrs. Carl Whipple, Detroit • Mrs. Morris J. White •
Whitney Family, Detroit • Mrs. James Whittemore, Detroit • Mrs. L. J. Whittemore,
Detroit • Margaret Faye Whittemore, Detroit • Marjorie M. Whittemore • Mrs. Wright
Nelson Whittemore, Detroit • Ora Wickersham, Detroit • Willamene Wilkes, Detroit •
Rev. Wilkowski, Detroit • Rt. Rev. Charles D. Williams, Detroit • Mrs. Charles D.
Williams, Detroit • Elizabeth Williamson, Detroit • Mrs. C. R. Wilson, Detroit • Mrs.
Phillip Wilson, Detroit • Adele Winslow • Mrs. George Wright, Detroit • Mrs. John Wright
Zaio A. Woodford, Detroit • Mrs. Edward F. Wunsch, Detroit • Ruby Zahn, Detroit •
Florence B. Ziegler, Detroit • Thomas Zoltowski, Detroit

WEXFORD COUNTY

Ella Thorn Burritt, Cadillac • Mrs. F. E. Cornwell, Cadillac • Mrs. Delos F. Diggins, Cadillac • Miles Hunt, Meauwataka • Lillian Kelley, Cadillac • Mrs. Earl McNitt, Cadillac • Mrs. H. E. McNitt, Cadillac • Mrs. William Mitchell, Cadillac • Hon. Perry F. Powers, Cadillac • Arista M. Wardell, Cadillac • Elizabeth Yost, Cadillac

NAMES NOT IDENTIFIED BY COUNTY

Marie B. Ames • Mrs. Dean Atcheson • N. Kate Bachus • Frances Baglels • Hon. Thomas Barkworth • Sen. John W. Belknap • Crystal Eastman Benedict • Mrs. T. Benson • Allaseba M. Bliss • Leonore Starker Bliss • Lila E. Bliss • J. B. Bloss • State Rep. Norris J. Brown • Sen. C. J. Brundage • Mary E. Burnett • Lt. Gov. Archibald Butters • Elizabeth Byers • Sen. Fremont G. Chamberlain • Annie D. Clark • B. F. Cocker • Mary Stuart Coffin • Ann Coleman • State Rep. Rowland Connor • Harriet A. Cook • State Rep. Dr. James B. F. Curtis • Father W. J. Dalton • Alice Danziger • Mrs. J. C. Dexter • Hon. John Donovan • Elizabeth Eaglesfield • Adam Elder • Wesley Emery • Hon. William S. Farmer Carrie C. Faxon • Rev. Richmond Fiske • D. M. Fox • Sen. Edwin G. Fox • Mrs. Wallace Frost • Charlotte J. Garrison • Sen. Arthur D. Gilmore • James B. Goff • State Rep. John V. B. Goodrich • Joseph Greusel • Edith Frances Hall • Elizabeth Boynton Harbert • Brent Harding • Dr. Isabella Holdum • Delisle P. Holmes • Sen. Samuel W. Hopkins • George B. Horton • Rep. Theodore G. Houk • Mrs. Andrew Howell • Margaret M. Huckins Grant M. Hudson • Mary A. Jewett • Dr. L. H. Jones • Jane M. Kinney • Mrs. Otto Kirchner • Judge Edwin Lawrence • Dr. Charlotte Levanway • Alice B. Locke • Rev. J. S. Loveland • Gov. Cyrus G. Luce • Florence Mayhew • Sen. Charles H. McGinley • Sen. Joseph R. McLaughlin • Rhea Miller • State Rep. Samuel Miller • Florence G. Mills • State Sen. Alfred Milnes • State Sen. Charles J. Monroe • Mrs. W. Morley • Mr. J. B. Mulliken • Mrs. Thomas Munger • Amos Musselman • Jessie Nicol • Gov. Chase Salmon Osborn • Frances Ostander • State Rep. Russell R. Pealer • Annie Smith Peck • Mrs. W. E. Praeger • State Rep. James A. Randall • Gov. John T. Rich • Frances Riddle • Meloin A. Root • Emma J. Rose • Elsie Russian • Dr. Walter H. Sawyer • Dr. E. L. Shirley • Sara Philleo Skinner • Grant Slocum • Minnie Smith • Laura Grover Smith • State Rep. Oliver S. Smith • Florence Jenkins Spalding • Lucy T. Stansell • Mrs. James Starkweather • Eloise C. Steele • Mrs. Charles Steele • Lt. Gov. John Strong • State Rep. Thomas C. Taylor • Miss M. Fitzhugh Thomas • State Sen. Edward H. Thompson • Charles Townsend • Lola C. Trax • Sen. James D. Turnbull • Coit Tyler • Mrs. Myron B. Vorce • Mr. Wait • Nellie Walker • Emily Ward • State Rep. Henry Watson • Sen. Dwight Web • Mrs. H. M. Wells • Carl Young

****

"Resolved, That it is the duty of the women of this country to secure to themselves their sacred right to the elective franchise."

**Ninth Resolution of the First Women's Rights Convention
Seneca Falls, New York, July 29, 1848**

****

"1. The right of citizens of the United States to vote shall not be denied or abridged by the United States or by any State on account of sex.

2. Congress shall have the power to enforce this Article by appropriate legislation."

**The Nineteenth Amendment to the Constitution
Ratified August 26, 1920**

****

LIST OF SOURCES

Sources for information in the biographical entries are symbolized by the following code numbers in the Reference sections of the entries.

BOOKS AND PERIODICALS

Code
Number

1   Agenda. Ann Arbor, Michigan.

2   Alger County: A Centennial History, 1885-1985. Munising: Alger County Historical Society, 1985.

3   Angus, Esther T. Wolfe. What's Past is Prologue: Swainsville and Brooklyn, 1832-1914. Brooklyn: The Exponent Press, 1962.

4   Ann Arbor News. Ann Arbor, Michigan.

5   Ann Arbor Observer. Ann Arbor, Michigan.

6   Argus Press. Owosso, Michigan.

7   Bernhardt, Marcia Webster. Carrie Jacobs-Bond: As Unpretentious As the Wild Rose. Caspian: Iron County Museum, 1978.

8   Black Women in America: An Historical Encyclopedia. Edited by Darlene Clark Hine. Two vols. Brooklyn, New York: Carlson Publishing, Inc., 1993.

9   Bob Miles' Charlevoix: A Century in Pictures. Charlevoix: Hillison and Etten Co.

10 Born From Iron: Iron Mountain, Michigan, 1879-1979. Iron Mountain, Michigan, 1979.

11 Bordin, Ruth. Washtenaw County: An Illustrated History. Northridge, California: Windsor Publications, 1988.

12 Bratt, James D. and Christopher H. Meehan. Gathered at the River: Grand Rapids, Michigan, and Its People of Faith. Grand Rapids: William B. Eerdmans Publishing Co., 1993.

13 Brinks, Herbert J. Pine Rest Christian Hospital: 75 Years, 1910-1985.

14 The Bulletin. Michigan Dental Hygienists Assocation.

15 Caruso, Virginia Ann Paganelli. "A History of Woman Suffrage in Michigan." Ph.D. dissertation, Michigan State University, 1986.

16 Christian Science Monitor. Boston, Massachusetts.

17 Citizens Quality Time. Ann Arbor: Citizens Insurance Company of America.

18 Clifford, Mary Louise and J. Candace Clifford. Women Who Kept the Lights: An Illustrated History of Female Lighthouse Keepers. Williamsburg, Virginia: Cypress Communications, 1993.

19 The Club Woman. Detroit: Detroit Federation of Women's Clubs.

20 Crathern, Alice Tarbell. Courage Was the Fashion: The Contribution of Women to the Development of Detroit from 1701 to 1951. Detroit: Wayne University Press, 1953.

21 Daily Telegram. Adrian, Michigan.

22 Detroit Free Press. Detroit, Michigan.

23 Detroit Free Press Magazine. Detroit, Michigan.

24 Detroit Metropolitan Woman. Southfield, Michigan.

25 Detroit News. Detroit, Michigan.

26 Detroit News Magazine. Detroit, Michigan.

27 Detroit Teacher. Detroit: Detroit Federation of Teachers.

28 Detroit Times. Detroit, Michigan.

29 Fedderson, Christian T. Scandinavians in Michigan, Vol. I. Romeo: 1968.

30 The Flint Journal Picture History of Flint. Edited by Lawrence R. Gustin. Grand Rapids: William B. Eerdmans Publishing Co., 1976.

31 Focus. Lansing: Women Lawyers Association of Michigan.

32 Focus: EMU. Ypsilanti: Eastern Michigan University.

33 Fox, Jean M., with John B. Cameron. A Farmington Childhood: The Watercolors of Lillian Drake Avery. Farmington Hills: Farmington Hills Historical Commission 1985.

34 Frames for the Future: Iron River Area. Edited by Marcia Webster Bernhardt. Iron River: Iron County Historical and Museum Society, 1981.

35 Frimodig, David Mac. Keweenaw Character: The Foundation of Michigan's Copper Country Lake Linden: John H. Forster Press, 1990.

36 Gauthier, Doris A. Alcona: The Women Pioneers. Harrisville, Michigan, n.d.

37 Gibson, Arthur Hopkin. Artists of Early Michigan. Detroit: Wayne State University Press, 1975.

38 Giese, Elizabeth Homer. Michigan Women's Suffrage: A Political History. Lansing: Michigan Political History Society and Michigan Women's Studies Association.

39 Grand Ledge Independent. Grand Ledge, Michigan.

40 Grand Rapids Magazine. Grand Rapids, Michigan.
41 Grand Rapids Press. Grand Rapids, Michigan.
42 Grand River Times. Grand Rapids, Michigan.
43 Grand River Valley History Grand Rapids, Michigan.
44 Harley, Rachel Brett and Betty MacDowell. Michigan Women: Firsts and Founders. Lansing: Michigan Women's Studies Association, 1992.
45 Headlight [Souvenir edition]: Sights and Scenes, Chicago to New York. Chicago: 1895-97.
46 Hill, Jack. History of Iron County, Michigan. Iron County: The Iron County Historical and Museum Society, n.d.
47 Hilton, Miriam. Northern Michigan University: The First 75 Years. Marquette: The Northern Michigan University Press, 1975.
48 Historic Michigan. Edited by George Newman Fuller and Byron Alfred Finney. Dayton, Ohio: National Historical Association, c. 1924.
49 A History of the Michigan State Federation of Women's Clubs, 1895-1953. Compiled by Blanche Blynn Maw. Ann Arbor: Ann Arbor Press, 1953.
50 Illustrated Detroit. Detroit, Michigan.
51 Inside Michigan. Ann Arbor, Michigan.
52 Katz, Irving I. and Jacob R. Marcus. The Beth-El Story. Detroit: Wayne University Press, 1955.
53 Kuhn, Madison. Michigan State: The First Hundred Years, 1855-1955. East Lansing: Michigan State University Press, 1955.
54 Lansing Magazine. East Lansing, Michigan.
55 Lansing Metropolitan Magazine. Lansing, Michigan.
56 Lansing Metropolitan Woman. East Lansing, Michigan.
57 Lansing State Journal. Lansing, Michigan.
58 Livingston County Press. Howell, Michigan.
59 Lochbiler, Don. Detroit's Coming of Age, 1873-1973. Detroit: Wayne State University Press, 1973.
60 Longcore, Kathleen. Chadwick-Munger: The Story of a House, 1892-1986. Hart: Oceana County Historical Society, 1986.
61 Lowe, Berenice Bryant. Tales of Battle Creek. The Albert L. and Louise B. Miller Foundation, 1976.
62 Ludington Daily News. Ludington, Michigan.
63 Lund, Robert. ABRACADABRA: Michigan and Magic. Ann Arbor: Historical Society of Michigan, 1991.

64   Mackinac Island Town Crier. Mackinac Island, Michigan.

65   Magoon, Johanna Meijer. "The First Meijer Stores." Unpublished manuscript. Ypsilanti, Michigan.

66   Markel, Robert and Nancy Brooks. For the Record. New York: World Almanac Publications, 1985.

67   Marlow, Joan. The Great Women. New York: A & W Publishers, Inc., 1979.

68   McGuigan, Dorothy Gies. A Dangerous Experiment: 100 Years of Women at the University of Michigan. Ann Arbor: Center for Continuing Education of Women, 1970.

69   Metropolitan Woman. Detroit, Michigan.

70   Michigan Bar Journal. Lansing: Michigan Bar Association.

71   Michigan Chronicle. Detroit, Michigan.

72   Michigan Counties. Lansing, Michigan.

73   Michigan Daily. Ann Arbor: University of Michigan.

74   Michigan History. Lansing: Michigan Department of State.

75   Michigan Manual of Freedmen's Progress. Compiled by Francis H. Warren. Detroit: 1915.

76   Michigan Monthly. Ann Arbor, Michigan.

77   Michigan Suffragist. Kalamazoo, Michigan.

78   Michigan Today   Ann Arbor: The University of Michigan.

79   Michigan Township News. Lansing, Michigan.

80   Michigan Voter. Lansing: Michigan League of Women Voters.

81   Michigan Woman. Detroit, Michigan.

82   Michigan Women. Lansing: Michigan Women's Commission.

83   Michigan Women in the Civil War. Michigan Civil War Centennial Observance Commission, 1963.

84   Michigan Women's Times. Kalamazoo, Michigan.

85   Miller, Ed. The Saginaw Hall of Fame. Saginaw: The Saginaw County Bicentennial Commission, 1976.

86   Mining Journal. Marquette, Michigan.

87   Monette, Clarence J. The History of Copper Harbor, Michigan. Lake Linden: Welden H. Curtin, 1976.

88   _____. The History of Eagle River, Michigan. Lake Linden: Welden H. Curtin, 1978.

89   Moon, Elaine Latzman. Untold Tales, Unsung Heroes: An Oral History of Detroit's African American Community, 1918-1967. Detroit: Wayne State University Press, 1994.

90   MSU Alumni Magazine. East Lansing: MSU Alumni Association.

91 MSU News Bulletin. East Lansing: Michigan State University.

92 MSU Today. East Lansing: Michigan State University.

93 Nagel, Elizabeth J. and Mary Jo Wilson. Peter Riley'
    Reserve: A Commemorative History of Carollton Township.
    Saginaw. Saginaw: Dornbos Press, 1976.

94 New Center News. Detroit, Michigan.

95 Notable Hispanic American Women. Edited by Diane Telgen
    and Jim Kamp. Detroit: Gale Research, Inc., 1993.

96 Olson, Gordon. In the Name of All Marys: A History of the
    Mary Free Bed Hospital and Rehabilitation Center. Grand
    Rapids: The Mary Free Bed Guild, 1991.

97 Outstanding Women of Barry County. Compiled, written and
    published by the Hastings Branch of the American
    Association of University Women. Hastings: 1976.

98 Pathways to Michigan's Black Heritage. Lansing: Michigan
    Department of State, 1988.

99 People Magazine. New York, New York.

100 Popular Photography. New York, New York.

101 Portrait and Biographical Album of Barry and Eaton Counties,
    Mich. Chicago: Chapman Bros, 1892.

102 "Profiles of Historic Women." Researched by the East Lansing
    Area Zonta Club. Compiled by Elizabeth Driscoll & Sue
    Neller. Unpublished manuscript.

103 Read, Phyllis J. and Bernard L. Witlieb. The Book of
    Women's Firsts. New York: Random House, 1992.

104 Salute to Ingham County Women of Accomplishment.
    Lansing: Ingham County Women's Commission, 1976.

105 Saginaw News. Saginaw, Michigan.

106 Scene Magazine. Battle Creek, Michigan.

107 Siegel, Beatrice. Murder On the Highway: The Viola Liuzzo
    Story. New York: Four Winds Press, 1993.

108 Smithsonian. Washington, D.C.: Smithsonian Associates.

109 Stephenson, O. W. Ann Arbor: The First 100 Years. Ann
    Arbor: The Alumni Press of the University of Michigan, 1927.

110 St. Louis Leader. St. Louis, Michigan.

111 The Swedish-Americans of the Year. Karlstad, Sweden: Press
    Forlag, 1982.

112 Towne Courier. Mason: Ingham Newspaper Company.

113 Traverse City Record-Eagle. Traverse City, Michigan.

114 Van Valkenburgh, Mills M. The American Legion in Michigan.
    Port Huron: Riverside Printing Co., 1930.

115 Ypsilanti Press. Ypsilanti, Michigan.
116 Wait, S. E. and W. S. Anderson. Old Settlers of the Grand
     Traverse Region. Traverse City: 1918. Reprinted, Grand
     Rapids: Black Letter Press, 1978.
117 Wayne State Magazine. Detroit: Wayne State University.
118 Woman. Grand Rapids, Michigan.
119 A Woman of the Century. Edited by Frances E. Willard and
     Mary E. Livermore. Charles Wells Moulton, 1893.
120 Woman's Art Journal. Knoxville, Tennessee.
121 Women of Bay County: 1809-1980. Edited by Joan Totten
     Musinsky Rezmer. Bay City: The Museum of the Great Lakes,
     1980.

OTHER SOURCES

122 Arnett, Alinda R. Kellogg's Archives. Kellogg
     Company/Corporate Headquarters. Battle Creek, Michigan.
123 Ash, Edith. Osseo, Michigan.
124 Bach Family Vertical File Folder. Bentley Historical Library.
     University of Michigan. Ann Arbor, Michigan.
125 Baker, Louise. Bethany Christian Services. Grand Rapids,
     Michigan.
126 Baxter, Melva J. East Lansing, Michigan.
127 Becker, Audrey. Palm Harbor, Florida.
128 Bernhardt, Marcia W. Iron County Historical and Museum
     Society. Caspian, Michigan.
129 Boving, Renee Laya. Northville, Michigan.
130 Brater, Elizabeth R. Ann Arbor, Michigan.
131 Brodbent, Mildred Carolyne. Florida.
132 Brotherton Papers, Florence Belle. State of Michigan
     Archives. Lansing, Michigan.
133 Brown, Esther M. Howell, Michigan.
134 Brown, Judith L. East Lansing, Michigan.
135 Brown, Mary Carney. Kalamazoo, Michigan.
136 Clarey, Jo Ellyn. Grand Rapids, Michigan.
137 Coha, Amy L. Portland, Maine.
138 Coir, Mark. Cranbrook Archives and Historical Collections.
     Bloomfield Hills, Michigan.
131 Collamer Bauman, Rosella E. Midland, Michigan.
140 Colone, Elizabeth. Pinckney, Michigan.
141 Copp, Charlotte Powers. Ann Arbor, Michigan.

142 Copper Range Historical Society. Houghton, Michigan.

143 Cowan, Belita. Silver Spring, Maryland.

144 Denning, Bernadine Newsom. Detroit, Michigan.

145 Douglas, Arlene. Monroe, Michigan.

146 Edmunds, Nathalie Elliott. Ypsilanti, Michigan.

147 Edut, Tali. Ann Arbor, Michigan.

148 Elk Rapids Area Historical Society. Elk Rapids, Michigan.

149 Estate Records. Keweenaw County Courthouse. Eagle River, Michigan.

150 Evans, Eva L. Lansing, Michigan.

151 Fagal, William. Ellen G. White Estate Branch Office. Andrews University, Berrien Springs, Michigan.

152 Fort Miami Heritage Society of Michigan. St. Joseph, Michigan.

153 Fron, Mary. Niles, Michigan.

154 Gardner Papers, Nannette B. Bentley Historical Library. University of Michigan. Ann Arbor, Michigan.

155 Geha, Suzanne. Grand Rapids, Michigan.

156 Gibson, Jo Ann. Detroit, Michigan.

157 Giese, Elizabeth Homer. Lansing, Michigan.

158 Greater Grand Rapids Women's History Council. Grand Rapids, Michigan.

159 Griffin, Larry. Michigan Department of State. Division of Museum, Archaeology & Publications. Lansing, Michigan.

160 Grimes Papers, Lucia Isabelle Voorhees. Bentley Historical Library. University of Michigan. Ann Arbor, Michigan.

161 Grosse Ile Historical Society. Grosse Ile, Michigan.

162 Gubbins, Roberta M. Ann Arbor, Michigan.

163 Haley, Charlotte. Bay City, Michigan.

164 Harbor Springs Area Historical Society. Harbor Springs, Michigan.

165 Historical Society of Bridgeport. Bridgeport, Michigan.

166 Jesse Besser Museum. Alpena, Michigan.

167 Johnson, Jeane A. Conlin. Jackson, Michigan.

168 Johnson, Mildred. Lapeer, Michigan.

169 Kelly, Marilee. Ann Arbor, Michigan.

170 Kerr, Mary P. Okemos, Michigan.

171 Keweenaw Historical Society. Eagle Harbor, Michigan.

172 Kian, Josephine. Grand Rapids, Michigan.

173 King, Lee Ann. Ann Arbor, Michigan.

174 Large, Katie. De Witt, Michigan.

175 Lathrop, Marion Bertsch Gray. Grand Rapids, Michigan.

176 Liepens, Joyce. Eaton County Historical Commission. Charlotte, Michigan.

177 Lindquist, Charles. Lenawee Historical Museum. Adrian, Michigan.

178 Livingston County Press. Howell, Michigan.

179 Loftis, Lynnea. Ella Sharp Museum. Jackson, Michigan.

180 McCracken, Marian. Farmington, Michigan.

181 McGee, Susan G. S. Ann Arbor, Michigan.

182 Mertz, Martha Mayhood. Okemos, Michigan.

183 Michigan Room. Grand Rapids Public Library.

184 Michigan Women's Historical Center & Hall of Fame. Lansing, Michigan.

185 Miller, Candice S. Michigan Department of State. Lansing, Michigan.

186 Miller, Margaret Ann. Edmore, Michigan.

187 Motown Collection. Eastern Michigan University Archives. Ypsilanti, Michigan.

188 Munsell, Susan Grimes. Howell, Michigan.

189 Nichols, Judy. Highland, Michigan.

190 Nuriel, R. Hedy. Huntington Woods, Michigan.

191 Oakland County Pioneer and Historical Society. Pontiac, Michigan.

192 Owen, Charlotte P. Ann Arbor, Michigan.

193 Panian, Linda K. John M. Longyear Research Library. Marquette County Historical Society. Marquette, Michigan.

194 Pollock, E. Jill. Orchard Lake, Michigan.

195 Poniatowski, Marge. City of Center Line. Center Line, Michigan.

196 Pugliesi, Edward. Henry Ford Museum. Dearborn, Michigan.

197 Port Huron Museum of Arts & History. Port Huron, Michigan.

198 Reading Room File. Burton Historical Collection. Detroit Public Library. Detroit, Michigan.

199 Reck, Susan L. Howell, Michigan.

200 Rockall, Diane M. Northville Historical Society. Northville, Michigan.

201 Rother, Helene. Metamora, Michigan.

202 Schmock, Helen Cloutier. Manistee, Michigan.

203 Scrapbook. Anna Botsford Bach Home. Ann Arbor, Michigan.

204 Selmon Papers, Bertha Eugenia Loveland. Bentley Historical Library. University of Michigan. Ann Arbor, Michigan.

205 Sieloff, Alice F. Brighton, Michigan.

206 Stakenas, Kay E. Rose Hawley Museum. Ludington, Michigan.

207 Stevenson, Jan. Farmington, Michigan.

208 Sutherland, Doris. East Lansing, Michigan.

209 Tischler, Sharon. Southfield Township. Birmingham, Michigan.

210 Tri-Cities Museum. Grand Haven, Michigan.

211 Trinklein, Lynda Litogot. Grand Ledge, Michigan.

212 Tuksal, Carmina Brooks. Franklin Historical Society. Franklin, Michigan.

213 Tulloch Scrapbook, Jean S. Grand Marais Historical Society. Grand Marais, Michigan.

214 Underwood, Mrs. Margaret. Ann Arbor, Michigan.

215 Van Pelt Library. Michigan Technological University. Houghton, Michigan.

216 Voss, B. Margaret. Rockford, Michigan.

217 Weston, Teresa and Joan McDowell. Korean Martial Arts Institute. Lapeer, Michigan.

218 White, Virginia L. Okemos, Michigan.

219 Widgeon, Betty R. Washtenaw County, Michigan.

220 Wilcox Papers, Lucinda Sexton. Bentley Historical Library. University of Michigan. Ann Arbor, Michigan.

GUIDE TO INDEX

The Index is organized into the following categories:

INDEX

WOMEN AS AUTHORS

Alvarado-Ortega, Yolanda G. H.
Avery, Lillian Drake
Bernhardt, Marcia Webster
Burgess, Lauren Cook
Coha, Amy L.
Cowan, Belita
Fisher, Mary
Gall, Elizabeth Babcock
Gentile, Judy Kay Taylor
Griffith, Roberta A.
Grimes, Lucia Isabelle Voorhees
Hawley, Rose Damaris Horne
Hine, Darlene Clark
Jackson, Nell Cecilia
Jeffers, Cora Doolittle
Jones, Irma Theoda Andrews
Kelly, Delta M. Hutchinson

Kennedy, Jessie Marie Carter
Lindquist Arndt, Lilly
Martin, Helen
Massingill, Alberta
McGee, Susan G. S.
Moore, Julia A. Davis
Nuriel, R. Hedy
Peck, Annie Smith
Pickett, Roberta McGuire
Putnam, Caroline Willard Williams
Rourke, Constance Mayfield
Schmock, Helen Cloutier
Selmon, Bertha Eugenia Loveland
Warsaw, Irene
White, Ellen G. Harmon
White, Virginia Converse

WOMEN IN AVIATION

Barber, Mary Isabel
DeRoo, Alta
Piccard, Jeannette Ridlon

Ruth, Marion "Babe" Weyant
Singletary, Sheryl
Wills-Merrell, Luanne

WOMEN IN BUSINESS, INDUSTRY & TRADES

Business Women

Aikey, Mary
Airriess, Mary
Angell, Alice
Avery Whitfield, Lucile
Barthwell, Gladys Whitfield
Bonde, Debra
Breitung, Charlotte G. Kaufman
Busby, Clara Caldwell
Campau, Sophie de Marsac
Currell, Anne-Marie J. Dalmasso
Denning, Bernadine Newsom
Draggoo, Sandra L.
Garza, Lila
Gearhart, Fern E. Briggs
Gibson, JoAnn
Heath, Lenora Cooper
Hubbard, Mary H. Green
Johnson, Jeane A. Conlin
Johnston, Susan

Kallen, Jackie
Lesnieski, Frances L.
Lucas, Teresa
Magoon, Johanna Meijer
Mertz, Martha Mayhood
Milford, Edna C. McNeely
Pollock, E. Jill
Prochnow, Ella Bareis
Rodgers, LaJune
Sareini, Suzanne
Saucedo-Smith, Irene
Schwannecke, Frances S.
Sjunneson, Siggan
Spears, Evelyn C.
Stevenson, Jan
Tufty, Esther Van Wagoner
Van Hoesen, Grace Ames
Warsaw, Irene
Yancheck, Gail

Industrial Women

Barber, Mary Isabel
Gerber, Dorothy Scott
Grimes, Lucia Isabelle Voorhees
Karlstrom, Signe
Miller, Linda

Nemeth, Valla Saltzsgiver
Oren, Martha Carlson
Pollock, E. Jill
Rother, Helene
Seabrooks, Nettie H.

Trades Women

Boldi, Lana
Hering, Barbara C.

McFall, Nancy

WOMEN AS CLUB LEADERS & MEMBERS

Ashbaugh, Delphine Dodge
Avery, Blanche
Avery, Lillian Drake
Avery Whitfield, Lucile
Bach, Anna Botsford
Ballard, L. Anne
Barnes, Amanda W. Fleming
Bates, M. E. Cram
Bates, Mrs. Morgan
Bolt, Mildred A.
Bower, Emma Eliza
Brunson, Rose T.
Bulson, Florence Breck
Burns, Frances Emily Sanford
Busby, Clara Caldwell
Campbell, Carina Bulkley
Colwell, Josephine French
Cowley, Mrs. B. P.
Dowd, Lucy Lockwood Stout
Duggan, Annie
Eggleston, Ella C. Mills Hecox
Evans, Eva L.
Farquharson, Rhoda Pamela
Farrand, Helen Wheaton
Gaines, Louisa
Gearhart, Fern E. Briggs
Gould, Josephine White
Graves, Ann E. Lapham
Grimes, Lucia Isabelle Voorhees
Haines, Blanche Moore
Hamilton, Rena Louise Tompkins
Hawley, Rose Damaris Horne
Hemmingsen, Christine
Hinsdale, Mary Louise
Hollister, Justina Hall Merrick
Jones, Irma Theoda Andrews
Jones, Mina C.

Keating, Martha Adalaide Cook
Keck, Christine M.
Kennedy, Jessie Marie Carter
Kingsford, Minnie Flaherty
Lee, Gertrude
Lewis, Emily
Longstreet, Martha
MacPherson, Ida Grout Rust
Majors, Ina
Massingill, Alberta R.
McLelland, Lilley
Mills, Florence Gertrude Balch
Morrison, Wealthy M.
O'Donnell, Sarah G.
Pearl, Dorothy Waite
Perkins, Della Foote
Perry, Belle McArthur
Pickett, Roberta McGuire
Pierce, Ella Matthews
Putnam, Caroline Willard Williams
Russell, Ellen P. Wells England
Rutson, Mrs. George
Schiller, Rose Krause
Selden, Anna Bell(e) Sears
Smith, Frances Wheeler
Toeppner, Sadie Drago
Towsley, Margaret Dow
Tulloch, Jean S.
Uhl, Alice Follett
Van Miller, Josephine McBride
Warner, Jeanette Shelly
Washington, Jacquelin Edwards
Waters, Florence Hills
Wells, Agnes Ermina
Whittemore, Susan
Williams, Lula Margaret Roberts
Withey, Marion Louise

WOMEN AS COMMUNITY VOLUNTEERS

Aikey, Mary
Ashbaugh, Delphine Dodge
Auberlin, Irene McGinnis
Avery, Lillian Drake
Bach, Anna Botsford
Ball, Lucy
Ballard, L. Anne
Barsamian, Gladys
Barthwell, Gladys Whitfield
Becker, Agnes Jane Gray
Bell, Mary A. Teaks
Bernhardt, Marcia Webster
Bignell, Ann H.
Breitung, Charlotte G. Kaufman
Brown, Esther M. Lynch
Bryant, Agnes Hardie
Bulson, Florence Breck
Durfee, Florence A. Nelson Mayer
Dye, Marie
Edmunds, Nathalie Elliott

Evans, Eva L.
Farquharson, Rhoda Pamela
Ferrier, Orpha Ray Lumsden
Frey, Mary Caroline
Glover, Sara
Heath, Lenora Cooper
Hering, Barbara C.
Hunt, Diann Marie Robinson
Karlstrom, Signe
Kelly, Delta M. Hutchinson
Kennedy, Jessie Marie Carter
Klaussen, Doris Dexter Davis
Lathrop, Marion Bertsch Gray
Lesnieski, Frances L.
Lipczynski, Valeria Glowczynska
Lucas, Teresa
Milford, Beth Wharton
Milonas, Maria Vasoulidis
Paul, Helen Longyear
Pearl, Dorothy Waite

WOMEN AS COMMUNITY VOLUNTEERS (CONTINUED)

Reck, Susan L.
Roscoe, Gladys Pelham
Rutherford, Clara Walls
Schiller, Rose Krause
Selden, Anna Bell(e) Sears
Shagonaby, Susan
Sjunneson, Siggan
Sloman, Lottie T.
Talley, Barbara

Toeppner, Sadie Drago
Towsley, Margaret Dow
Voss, B. Margaret
Walker, Flora
Waters, Florence Hills
Whittemore, Susan
Williams, Lula Margaret Roberts
Wood, Jane Lundell

WOMEN AS CONSERVATIONISTS & ENVIRONMENTALISTS

Dockeray, Mary Jane
Edmunds, Nathalie Elliott
Graunstadt, Cheryl
Humphries, Becky
Kelly, Delta M. Hutchinson
Leggett, Elizabeth Seaman

Martin, Helen
Munger, Edith Gotts
Paul, Helen Longyear
Smith, Marie Doan
Toeppner, Sadie Drago
Walker, Janet

WOMEN IN EDUCATION

Elementary & Secondary Teachers & Administrators

Aldinger, Ella Hough
Avery, Blanche
Ballard, L. Anne
Barthwell, Gladys Whitfield
Benane, Anna
Bergh, Ida Jarve
Bergt, Marilyn
Bernhardt, Marcia Webster
Blackwell, Catherine Carter
Boyse, Alice
Buchalter, Alice
Burns, Frances Emily Sanford
Bush, Eliza Powell
Calvert-Baker, Gwendolyn
Carter, Mary L.
Chalou, Margaret (Peggy) Risk
Clark, Chloe A.
Clark, Mary H.
Clark, Roby
Coryell McBain, Eva Diann
Denning, Bernadine Newsom
Durfee, Florence A. Nelson Mayer
Eggleston, Ella C. Mills Hecox
Evans, Eva L.
Faith
Fay, Maureen
Ferguson, Joan
Ferrier, Orpha Ray Lumsden
Ford, Caroline L.
Frey, Mary Caroline
Giese, Elizabeth Homer
Goodale Hitchcock, Helen R.
Goss, Josephine Ahnefeldt
Gould, Josephine White
Graves, Ann E. Lapham
Green, Mary E.
Grimes, Lucia Isabelle Voorhees
Gubbins, Roberta M.

Hendricks, Jennie Maria Burnett
Heth, Cynthia H.
Horowitz, June
Hunt, Diann Marie Robinson
Jasinski, Lucille
Jeffers, Cora Doolittle
Jerome Fox, Mary Ruth
Jones, Irma Theoda Andrews
Kelly, Delta M. Hutchinson
Kennedy, Jessie Marie Carter
Killgore Wertman, Sarah
Kingsford, Minnie Flaherty
Klaussen, Doris Dexter Davis
Leavey, Kathleen
Leonard, Viola
Lindquist Arndt, Lilly
Magoon, Johanna Meijer
Milford, Beth Wharton
Milford, Edna C. McNeely
Miller, Linda
Munger, Edith Gotts
Murtland, Cleo
Palmer, Alice Freeman
Paul, Sarah
Peck, Annie Smith
Pickett, Roberta McGuire
Prochnow, Ella Bareis
Putnam, Caroline Willard Williams
Riesterer, Jeanne
Riseman, Meta Rosenberg
Roscoe, Gladys Pelham
Rourke, Constance Davis
Sharpe, Eva Alma
Smith, Frances Wheeler
Smith, Marie Doane
Stockman, Lottie
Strong, Martha Cochrane
Sweeney, Florence

Women in Other Educational Roles

Allison, Janice
Ball, Lucy
Becker, Agnes Jane Gray
Bolt, Mildred A.
Calvert-Baker, Gwendolyn
Collamer Bauman, Rosella E.
Currell, Anne-Marie J. Dalmasso
Doan, Donalda
Giese, Elizabeth Homer
Goggin, Flora
Griffin, Jean
Griffith, Roberta A.
Hamer, Sylvia J. Cole
Hendricks, Jennie Maria Burnett
Hommel, Flora Suhd

Kelly, Delta M. Hutchinson
Milonas, Maria Vasoulidis
Niedzielski, Eleanore Craves
Pearl, Dorothy Waite
Preston, Mrs. E. J.
Reyes, Angie
Riseman, Meta Rosenberg
Rourke, Constance Davis
Rouse, Rosamund R.
Ruth, Marion "Babe" Weyant
Saarinen, Loja (Louise) Gesellius
Shagonaby, Susan
Spears, Evelyn C.
Toeppner, Sadie Drago
Towsley, Margaret Dow

WOMEN AS ENGINEERS

Moore, Willie Hobbs

Sloan, Martha

WOMEN ON THE GREAT LAKES

Boynton, Marcia
Brawn Way, Julia Toby
Carlson, Annie M.
Carlton, S. B.
Ferguson, Joan
Garraty, Anne
Griswold, Mrs. John
Harrison, Mrs. Donald E.
Litogot Antaya, Caroline A. Taylor

Marvin, Kate
McGuire, Annie
Monroe, Mrs. William M.
Omalley, Mrs. Charles M.
Papa, Eva
Smith, Lydia
Terry, Mary L.
Truckey, Eliza
Wheatley, Mary A.

WOMEN IN HEALTH CARE

Nurses

Brewer, Mabel E. Overett
Gall, Elizabeth Babcock
Glover, Sara
Goodwin, Della Mae McGraw
Hayes, Jennie
Hendricks, Jennie Maria Burnett
Hommel, Flora Suhd

Knapp, Ruth Margaret
Munger, Edith Gotts
Taubert, Gertude M.
Tuanquin, Adoracion B.
Williams, Charlotte
Williams, Regina

Physicians

Adelman, Susan Hershberg
Ballard, L. Anne
Becker, Cristie J.
Bower, Emma Eliza
Brunson, Rose T.
Carter, Sarah L.
Decker, Emma Amy Adams
Evangelista, Stella
Farquharson, Rhoda Pamela
Gendzwill, Joyce A.
Green, Mary E.
Haines, Blanche Moore

Hamilton, Alice
Longstreet, Martha
Lucas, Teresa
Rann, Betty J. Wright
Ross-Lee, Barbara
Schuman, Paula
Selmon, Bertha Eugenia Loveland
Strong, Martha Cochrane
Walshaw, Sally
Wilcox, Lucinda Sexton
Wolfe, Delight J.

Other Contributors to Health Care

WOMEN IN THE LABOR MOVEMENT

WOMEN IN LAW

WOMEN AS LIBRARY & MUSEUM PERSONNEL

WOMEN IN THE MEDIA

Alvarado-Ortega, Yolanda G. H.
Ashbaugh, Delphine Dodge
Bates, M. E. Cram
Bell, Mary L. Teaks
Bignell, Ann H.
Bower, Emma Eliza
Carlton, Ruth
Cowan, Belita
Dieterle, Lorraine
Dowd, Lucy Lockwood Stout
Edut, Ophira
Edut, Tali
Geha, Suzanne
Gerber, Dorothy Scott
Hawley, Rose Damaris Horne
Hilliard, Wendy
Hubbard, Merry H. Green
Jones, Irma Theoda Andrews
Jurney, Dorothy Misener
Kallen, Jackie

Lipczynski, Valeria Glowczynska
Logwood, Dyann
Perry, Belle McArthur
Phillips, Leonora
Prater, Constance C.
Rabbers, Jan
Schmock, Helen Cloutier
Shook, Frances
Sieloff, Alice F.
Spears, Evelyn C.
Strahl, Marion
Taylor, Kristin Clark
Thomas, Jacqueline
Torre, Susana
Tufty, Esther Van Wagoner
Ward, Margaret McCall Thomas
Watson, Susan
White, Virginia Converse
White, Zae Robinson
Whittemore, Susan

WOMEN IN THE MILITARY

Brewer, Mabel E. Overett
Brodbent, Mildred C. Young
DeRoo, Alta
Dhaene, Margaret
Dieterle, Lorraine
Hayes, Jennie
Hogue, Micki King

Knapp, Ruth Margaret
Meter, Ethelyn
Owen, Charlotte Plummer
Rathbun-Nealy Coleman, Melissa
Shook, Frances
Williams, Regina

WOMEN AS PEACE ACTIVISTS

Alvarado-Ortega, Yolanda G. H.
Bryant, Agnes Hardie
Dollinger, Genora Johnon
Hommel, Flora Suhd

Johnston, Susan
MacPherson, Ida Grout Rust
Magoon, Johanna Meijer
Riseman, Meta Rosenberg

WOMEN AS PHILANTHROPISTS

Bates, Octavia
Bell, Mary L. Teaks
Breitung, Charlotte G. Kaufman
Frey, Mary Caroline
Gerber, Dorothy Scott
Kennedy, Jessie Marie Carter
MacPherson, Ida Grout Rust

Morrison, Wealthy M.
Perkins, Della Foote
Paul, Helen Longyear
Pulte, Mary Jo
Towsley, Margaret Dow
Waters, Florence Hills

WOMEN PIONEERS & EARLY SETTLERS

Barnes, Amanda Watson Fleming
Bates, M. E. Cram
Bates, Mrs. Morgan
Benane, Anna
Burton, Harriet Guild
Bush, Eliza Powell
Campau, Sophie de Marsac
Carter, Mary L.
Carter, Sarah L.
Clark, Chloe A.
Clark, Mary H.
Clark, Roby
Ferry, Amanda White

Ford, Caroline L.
Goodale Hitchcock, Helen R.
Green, Mary E.
Johnston, Susan
Paul, Sarah
Phillips, Leonora
Sagatoo, Mary Henderson Cabay
Thomas, Pamela Brown
Warren Hill, Susan
Watkins Thompson, Ruth Maria
White, Mary A.
Worden Lathrop, Samantha

WOMEN IN POLITICS & GOVERNMENT SERVICE

Appointed Officials

Alvarado-Ortega, Yolanda G. H.
Ashbaugh, Delphine Dodge
Barber, Mary Isabel
Boyse, Alice
Bryant, Agnes Hardie
Bulson, Florence Breck
Burns, Frances Emily Sanford
Calvert-Baker, Gwendolyn
Denning, Bernadine Newsom
Eggleston, Ella C. Mills Hecox
Evans, Eva L.
Fisher, Mary
Forhan, Elizabeth
Haines, Blanche Moore

Ingalls, Blanche
Johnson, Jeane A. Conlin
King, Rosalie Grandelis
Leavey, Kathleen
Micklow, Patricia Lenore Johnson
Pearl, Dorothy Waite
Reynolds, Nanette Lee
Sareini, Suzanne
Seabrooks, Nettie H.
Viventi, Carol
Wanger, Marilyn Morris
Webster-Maier, Carlene L.
Withrow, Pamela K.

Elected Officials

Adams, Frances Harris
Airriess, Mary
Avery Whitfield, Lucile
Barsamian, Gladys
Bergh, Ida Jarve
Boyse, Alice
Brater, Elizabeth S.
Brown. Esther M. Lynch
Brown, Mary Carney
Cargo. Ruth
Chalou. Margaret (Peggy) Risk
Colone, Elizabeth
Forhan, Elizabeth
Goodwin, Della Mae McGraw
Houston, Fannie Kanter Hubbard
Jackson, Gail George
Lamberts, Evangeline
Micklow, Patricia Lenore Johnson
Miller, Candice Snider
Munsell, Susan Grimes
Neuenfelt, Lila M.
Palmer, Alice Freeman

Ray, Bertha
Reck, Susan L.
Riesterer, Jeanne
Ritchie, Catherine Campbell
Roberts, Estelle
Robinson, Glenda
Sareini, Suzanne
Snyder, Ruth
Talley, Barbara
Tinsley-Williams, Alberta
Towsley, Margaret Dow
Trinklein, Lynda Litogot
Van Hoesen, Grace Ames
Viventi, Carol
Webster-Maier, Carlene L.
White, Virginia Converse
White, Zae Robinson
Whitmyer, Naomi Wilkins
Widgeon, Betty R.
Williams, Charlotte
Zielinski, Mary Ann

Women in Fire Protection

Oakes, Pam
Singletary, Sheryl

Wilcox, Laura

Women in Law Enforcement

Bergh, Ida Jarve
Busby, Clara Caldwell
Chalou, Margaret (Peggy) Risk
Gauchey, Nancy
Ghougoian, Joan
Hill, Harriet

Hillary Earhart, Noreen E.
Knox, Dorothy D.
Moore, Marilyn
Nichols, Judy
Tapp, Ann Schweizer
Whitfield McEntee, Kay

WOMEN AS RELIGIOUS LEADERS

Andrews, Barbara
Barney, Violet Jane Lockwood
Bergt, Marilyn
Busby, Clara Caldwell
Fay, Maureen
Feldner, Mary Baptist
Ferry, Amanda White
Jones, Irma Theoda Andrews
Kostielney, Monica
McCord, Mary Ignatius
McMullen, Mary Anthony

Piccard, Jeannette Ridlon
Reeves, Martha
Sagatoo, Mary Henderson Cabay
Schwannecke, Frances S.
Selmon, Bertha Eugenia Loveland
Sloman, Lottie T.
Tuanquin, Adoracion B.
Voss, B. Margaret
White, Ellen G. Harmon
Williams, Charlotte

WOMEN AS SCIENTISTS & INVENTORS

Boving, Renee Laya
Hampton, Christine
Humphries, Becky
Hwaleck, Melanie
Neale, Victoria

Oren, Martha Carlson
Saunders, Patricia McNaughton
Schultz, Lonnie
Swanson, G. Marie
Tilley, Barbara

WOMEN AS SOCIAL ACTIVISTS

Alvarado-Ortega, Yolanda G. H.
Ballard, L. Anne
Barfield, Clementine
Blaquiere, Theresa
Brown, Mary Carney
Bryant, Agnes Hardie
Burgess, Lauren Cook
Busby, Clara Caldwell
Carlton, Ruth
Coha, Amy L.
Collamer Bauman, Rosella E.
Cowan, Belita
DeYoung, Lisa
Dominic, Waunetta McClellan
Faith
Fisher, Mary
Gentile, Judy Kay Taylor
Giese, Elizabeth Homer
Gorrecht, Freida
Graunstadt, Cheryl
Griffith, Roberta A.
Hamilton, Alice
Hommel, Flora Suhd
Jerome Fox, Mary Ruth

Josaitis, Eleanor M.
Leggett, Elizabeth Seaman
Liuzzo, Viola Gregg
MacPherson, Ida Grout Rust
Magoon, Johanna Meijer
Manning, Lois
Marx, Jean
McGee, Susan G. S.
McGlendon, Mary Upshaw
McPherson, Joanne
Mertz, Martha Mayhood
Micklow, Patricia Lenore Johnson
Nuriel, R. Hedy
Pries, Mrs. J. F.
Riseman, Meta Rosenberg
Ross, Marjorie A.
Spears, Evelyn C.
Stearns, Sarah Burger
Stebbins, Catharine A. Fish
Stevenson, Jan
Thomas, Pamela Brown
Tinsley-Williams, Alberta
Washington, Jacquelin Edwards
Whitten, Eloise Culmer

WOMEN AS SOCIAL WORKERS & HUMANITARIANS

Bach, Anna Botsford
Barfield, Clementine
Barney, Violet Jane Lockwood
Barthwell, Gladys Whitfield
Bergt, Marilyn
Bonde, Debra
Bonnema, Marguerite
Burton, Harriet Guild
Carlton, Ruth
Coha, Amy L.
Comey, Louise
Cory, Jerre

DeBoer VandenBosch, Mary
DeYoung, Lisa
Fron, Mary
Gauchey, Nancy
Gorrecht, Freida
Heth, Cynthia H.
Hillary Earhart, Noreen E.
Hunt, Diann Marie Robinson
Lathrop, Marion Bertsch Gray
Lipczynski, Valeria Glowczynska
Longstreet, Martha
McGee, Susan G. S.

WOMEN'S ORGANIZATIONS

(REPRESENTED BY WOMEN LISTED IN THIS VOLUME)

Activist Organizations

Detroit Women for Peace: (Dollinger)

Mothers Against Drunk Driving (MADD): (Nichols)

National Organization for Women (NOW): (Brown, M. • Coha • Collamer Bauman • Giese • McGee • Nemeth • Washington)

National Women's Health Network: (Cowan)

Planned Parenthood: (Magoon • Munger • Towsley • Washington • Whitten)

Woman Suffrage Associations:
(Angell • Ashbaugh • Avery, L.• Burns • Graves • Grimes • Haines • Hendricks • Ketcham • Munger • Perry • Sanders • Stearns • Van Hoesen)

Women for Meaningful Summits: (Alvarado-Ortega)

Women Involved In Giving Support (WINGS): (Washington)

Women's Christian Temperance Union (WCTU):
(Ballard • Hendricks • Jones, I. • Perry • Seldon)

Women's Civic Improvement League: (Mills)

Women's International League for Peace and Freedom:
(Bryant • Riseman)

Women's Strike for Peace: (Hommel)

Associations of Women's Clubs

General Federation of Women's Clubs (including local chapters):
(Aldinger • Ashbaugh • Avery, L. • Ballard • Barnes • Bulson • Burns • Dowd • Gearhart • Gould • Graves • Haines • Hamilton, R. Hawley • Jones, I. • Keating • Kelly • Kingsford • Knapp • Mills • O'Donnell • Perkins • Perry • Seldon • Smith, F. • Toeppner • Tulloch)

National Association of Colored Women's Clubs (including local chapters):
(Brunson • Lee • Majors)

Benevolent & Service Organizations

Big Sisters: (Webster)

Female Union Charitable Association (United Benevolent Association):
(Bach • Morrison)

Girls Protective League: (Sloman)

Hadassah: (Schiller)

Hastings Ladies Aid Society: (Eggleston)

Industrial Aid Society: (Ballard • Jones, I.)

The Links: (Kennedy • Moore, W.)

Mary Free Bed Guild: (Rouse)

Old Ladies Home Society: (Bach • Bower)

Original Willing Workers Society: (Roscoe)

PEO Sisterhood: (Houston • Magoon • Towsley)

Benevolent & Service Organizations (continued)

Salvation Army Women's Auxiliary: (Ashbaugh)

Union Benevolent Association: (Burton • Withey)

Women's Benefit Association: (Burns)

Women's Hospital Association: (Barnes)

Zonta International:
(Collamer Bauman • Edmunds • Houston • Lesnieski • Longstreet • Massingill • Mertz • Towsley)

Labor Organizations

Coalition of Labor Union Women (CLUW): (Hering • Nemeth)

Household Workers Organization: (McGlendon)

International Glove Workers Union: (Nestor)

National Women's Trade Union League: (Nestor)

UAW Women's Auxiliary: (Dollinger)

Women's Emergency Brigade: (Dollinger)

Political Organizations

Democratic Women's Caucus and Clubs: (Brown, M. • Giese)

League of Women Voters:
(Aldinger • Avery Whitfield • Brown, E. Brown, M. • Bryant • Ferrier Giese • Gubbins • Hinsdale •Hollister • Keck • Lamberts • MacPherson • Mills • Munger • Munsell • Reck • Talley • Van Hoesen Warner • Whittemore)

Legislative Council of Michigan Women: (Grimes)

National Woman's Party:
(Aldinger • Breitung • Grimes • Hendrie • Reyneau • Wells)

National Women's Political Caucus: (Nemeth)

Republican Women's Caucus and Clubs:
(Grimes • Milford, B. • White, V.)

Women Citizen's League: (Greenwood • Grimes)

Professional Organizations

American Association of Deans of Women: (Wells)

American Home Economics Association: (Barber • Dye • Raven)

American Newspaper Women's Club: (Tufty)

American Women in Radio and Television: (Bignell • Tufty)

American Women's Medical Association: (Haines • Selmon)

Association for Women in Science:
(Boving • Hampton • Hwaleck • Neale • Schultz • Tilley)

Association of Women Deans, Administrators, and Counselors:
(Brown, M.)

Business and Professional Women's Clubs:
(Farquharson • Giese • Johnson • Knapp • Massingill • Milford, B. • Selmon • Strong • Washington • Wells)

Delta Kappa Gamma: (Bernhardt • Knapp)

Dental Hygienists Association (state and national): (Shook)

Professional Organizations (continued)

Detroit Women Writers: (Warsaw)

Dietetic Associations (state and national): (Barber)

Eta Phi Beta Business and Professional Sorority: (Hubbard)

Michigan Women Realtors: (Milford, E.)

Michigan Women's Press Association:
(Bower • Burns • Hamilton, R. • Jones, I. • Perry)

National Association for Female Executives: (Gibson)

National Association of Women Business Owners:
(Gibson • Pollock • Sieloff)

National Federation of Press Women: (Carlton, R.)

National League of American Pen Women: (Warsaw)

Nurses Clubs and Associations (local and state):
(Goodwin • Taubert • Tuanquin • Williams, R.)

Society of Women Engineers: (Sloan)

Women Band Directors National Association: (Owen)

Women in Communications: (Carlton, R.)

Women in Public Administration: (Martin, D.)

Women Lawyers Association of Michigan:
(Brown, M. • Gubbins • Neuenfelt • Ranucci • Washington)

Women's Economic Club of Detroit: (Bryant • Sieloff • Washington)

Women's National Press Club: (Tufty)

Sports Organizations

Ladies of the Unique Cycle Club: (Pries)

Lady Bass Anglers of West Michigan: (Hawkins)

Michigan Women's Golf Association: (Hilding)

National Association for Girls and Women in Sports: (Jackson, N.)

99's: (Ruth)

Women's Sports Foundation: (Hilliard • Hogue, M. • Krone)

Study Organizations

Friends in Council (Monroe): (Campbell, C. • Lewis • Van Miller)

Grand Rapids Study Club: (Gaines)

Greater Grand Rapids Women's History Council: (Frey)

Hypatia Study Club (Detroit): (Grimes)

Local Literary Clubs and Societies:
(Avery, L. • Colwell • Cowley • Duggan • Gould • McLelland •
Munger • Putnam • Rutson • Withey)

Owosso Current Topic Club: (Gould)

The Reviewers (Grand Rapids): (Perkins)

Shakespeare Study Club (Detroit): (Bolt)

Women's Studies Association (state and national): (Collamer Bauman • Giese)

Other Organizations

Alpha Kappa Alpha: (Evans • Kennedy • Washington)

American Association of University Women (AAUW): (Aldinger • Avery, B. • Brown, M. • Collamer Bauman • Haines • Longstreet • Martin, H. • Palmer • Strong • Wells • Whittemore)

American Legion Auxiliary: (Pearl)

Art Clubs and Associations: (Graves • MacPherson • Perkins)

Battle Creek Women's League: (Graves • Hamilton, R.)

Bay City Civic League: (Toeppner)

Campfire Girls: (Becker, A.)

Century Club (Charlotte): (Perry)

Church Women United: (Williams, C.)

Danish Sisterhood of America: (Hemmingsen)

Daughters of Colonial Wars: (Haines)

Daughters of 1812: (Russell • Wells)

Daughters of Founders and Patriots of America: (Grimes)

Daughters of the American Revolution (DAR): (Aldinger • Avery, L. • Bulson • Gould • Haines • Hamilton, R. • Houston • Knapp • Longstreet • Perkins • Uhl • Wells)

Delta Sigma Theta: (Barthwell • Moore • Pickett)

Detroit Women's Club: (Stebbins)

Dorcas Club (Kalamazoo): (Williams, L.)

Free Kindergarten Association: (MacPherson)

Garden Clubs (national, state and local); (Hamilton, R. • Hawley • Martin, H. • Toeppner)

Girl Scouts: (Barthwell • Durfee • Kelly • Munsell • Washington)

Hispanic Women in the Network: (Alvarado-Ortega)

Home Extension Clubs: (Becker, A. • Raven)

Kalamazoo Women's Network: (Brown, M.)

Kappa Alpha Phi: (Avery, B.)

Ladies' Library Associations: (Bach • Barnes • Bates, M. E. • Bates, Mrs. Morgan • Cornell • Farrand • Graves • Mills)

Ladies of the Maccabees: (Bower • Burns • Haines)

La Leche League: (Gall)

Lansing Unity Club: (Jones, I.)

Let Us Be Friends Club: (Williams, L.)

Michigan State Federation of Temple Sisterhoods: (Sloman)

Michigan Women's Assembly: (Giese)

Michigan Women's Forum: (Barsamian, Bryant)

Minority Women's Network: (Walker, F.)

Mujeres Unidas de Michigan: (Alvarado-Ortega)

National Council of Negro Women: (Pickett)

National Council of Women: (Burns)

Other Organizations (continued)

Order of Eastern Star:
(Becker, A. • Burns • Farquharson • Grimes • Taubert)

Phi Delta Kappa: (Roscoe)

Society of Polish Ladies: (Lipczynski)

St. Cecilia Society (Grand Rapids): (Pierce • Uhl)

Top Ladies of Distinction: (Pickett • Washington)

Twentieth Century Club (Iron River): (Bernhardt • Jones, M.)

U and I Club (Lansing): (Barnes)

United Mothers Club of Greater Lansing: (Busby)

Women's Association for the Detroit Symphony: (Karlstrom)

Women's City Clubs (local clubs):
(Lathrop • Pearl • Perkins • Towsley • Waters)

Women's Civil Defense: (Pearl)

Women's Conference of Concerns:
(Bryant • Giese • Hommel • Talley)

Women's Liberty Loan Committee: (Bulson)

Women's Outreach Network: (Gerus)

Women's Relief Corps: (Edmunds • Strong)

Young Women's Christian Association (YWCA):
(Aikey • Alvarado-Ortega • Bach • Ballard • Bell • Breitung •
Brown, M. • Bryant • Calvert-Baker • Cory • Ferrier • Hamilton, R.
Hering • Lesnieski • MacPherson • Nemeth • Selmon • Williams, L.)

****

*"1. The right of citizens of the United States to vote
shall not be denied or abridged by the United States
or by any State on account of sex.*

*2. Congress shall have the power to enforce this
Article by appropriate legislation."*

The Nineteenth Amendment to the Constitution
Ratified August 26, 1920

****